Maulana Abul Kalam Azad

Maulana Abul Kalam Azad

Dr. C.P. Raj
Dr. Ved Prakash

AMIGA PRESS. INC
Delhi -110051

AMIGA
PRESS INC.
AMIGA PRESS INC.
Registered Office:
19 DBS Building, Ansari Road, Darya Ganj, Delhi. 110002, India
Phone: +91-11-23283333 Email: amigapress@gmail.com

This edition is published by Amiga Press.Inc

ISBN : 978-93-84533-29-8

First Published 2018

Reprint 2024

PRINTED : Replika Press Pvt. Ltd.

Preface

On February 22, 1958 Maulana Abul Kalam Azad, one of the foremost leaders of the Indian freedom struggle passed away. For his invaluable contribution to the nation, Maulana Abul Kalam Azad was posthumously awarded India's highest civilian honor, the 'Bharat Ratna' in 1992.

Journalist, Scholar, author, freedom fighter, and the first minister for education in the first ministry of independent India, Abul Kalam Mohiyuddin Ahmed was born in Mecca in 1888. His father was Maulana Muhamed Khairuddin, a great Islamic scholar. He migrated to Mecca after the First Independence Struggle of India of 1857. He came into the attention of Muhamed Zahir Vatri, a renowned scholar of Medina and married his daughter Aeli. They had five kids, including Abul Kalam. The sudden demise of his wife made Sheikh Khairuddin decide to return to India and he settled in Calcutta with his kids.

As a young man, Azad composed poetry in Urdu language, as well as treaties on religion and philosophy. He rose to prominence through his work as a journalist, publishing works critical of the British Raj and espousing the causes of Indian nationalism. Azad became the leader of the Khilafat Movement, during which he came into close contact with the Indian leader Mahatma Gandhi. Azad became an enthusiastic supporter of Gandhi's ideas of non-violent civil disobedience, and worked to organise the non-co-operation movement in protest of the 1919 Rowlatt Acts. Azad committed himself to Gandhi's ideals, including promoting *Swadeshi* (indigenous) products and the cause of *Swaraj* (*Self-rule*) for India. In 1923, at an age of 35, he became the youngest person to serve as the President of the Indian National Congress.

Azad was a penname he assumed and he began writing poems in that pseudonym. When he was only fifteen, he started a weekly in Urdu, styled 'the voice of truth'. Then he started another weekly in which he interpreted the Quran in an independent style. Thus he grew up into a courageous fighter for freedom and came into contact with the sage, Aurobindo Ghosh. This led him to a group of revolutionaries and he took the leadership in organizing branches of their outfit all over north India.

Azad paid special attention to the importance of communication through newspapers. His attempts at this field invited the anger of the government and the newspaper he started was banned and he launched another one within the next five months. The government banished Azad from Bengal. He was declared a persona non grata in several other provinces like Bombay, Punjab and Uttar Pradesh and so he migrated to a tribal village in Bihar and beamed article after article in a torrential flow.

The great patriot, the great secularist, the great educationist and writer, and the one who was deadly against the division of India into two countries, Maulana Abul Kalam Azad breathed his last in 1958. 'India Wins Freedom', his magnum opus remains the best memorial for this great man of modern India.

The book on Maulana Abul Kalam Azad as nationalist Muslim, fore-runners of India's freedom struggle, a reformist and as the first education minister of India's is of great importance for the scholars, researchers, students, teachers and historians as well pertaining to this sphere.

—*Editor*

Contents

Preface (*v*)

1. **Biography** 1
Literary works; Non-co-operation; Nonviolent Non-Cooperation; Congress leader; Quit India; Partition of India; Post-Independence; Legacy and influence; Maulana and his philosophy; Remembering Maulana Abul Kalam Azad

2. **Maulana Azad : A Revolutionary Journalist** 21
Maulana Abul Kalam Azad; Opinion: Maulana Azad: An Eminent Educationist; Role of journalism; Role of Muslim leaders in Journalism in Subcontinent

3. **Maulana Azad and Education System in India** 35
Maulana Azad's Educational Leadership; Educational Leadership of Maulana Azad as Education Minister; Azad's efforts in shaping the Indian Education Policy; Maulana Abul Kalam Azad and Education; Azad and Education in India; Consists of Real Education; Azad : Educationist & Scholar Extraordinary

4. **Maulana Azad and Role in National Movement** 61
About Maulana Abul Kalam; Maulana Azad in India Wins Freedom; Maulana Azad as Freedom Fighter; The Swarajist Strategy; Maulana Abul Kalam Azad , Indian Freedom Fighter; Maulana Abul Kalam Azad The Freedom Fighter

5. **Azad on Nehru's 'Blunders' Leading to the Partition of India** 81
Abul Kalam Azad; Pakistan Without Partition: Let's Revive The Buried Idea Of Indo-Pak Confederation; The age of unmixing; Pandit Jawaharlal Nehru; Maulana Azad and partition; Partition and dislocation in the East India; 'Government of Agitation' and Jabar Dakhal Colonies

6. **Abul Kalam Azad and Mahatma Gandhi** 133
Maulana Abul Kalam Azad; Azad, Congress and Gandhi; Gandhi and Indian Muslims: Overlaps and Conflicts; The Gandhi Era; Principles of Swadeshi; Congress and 'nationalist' Muslims; Indian National Congress ; Freedom and Partition of India

7. **Azad, Jinnah and Cabinet Mission Plan** 171
1946 Cabinet Mission to India; Jinnah, in a Class of His Own; British Strategic Interests in India and The Cabinet Mission

Bibliography 217

Index 219

1

Biography

Maulana Sayyid Abul Kalam Ghulam Muhiyuddin Ahmed Azad (pronunciation (help·info); 11 November 1888 – 22 February 1958) was an Indian scholar and the senior Muslim leader of the Indian National Congress during the Indian independence movement. Following India's independence, he became the first Minister of Education in the Indian government. He is commonly remembered as Maulana Azad; the word Maulana is an honorific meaning 'Our Master', and he had adopted *Azad* (*Free*) as his pen name. His contribution to establishing the education foundation in India is recognised by celebrating his birthday as "National Education Day" across India.

As a young man, Azad composed poetry in Urdu language, as well as treaties on religion and philosophy. He rose to prominence through his work as a journalist, publishing works critical of the British Raj and espousing the causes of Indian nationalism. Azad became the leader of the Khilafat Movement, during which he came into close contact with the Indian leader Mahatma Gandhi. Azad became an enthusiastic supporter of Gandhi's ideas of non-violent civil disobedience, and worked to organise the non-co-operation movement in protest of the 1919 Rowlatt Acts. Azad committed himself to Gandhi's ideals, including promoting *Swadeshi* (indigenous) products and the cause of *Swaraj* (*Self-rule*) for India. In 1923, at an age of 35, he became the youngest person to serve as the President of the Indian National Congress.

In October 1920, Maulana Abul Kalam Azad was elected as a member of foundation committee to establish Jamia Millia Islamia at Aligarh in U. P. without taking help from British colonial government. He helped a lot in shifting of the campus of the university to New Delhi from Aligarh in 1934. The main gate (Gate No. 7) to main campus of the university is named after him.

Azad was one of the main organisers of the Dharasana Satyagraha in 1931, and emerged as one of the most important national leaders of the time, prominently leading the causes of Hindu-Muslim unity as well as espousing secularism and socialism. He served as Congress president from 1940 to 1945, during which the *Quit India* rebellion was launched. Azad was imprisoned, together with the entire Congress leadership, for three years.

Amidst communal turmoil following the partition of India, he worked for religious harmony. As India's Education Minister, Azad oversaw the establishment of a national education system with free primary education and modern institutions of higher education. He is also credited with the establishment of the Indian Institutes of Technology and the foundation of the University Grants Commission, an important institution to supervise and advance the higher education in the nation.

National Education Day (India) an annual observance in India to commemorate the birth anniversary of Maulana Abul Kalam Azad, the first education minister of independent India, who served from 15 August 1947 until 2 February 1958. National Education Day of India is celebrated on 11 November every year in India. He also worked for Hindu-Muslim unity through the *Al-Hilal* newspaper.

Early life

Azad was born on 11 November 1888 in Mecca, Saudi Arabia. His real name was Sayyid Abul Kalaam Ghulam Muhiyuddin Ahmed who eventually became known as Maulana Azad. Azad's father was a scholar.He lived in Delhi with his maternal grandfather, as his father had died at a very young age. During Sepoy Mutiny he left India and settled in Mecca. Maulana Sayyid Muhammad Khairuddin bin Ahmed AlHussaini,authored a dozen of books and had thousands of disciples as well as claiming his ancestry to Imam Hussain, while his mother was Sheikha Alia bint Mohammad, the daughter of Sheikh Mohammad bin Zaher AlWatri, himself a reputed scholar from Medina who had a reputation that extended even outside of Arabia.

In Mecca, where Maulana Azad was born, but returned to Calcutta with his family in 1890. Azad began to master several languages, including Urdu, Hindi, Persian, Bengali, Arabic, and English. He was also trained in the Mazahibs of Hanafi, Maliki, Shafi'i and Hanbali fiqh, Shariat, mathematics, philosophy, world history and science by reputed tutors hired by his family. An avid and determined student, the precocious Azad was running a library, a reading room, a debating society before he was twelve, wanted to write on the life of Ghazali at twelve, was contributing learned articles to *Makhzan* (A literary magazine) at fourteen, was teaching a class of students, most of whom were twice his age, when he was merely fifteen and succeeded in completing the traditional course of study at the young age of sixteen, nine years ahead of his contemporaries, and brought out a magazine at the same age. In fact, in the field of journalism, he was publishing a poetical journal (*Nairang-e-Aalam*) and was already an editor of a weekly (*Al-Misbah*), in 1900, at the age of twelve and, in 1903, brought out a monthly journal, *Lissan-us-Sidq*, which soon gained popularity. At the age of thirteen, he was married to a young Muslim girl, Zulaikha Begum. Azad compiled many treatises interpreting the Qur'an, the *Hadis*, and the principles of *Fiqh* and *Kalam*.

Revolutionary and journalist

Azad developed political views considered radical for most Akbad Muslims of the time and became a full-fledged Indian nationalist. He fiercely criticised the British for racial discrimination and ignoring the needs of common people across India. He also criticised Muslim politicians for focusing on communal issues before the national interest and rejected the All India Muslim League's communal separatism. Azad developed curiosity and interest in the pan-Islamic doctrines of Jamal al-Din al-Afghani and visited Afghanistan, Iraq, Egypt, Syria and Turkey. But his views changed considerably when he met revolutionary activists in Iraq and was influenced by their fervent anti-imperialism and nationalism. Against common Muslim opinion of the time, Azad opposed the partition of Bengal in 1905 and became increasingly active in revolutionary activities, to which he was introduced by the prominent Hindu revolutionaries Aurobindo Ghosh and Shyam Sundar Chakravarty. Azad initially evoked surprise from other revolutionaries, but Azad won their praise and confidence by working secretly to organise revolutionaries activities and meetings in Bengal, Bihar and Bombay (now called Mumbai).

Azad's education had been shaped for him to become a cleric, but his rebellious nature and affinity for politics turned him towards journalism. He established an Urdu weekly newspaper in 1912 called Al-Hilal, and openly attacked British policies while exploring the challenges facing common people, but it was banned in 1914. Espousing the ideals of Indian nationalism, Azad's publications were aimed at encouraging young Muslims into fighting for independence and Hindu-Muslim unity. His work helped improve the relationship between Hindus and Muslims in Bengal, which had been soured by the controversy surrounding the partition of Bengal and the issue of separate communal electorates.

With the onset of World War I, the British stiffened censorship and restrictions on political activity. Azad's *Al-Hilal* was consequently banned in 1914 under the *Press Act*. Azad started a new journal, the *Al-Balagh*, which increased its active support for nationalist causes and communal unity. In this period Azad also became active in his support for the Khilafat agitation to protect the position of the Sultan of Ottoman Turkey, who was considered the

Caliph or Khalifa for Muslims worldwide. The Sultan had sided against the British in the war and the continuity of his rule came under serious threat, causing distress amongst Muslim conservatives. Azad saw an opportunity to energise Indian Muslims and achieve major political and social reform through the struggle. With his popularity increasing across India, the government outlawed Azad's second publication under the *Defence of India Regulations Act* and arrested him.

The governments of the Bombay Presidency, United Provinces, Punjab and Delhi prohibited his entry into the provinces and Azad was moved to a jail in Ranchi, where he was incarcerated until 1 January 1920.

LITERARY WORKS

Maulana Azad is considered one of the greatest Urdu writers of the 20th century. He has written many books including *India Wins Freedom*, Ghubar-e-Khatir, Tazkirah, Tarjumanul Quran, etc.

Ghubar-e-Khatir

Ghubar-e-Khatir is one of the most important works of Maulana Abul Kalam Azad, written primarily during 1942 to 1946 when he was imprisoned in Ahmednagar Fort in Maharashtra by British Raj while he was in Bombay (now Mumbai) to preside over the meeting of All India Congress Working Committee.

The book is basically a collection of 24 letters he wrote addressing his close friend Maulana Habibur Rahman Khan Sherwani. These letters were never sent to him because there was no permission for that during the imprisonment and after the release in 1946, he gave all these letters to his friend Ajmal Khan who let it published for the first time in 1946.

Although the book is a collection of letters but except one or two letters, all other letters are unique and most of the letters deal with complex issues such as existence of God, the origin of religions, the origin of music and its place in religion, etc.

The book is primarily an Urdu language book; however, there are over five hundred of couplets, mostly in Persian and Arabic languages. It is because, Maulana was born in a family where Arabic and Persian were used more frequently than Urdu. He was born in Mekkah, given formal education in Persian and Arabic languages but he was never taught Urdu.

It is often said that his book India wins Freedom is about his political life and Ghubar-e-Khatir deals with his social and spiritual life.

NON-CO-OPERATION

Upon his release, Azad returned to a political atmosphere charged with sentiments of outrage and rebellion against British rule. The Indian public had been angered by the passage of the Rowlatt Acts in 1919, which severely restricted civil liberties and individual rights. Consequently, thousands of political activists had been arrested and many publications banned. The killing of unarmed civilians at Jallianwala Bagh in Amritsar on 13 April 1919 had provoked intense outrage all over India, alienating most Indians, including long-time British supporters, from the authorities. The Khilafat struggle had also peaked with the defeat of the Ottoman Empire in World War I and the raging Turkish War of Independence, which had made the caliphate's position precarious. India's main political party, the Indian National Congress came under the leadership of Mahatma Gandhi, who had aroused excitement all over India when he led the farmers of Champaran and Kheda in a successful revolt against British authorities in 1918. Gandhi organised the people of the region and pioneered the art of *Satyagraha*— combining mass civil disobedience with complete non-violence and self-reliance.

Taking charge of the Congress, Gandhi also reached out to support the Khilafat struggle, helping to bridge Hindu-Muslim political divides. Azad and the Ali brothers - Maulana Mohammad Ali and Shaukat Ali - warmly welcomed Congress support and began working together on a programme of *non-co-operation* by asking all Indians to boycott British-run schools, colleges, courts, public services, the civil service, police and military. Non-violence and Hindu-Muslim unity were universally emphasised, while the boycott of foreign goods, especially clothes were organised. Azad joined the Congress and was also elected president of the All India Khilafat Committee. Although Azad and other leaders were soon arrested, the movement drew out millions of people in peaceful processions, strikes and protests.

This period marked a transformation in Azad's own life. Along with fellow Khilafat leaders Dr. Mukhtar Ahmad Ansari, Hakim Ajmal Khan and others, Azad grew personally close to Gandhi and his philosophy. The three men founded the Jamia Millia Islamia in Delhi as an institution of higher education managed entirely by Indians without any British support or control. Both Azad and Gandhi shared a deep passion for religion and Azad developed a close friendship with him. He adopted the Prophet Muhammad's ideas by living simply, rejecting material possessions and pleasures. He began to spin his own clothes using *khadi* on the *charkha,* and began frequently living and participating in the ashrams organised by Gandhi. Becoming deeply committed to *ahimsa* (*non-violence*) himself, Azad grew close to fellow nationalists like Jawaharlal

Nehru, Chittaranjan Das and Subhas Chandra Bose. He strongly criticised the continuing suspicion of the Congress amongst the Muslim intellectuals from the Aligarh Muslim University and the Muslim League.

The movement had a sudden decline with rising incidences of violence; a nationalist mob killed 22 policemen in Chauri Chaura in 1922. Fearing degeneration into violence, Gandhi asked Indians to suspend the revolt and undertook a five-day fast to repent and encourage others to stop the rebellion. Although the movement stopped all over India, several Congress leaders and activists were disillusioned with Gandhi. The following year, the caliphate was overthrown by Mustafa Kemal Atatürk and the Ali brothers grew distant and critical of Gandhi and the Congress. Azad's close friend Chittaranjan Das co-founded the Swaraj Party, breaking from Gandhi's leadership. Despite the circumstances, Azad remained firmly committed to Gandhi's ideals and leadership. In 1923, he became the youngest man to be elected Congress president. Azad led efforts to organise the Flag Satyagraha in Nagpur. Azad served as president of the 1924 Unity Conference in Delhi, using his position to work to re-unite the Swarajists and the Khilafat leaders under the common banner of the Congress. In the years following the movement, Azad travelled across India, working extensively to promote Gandhi's vision, education and social reform.

NONVIOLENT NON-COOPERATION

The programme of "nonviolent noncooperation" included the boycott of councils, courts and schools, set up by the British and of all foreign cloth. With some naivete Gandhi claimed that his movement was not unconstitutional: In his dictionary, constitutional and moral were synonymous terms. The British saw that the success of "noncooperation" would paralyse their administration. Lord Chelmsford, the Viceroy, tried to kill with ridicule "the most foolish of all foolish schemes", which would "bring ruin to those who had any stake in the country". A number of eminent "moderate" politicians joined official critics in underlining the risks of mass noncooperation as proposed by Gandhi.

That a political programme had no chance of success without an adequate organization to implement it, Gandhi had realized at the age of twenty-five, when he had founded the Natal Indian Congress to fight for the rights of Indians in Natal. The Indian National Congress, had, therefore, to be refashioned, if it was to prove an efficient instrument of nonviolent noncooperation. Gandhi saw that what the country needed was not a forum for an annual pageant and feast of oratory, but a militant organization in touch with the masses. Under the new constitution, the Congress was given a broad-based pyramidal structure by formation of village, taluka, district and provincial committees, with the All India Congress Committee and the Working Committee at the apex. The Congress was thus reorganized not only on a more representative basis, but in such a way that it could function efficiently between its annual sessions. It ceased to be a preserve of the upper and middle classes; its doors were opened to the masses in the small towns and villages whose political consciousness Gandhi himself was quickening.

Gandhi was swept to the top of Indian politics in 1919-20 because he had caught the imagination of the people. He was loved and respected as the Mahatma, the great soul; with voluntary poverty, simplicity, humility and saintliness, he seemed a rishi (sage) of old who had stepped from the pages of an ancient epic to bring about the liberation of his country. Nay, to millions he was the incarnation of God. It was not only for his message that people came to him, but for the merit of seeing him. The sacred sight of the Mahatma-his darshan-was almost equivalent to a pilgrimage to holy Benares. The unthinking adoration of the multitude sometimes made Gandhi feel sick. "The woes of the Mahatma", he wrote, "are known only to the Mahatma". But this adoration was the mainspring from which was drawn the immense influence he exercised over Indian public life.

Gandhi had struck some of the inner chords of Indian humanity; his appeal for courage and sacrifice evoked a ready response because he was himself the epitome of these qualities. It was because he was, to use Churchill's epithet, a "naked fakir", because his life was one of austerity and self-sacrifice that a great emotional bond grew between him and the Indian people. The number of such "fakirs" was to multiply fast. Among those who gave up their lucrative careers and queued up for prison under Gandhi's leadership were Motilal Nehru, Rajendra Prasad, C.R. Das, Vallabhbhai Patel, and C. Rajagopalachari. Life acquired a new meaning for them. Abbas Tyabji, a former Chief Justice of Baroda, wrote from a village that he was feeling twenty years younger. "God?" he exclaimed, "what an experience ! We have so much love and affection for the common folk to whom it is now an honour to belong. It is the fakir's dress that has broken down all barriers." It is of this period that Jawaharlal Nehru has written in his autobiography that the movement absorbed him so wholly that he "gave up all other associations and contacts, old friends, books, even newspapers except in so far as they dealt with the work in hand.... I almost forgot my family, my wife, my daughter."

From the autumn of 1920, the noncooperation movement gathered momentum. The attitude of the Government at first was one of caution. It was reluctant to launch a drastic repression, as it did not want to alienate moderate

Indian opinion. Soon after his arrival in India in April, 1921, Lord Reading, the new Viceroy, met Gandhi. In a private letter to his son, the Viceroy confessed to a feeling of excitement, almost a thrill, in meeting his unusual visitor and described his religious and moral views as admirable, though he found it difficult to understand his practice of them in politics.

Throughout 1921, the tension between the Congress and the Government was steadily mounting. There was no meeting of minds between Gandhi and Reading. The Ali Brothers, the principal leaders of the Khilafat, were arrested in September 1921 on a charge of inciting the army to disloyalty; their offence was repeated by a number of Indian leaders including Gandhi. This was a challenge which was difficult for the Government not to accept. The official optimism that the movement would melt away by internal differences or popular apathy proved to be misplaced. Nearly thirty thousand non-cooperators were arrested.

The Government was reluctant to touch Gandhi until a favourable opportunity came. Indeed as late as December 1921, Lord Reading seemed willing to hold a round table conference with Gandhi and other Indian leaders to reach an understanding and to avoid unseemly scenes during the visit to India of the Prince of Wales. Lord Reading was, however, hardly in a position to make any substantial political concessions. Meanwhile, Gandhi was under increasing pressure from his adherents to launch a civil disobedience campaign. The Ahmedabad Congress in December 1921 invested him with authority to launch a mass movement. Mass civil disobedience was, in the words of Gandhi, "an earthquake, a sort of general upheaval on the political plane-the Government ceases to function... the police stations, the courts, offices, etc., all cease to be Government property and shall be taken charge of by the people." He proposed to proceed cautiously. His plan was to launch civil disobedience in one district; if it succeeded he proposed to extend it to the adjacent districts, and so on, until the whole of India was liberated. But he gave a clear warning that if violence broke out in any form in any part of the country, the movement would lose its character as a movement of peace, "even as a lute would begin to emit notes of discord the moment a single string snaps."

A riot which disfigured Bombay during the visit of Prince of Wales in November 1921 had led Gandhi to postpone civil disobedience. Nevertheless, two months later, under growing pressure from his colleagues, he decided to launch a no-tax campaign in Bardoli taluka in Gujarat. He communicated the step he contemplated, with his reasons for it, in a letter to the Viceroy. This was taken by the Government of India as an ultimatum. A head-on collision between the Government on the one hand and the nationalist forces on the other seemed imminent. Gandhi's letter to the Viceroy was dated February 1,1922. Three days later, there was a clash between a procession and the police at Chauri Chaura, a small village in the United Province, in which the police station was set on fire and 22 policemen were killed.

Gandhi viewed the Chauri Chaura tragedy as a red signal, a warning that the atmosphere in the country was too explosive for a mass movement. He decided to retrace his steps, to cancel the plans for civil disobedience in Bardoli, to suspend the aggressive part of the noncooperation campaign, and to shift the emphasis to the 'constructive' programme of hand-spinning, communal unity, abolition of untouchability, etc. His action shocked and bewildered his closest colleagues. Their reaction is best expressed in Romain Rolland's words: "It was dangerous to assemble all the forces of a nation and to hold the nation panting before a prescribed movement, to lift one's arm to give the final command, then at the last moment, let one's arm drop and thrice call a halt just as the formidable machinery has been set in motion. One risks ruining the brakes and paralysing the impetus." The Viceroy, Lord Reading, cheerfully confided to his son that Gandhi "had pretty well run himself to the last ditch as a politician by extraordinary manifestation in the last month or six weeks before his arrest".

CONGRESS LEADER

Azad became an inspiring personality in the field of politics. Azad became an important national leader, and served on the Congress Working Committee and in the offices of general secretary and president many times. The political environment in India re-energised in 1928 with nationalist outrage against the Simon Commission appointed to propose constitutional reforms. The commission included no Indian members and did not even consult Indian leaders and experts. In response, the Congress and other political parties appointed a commission under Motilal Nehru to propose constitutional reforms from Indian opinions. In 1928, Azad endorsed the Nehru Report, which was criticised by the Ali brothers and Muslim League politician Muhammad Ali Jinnah. Azad endorsed the ending of separate electorates based on religion, and called for an independent India to be committed to secularism. At the 1928 Congress session in Guwahati, Azad endorsed Gandhi's call for dominion status for India within a year. If not granted, the Congress would adopt the goal of complete political independence for India. Despite his affinity for Gandhi, Azad also drew close to the young radical leaders Jawaharlal Nehru and Subhash Bose, who had criticised the delay in demanding full independence. Azad developed a close friendship with Nehru and began espousing socialism as the means to fight inequality, poverty and other national challenges. Azad decided the name of Muslim political party Majlis-e-Ahrar-ul-Islam. He was also a friend of Syed Ata Ullah Shah Bukhari, founder of All India Majlis-e-Ahrar. When Gandhi embarked on the Dandi Salt March that inaugurated the Salt Satyagraha in 1930, Azad organised and led the nationalist raid, albeit non-violent on the Dharasana salt works to protest the salt tax and restriction of its production and sale. The biggest nationalist upheaval in a decade, Azad was imprisoned along with millions of people, and would frequently be jailed from 1930 to 1934 for long periods of time. Following the Gandhi-Irwin Pact in 1931, Azad was amongst millions of political prisoners released. When elections were called under the Government of India Act 1935, Azad was appointed to organise the Congress election campaign, raising funds, selecting candidates and organising volunteers and rallies across India. Azad had criticised the Act for including a high proportion of un-elected members in the central legislature, and did not himself contest a seat. He again declined to contest elections in 1937, and helped head the party's efforts to organise elections and preserve co-ordination and unity amongst the Congress governments elected in different provinces.

At the 1936 Congress session in Lucknow, Azad was drawn into a dispute with Sardar Vallabhbhai Patel, Dr. Rajendra Prasad and Chakravarthi Rajagopalachari regarding the espousal of socialism as the Congress goal. Azad had backed the election of Nehru as Congress president, and supported the resolution endorsing socialism. In doing so, he aligned with Congress socialists like Nehru, Subhash Bose and Jayaprakash Narayan. Azad also supported Nehru's re-election in 1937, at the consternation of many conservative Congressmen. Azad supported dialogue with Jinnah and the Muslim League between 1935 and 1937 over a Congress-League coalition and broader political co-operation. Less inclined to brand the League as obstructive, Azad nevertheless joined the Congress's vehement rejection of Jinnah's demand that the League be seen exclusively as the representative of Indian Muslims.

QUIT INDIA

In 1938, Azad served as an intermediary between the supporters of and the Congress faction led by Congress president Subhash Bose, who criticised Gandhi for not launching another rebellion against the British and sought to move the Congress away from Gandhi's leadership. Azad stood by Gandhi with most other Congress leaders, but reluctantly endorsed the Congress's exit from the assemblies in 1939 following the inclusion of India in World War II. Nationalists were infuriated that Viceroy Lord Linlithgow had entered India into the war without consulting national leaders. Although willing to support the British effort in return for independence, Azad sided with Gandhi when the British ignored the Congress overtures. Azad's criticism of Jinnah and the League intensified as Jinnah called Congress rule in the provinces as "Hindu Raj", calling the resignation of the Congress ministries as a "Day of Deliverance" for Muslims. Jinnah and the League's separatist agenda was gaining popular support amongst Muslims. Muslim religious and political leaders criticised Azad as being too close to the Congress and placing politics before Muslim welfare. As the Muslim League adopted a resolution calling for a separate Muslim state (Pakistan) in its session in Lahore in 1940, Azad was elected Congress president in its session in Ramgarh. Speaking vehemently against Jinnah's *Two-Nation Theory*—the notion that Hindus and Muslims were distinct nations—Azad lambasted religious separatism and exhorted all Muslims to preserve a united India, as all Hindus and Muslims were Indians who shared deep bonds of brotherhood and nationhood. In his presidential address, Azad said:

"... Full eleven centuries have passed by since then. Islam has now as great a claim on the soil of India as Hinduism. If Hinduism has been the religion of the people here for several thousands of years Islam also has been their religion for a thousand years. Just as a Hindu can say with pride that he is an Indian and follows Hinduism, so also we can say with equal pride that we are Indians and follow Islam. I shall enlarge this orbit still further. The Indian Christian is equally entitled to say with pride that he is an Indian and is following a religion of India, namely Christianity."

In face of increasing popular disenchantment with the British across India, Gandhi and Patel advocated an all-out rebellion demanding immediate independence. The situation had grown precarious as the Japanese conquered Burma and approached India's borders, which left Indians insecure but resentful of the British inability to protect India. Azad was wary and sceptical of the idea, aware that India's Muslims were increasingly looking to Jinnah and had supported the war. Feeling that a struggle would not force a British exit, Azad and Nehru warned that such a campaign would divide India and make the war situation even more precarious. Intensive and emotional debates took place between Azad, Nehru, Gandhi and Patel in the Congress Working Committee's meetings in May and June 1942. In the end, Azad became convinced that decisive action in one form or another had to be taken, as the Congress had to provide leadership to India's people and would lose its standing if it did not.

Supporting the call for the British to "Quit India", Azad began exhorting thousands of people in rallies across the nation to prepare for a definitive, all-out struggle. As Congress president, Azad travelled across India and met with local and provincial Congress leaders and grass-roots activists, delivering speeches and planning the rebellion. Despite their previous differences, Azad worked closely with Patel and Dr. Rajendra Prasad to make the rebellion as effective as possible. On 7 August 1942 at the Gowalia Tank in Mumbai, Congress president Azad inaugurated the struggle with a vociferous speech exhorting Indians into action.

Just two days later, the British arrested Azad and the entire Congress leadership. While Gandhi was incarcerated at the Aga Khan Palace in Pune, Azad and the Congress Working Committee were imprisoned at a fort in Ahmednagar, where they would remain under isolation and intense security for nearly four years. Outside news and communication had been largely prohibited and completely censored. Although frustrated at their incarceration and isolation, Azad and his companions attested to feeling a deep satisfaction at having done their duty to their country and people.

Azad occupied the time playing bridge and acting as the referee in tennis matches played by his colleagues. In the early mornings, Azad began working on his classic Urdu work, the *Ghubhar-i-Khatir*. Sharing daily chores, Azad also taught the Persian and Urdu languages, as well as Indian and world history to several of his companions. The leaders would generally avoid talking of politics, unwilling to cause any arguments that could exacerbate the pain of their imprisonment. However, each year on 26 January, which was then considered *Poorna Swaraj* (Complete Independence) Day, the leaders would gather to remember their cause and pray together. Azad, Nehru and Patel would briefly speak about the nation and the future. Azad and Nehru proposed an initiative to forge an agreement with the British in 1943. Arguing that the rebellion had been mistimed, Azad attempted to convince his colleagues that the Congress should agree to negotiate with the British and call for the suspension of disobedience if the British agreed to transfer power. Although his proposal was overwhelmingly rejected, Azad and a few others agreed that Gandhi and the Congress had not done enough. When they learnt of Gandhi holding talks with Jinnah in Mumbai in 1944, Azad criticised Gandhi's move as counter-productive and ill-advised.

PARTITION OF INDIA

With the end of the war, the British agreed to transfer power to Indian hands. All political prisoners were released in 1946 and Azad led the Congress in the elections for the new Constituent Assembly of India, which would draft India's constitution. He headed the delegation to negotiate with the British

Cabinet Mission, in his sixth year as Congress president. While attacking Jinnah's demand for Pakistan and the mission's proposal of 16 June 1946 that envisaged the partition of India, Azad became a strong proponent of the mission's earlier proposal of 16 May. The proposal advocated a federal system with a limited central government and autonomy for the provinces. The central government would have Defence, Foreign Affairs and Communication while the provinces would win all other subjects unless they voluntarily relinquished selected subjects to the Central Government. Additionally, the proposal called for the "grouping" of provinces on religious lines, which would informally band together the Muslim-majority province in the West as Group B, Muslim-majority provinces of Bengal and Assam as Group C and the rest of India as Group A. While Gandhi and others expressed scepticism of this clause, Azad argued that Jinnah's demand for Pakistan would be buried and the concerns of the Muslim community would be assuaged. Under Azad and Patel's backing, the Working Committee approved the resolution against Gandhi's advice. Azad also managed to win Jinnah's agreement to the proposal citing the greater good of all Indian Muslims.

Azad had been the Congress president since 1939, so he volunteered to resign in 1946. He nominated Nehru, who replaced him as Congress president and led the Congress into the interim government. Azad was appointed to head the Department of Education. However, Jinnah's *Direct Action Day* agitation for Pakistan, launched on 16 August sparked communal violence across India. Thousands of people were killed as Azad travelled across Bengal and Bihar to calm the tensions and heal relations between Muslims and Hindus. Despite Azad's call for Hindu-Muslim unity, Jinnah's popularity amongst Muslims soared and the League entered a coalition with the Congress in December, but continued to boycott the constituent assembly. Later in his autobiography, Azad indicated Patel having become more pro-partition than the Muslim League, largely due to the League's not co-operating with the Congress in the provisional government on any issue.

Azad had grown increasingly hostile to Jinnah, who had described him as the "Muslim Lord Haw-Haw" and a "Congress Showboy." Muslim League politicians accused Azad of allowing Muslims to be culturally and politically dominated by the Hindu community. Azad continued to proclaim his faith in Hindu-Muslim unity:

"I am proud of being an Indian. I am part of the indivisible unity that is Indian nationality. I am indispensable to this noble edifice and without me this splendid structure is incomplete. I am an essential element, which has gone to build India. I can never surrender this claim."

Amidst more incidences of violence in early 1947, the Congress-League coalition struggled to function. The provinces of Bengal and Punjab were to be partitioned on religious lines, and on 3 June 1947 the British announced a proposal to partition India on religious lines, with the princely states free to choose between either dominion. The proposal was hotly debated in the All India Congress Committee, with Muslim leaders Saifuddin Kitchlew and Khan Abdul Ghaffar Khan expressing fierce opposition. Azad privately discussed the proposal with Gandhi, Patel and Nehru, but despite his opposition was unable to deny the popularity of the League and the unworkability of any coalition with the League. Faced with the serious possibility of a civil war, Azad abstained from voting on the resolution, remaining silent and not speaking throughout the AICC session, which ultimately approved the plan.

POST-INDEPENDENCE

India's partition and independence on 15 August 1947 brought with it a scourge of violence that swept the Punjab, Bengal, Bihar, Delhi and many other parts of India. Millions of Hindus and Sikhs fled the newly created Pakistan for India, and millions of Muslims fled for West Pakistan and East Pakistan, created out of East Bengal. Violence claimed the lives of an estimated one million people. Azad took up responsibility for the safety of Muslims in India, touring affected areas in Bengal, Bihar, Assam and the Punjab, guiding the organisation of refugee camps, supplies and security.

Azad gave speeches to large crowds encouraging peace and calm in the border areas and encouraging Muslims across the country to remain in India and not fear for their safety and security. Focusing on bringing the capital of Delhi back to peace, Azad organised security and relief efforts, but was drawn into a dispute with the Deputy prime minister and Home Minister Sardar Vallabhbhai Patel when he demanded the dismissal of Delhi's police commissioner, who was a Sikh accused by Muslims of overlooking attacks and neglecting their safety. Patel argued that the commissioner was not biased, and if his dismissal was forced it would provoke anger amongst Hindus and Sikhs and divide the city police. In Cabinet meetings and discussions with Gandhi, Patel and Azad clashed over security issues in Delhi and Punjab, as well as the allocation of resources for relief and rehabilitation. Patel opposed Azad and Nehru's proposal to reserve the houses vacated by Muslims who had departed for Pakistan for Muslims in India displaced by the violence. Patel argued that a secular government could not offer preferential treatment for any religious community, while Azad remained anxious to assure the rehabilitation of Muslims in India, secularism, religious freedom and equality for all Indians. He supported provisions for Muslim citizens to make avail of Muslim personal law in courts.

Azad remained a close confidante, supporter and advisor to prime minister Nehru, and played an important role in framing national policies. Azad masterminded the creation of national programmes of school and college construction and spreading the enrolment of children and young adults into schools, to promote universal primary education. Elected to the lower house of the Indian Parliament, the Lok Sabha in 1952 and again in 1957, Azad supported Nehru's socialist economic and industrial policies, as well as the advancing social rights and economic opportunities for women and underprivileged Indians. In 1956, he served as president of the UNESCO General Conference held in Delhi. Azad spent the final years of his life focusing on writing his book *India Wins Freedom*, an exhaustive account of India's freedom struggle and its leaders, which was published in 1957.

As India's first Minister of Education, he emphasised on educating the rural poor and girls. As Chairman of the Central Advisory Board of Education, he gave thrust to adult literacy, universal primary education, free and compulsory for all children up to the age of 14, girls *education, and diversification of secondary education and vocational training.* Addressing the conference on All India Education on 16 January 1948, Maulana Azad emphasised,

We must not for a moment forget, it is a birthright of every individual to receive at least the basic education without which he cannot fully discharge his duties as a citizen.

He oversaw the setting up of the Central Institute of Education, Delhi, which later became the Department of Education of the University of Delhi as "a research centre for solving new educational problems of the country". Under his leadership, the Ministry of Education established the first Indian Institute of Technology in 1951 and the University Grants Commission in 1953., He also laid emphasis on the development of the Indian Institute of Science, Bangalore and the Faculty of Technology of the Delhi University. He foresaw a great future in the IITs for India:

I have no doubt that the establishment of this Institute will form a landmark in the progress of higher technological education and research in the country.

Criticism

During his life and in contemporary times, Maulana Azad has been criticised for not doing enough to prevent the partition of India although he was committed to united India till his last attempt. He was condemned by the advocates of Pakistan, especially Muslim League.

LEGACY AND INFLUENCE

Azad is remembered as one of the leading Indian nationalists of his time. His firm belief in Hindu-Muslim unity earned him the respect of the Hindu community and he still remains one of the most important symbols of communal harmony in modern India. His work for education and social uplift in India made him an important influence in guiding India's economic and social development.

The Ministry of Minority Affairs of the central Government of India set up the Maulana Azad Education Foundation in 1989 on the occasion of his birth centenary to promote education amongst educationally backward sections of the Society. The Ministry also provides the Maulana Abul Kalam Azad National Fellowship, an integrated five-year fellowship in the form of financial assistance to students from minority communities to pursue higher studies such as M. Phil and PhD

Numerous institutions across India have also been named in his honour. Some of them are the Maulana Azad Medical College in New Delhi, the Maulana Azad National Institute of Technology in Bhopal, the Maulana Azad National Urdu University in Hyderabad, Maulana Azad Centre for Elementary and Social Education (MACESE Delhi University), the Maulana Azad College, Maulana Abul Kalam Azad Institute of Asian Studies, and Maulana Abul Kalam Azad University of Technology, in Kolkata, Bab - e - Maulana Abul Kalam Azad (Gate No. 7), Jamia Millia Islamia, A Central (Minority) University in New Delhi, the Maulana Azad library in the Aligarh Muslim University in Aligarh and Maulana Azad Stadium in Jammu. His home housed the Maulana Abul Kalam Azad Institute of Asian Studies earlier, and is now the Maulana Azad Museum.

He is celebrated as one of the founders and greatest patrons of the Jamia Millia Islamia. Azad's tomb is located next to the Jama Masjid in Delhi. In recent years great concern has been expressed by many in India over the poor maintenance of the tomb. On 16 November 2005 the Delhi High Court ordered that the tomb of Maulana Azad in New Delhi be renovated and restored as a major national monument. Azad's tomb is a major landmark and receives large numbers of visitors annually.

Jawaharlal Nehru referred to him as *Mir-i- Karawan* (the caravan leader), "a very brave and gallant gentleman, a finished product of the culture that, in these days, pertains to few".Mahatma Gandhi remarked about Azad by counting him as "a person of the calibre of Plato, Aristotle and Pythagorus". Azad was portrayed by actor Virendra Razdan in the 1982 biographical film,

Gandhi, directed by Richard Attenborough. His birthday, 11 November is celebrated as National Education Day in India.

MAULANA AND HIS PHILOSOPHY

National Education Day could best be utilised to analyse the causes that have resulted in the dilution of quality and skill acquisition. After the partition of India, the expectation from the ruling dispensation was of strict adherence to the principles and guidelines given by Mahatma Gandhi that could alone ensure respect for diversity and social and religious cohesion.

Universalising education was the master key. India needed an education that was 'rooted to its culture and committed to progress'. Great stalwarts around Mahatma Gandhi realised the criticality of ensuring the best features of Indian tradition: Equal respect for all religions, beliefs and diverse practices gets its traditional due. Muslims, who refused to migrate to the promised paradise called Pakistan, loved India and its tradition of unity in diversity. Maulana Abul Kalam Azad, one of the stalwarts of the freedom struggle and a great scholar of international repute in matters of religions and spirituality, elaborates it: "The acceptance of unity in diversity has been (India's) motto throughout the ages. The essence of this principle is a large and wide-hearted

toleration in which differences are recognised and given their due. The Indian genius has always recognised that truth as many faces and conflict and hatred have arisen because people claim a monopoly of truth and virtue." One wonders why India has not paid due attention to the perception of the Maulana who had, in his own way, strived hard to prepare people who understood the Indian diversity in its full glory and glare. Maulana's concern to see India as a nation of people proud of their heritage and, simultaneously, also of their readiness to accept and acknowledge all that contributes to the growth and well-being of India and its people.

There are occasions when, one single sentence or a small statement could project the total personality of a visionary leader. Here is an example from his presidential address delivered in the 1940 annual session of the Indian National Congress: "I am a part of this indivisible unity that is Indian nationality. I am indispensible to the noble edifice and without me, this splendid structure of India is incomplete. I am an essential element which has gone to build India. I can never surrender this claim." Sadly enough, India was partitioned but Maulana remained steadfast in his views. He became the first Education Minister of India. Apart from the formal celebrations of the National Education Day every year on November 11, it would be prudent that the contemporary relevance of Maulana's views is thoroughly discussed and incisively debated amongst the policy makers and implementers. Education, in its present shape, is certainly not 'bringing out the best from the body, mind and spirit'!

During the last over-six decades, India has much to project as its achievements are under progress and development. This includes the international chorus about India being a young nation that could provide skilled manpower to the nations facing 'ageing societies'! We have a far-more literate, modern and forward-looking India today than in Maulana's times. There is the other side as well: We have far more violence, bigotry, distrust and unrest in the country today than fifty years ago. The dream — post-independence — was that things would just be the other way round: More peace, intense social cohesion, ever-increasing religious harmony, peace, mutual trust and equal distribution of the fruits of progress and development. Obviously, something has gone wrong during the intervening period. It deserves to be analysed and pragmatic remedial steps should be initiated to redress the situation.

Did Maulana anticipate the negative developments of tomorrow in his times? A couple of instances would indicate that he was a visionary scholar who understood and contributed effectively in the freedom struggle and in the much-needed transformation towards a fully literate India comprising of a just and value-based society. Addressing a meeting of the vice-chancellors of Indian universities in Delhi on November 3, 1951, Maulana said: "The basis of our life is still agriculture and a vast majority of our people depend on agriculture for their livelihood....Our agriculture graduates are fit for almost everything except becoming agriculturists themselves." Even in times of globalisation, vast number of Indians remain dependent on agriculture, which has continuously remained ignored. The growth rate in this sector is abysmally low.

The result: Young persons are migrating to cities and towns and often leading a far miserable life which they could have improved upon if agricultural operations were given the much needed support. He had suggested a way out to overcome the deficiency by giving an extra bias to agriculture in school education and introducing agricultural education in the universities: "In addition, schools and colleges in the rural and semi-rural areas must encourage all students — whatever may be their subjects of study — to devote a part of their normal scholastic routine to work on land. For schools and colleges in cities and towns, I would suggest their adoption of villages where students may participate in a programme of complete reconstruction of village life."

The Maulana gave a great and scholarly speech while inaugurating the symposium on the Concept of Man and Philosophy of Education in East and West, New Delhi, December 13, 1951: "The Greek approached the concept of man from an external point of view. Hence we find that, from the early times, Greek philosophy devotes far greater attention to what man does than what man is."

REMEMBERING MAULANA ABUL KALAM AZAD

Maulana Abul Kalam Azad's real name was Abul Kalam Ghulam Muhiyuddin. He was popularly known as Maulana Azad. Maulana Abul Kalam Azad was one of the foremost leaders of Indian freedom struggle. He was also a renowned scholar, and poet. Maulana Abul Kalam Azad was well versed in many languages viz. Arabic, English, Urdu, Hindi, Persian and Bengali. Maulana Abul Kalam Azad was a brilliand debater, as indicated by his name, Abul Kalam, which literally means "Lord of dialogue" He adopted the pen name Azad as a mark of his mental emancipation from a narrow view of religion and life.

Maulana Abul Kalam Azad was born on November 11, 1888 in Mecca. His forefathers came from Herat (a city Afghanistan) in Babar's days. Azad was a descendent of a lineage of learned Muslim scholars, or maulanas. His mother was an Arab and the daughter of Sheikh Mohammad Zaher Watri and his father, Maulana Khairuddin, was a Bengali Muslim of Afghan origins. Khairuddin left India during tile Sepoy Mutiny and proceeded to Mecca and settled there. He came back to Calcutta with his family in 1890.

Because of his orthodox family background Azad had to pursue traditional Islamic education. He was taught at home, first by his father and later by appointed teachers who were eminent in their respective fields. Azad learned Arabic and Persian first and then philosophy, geometry, mathematics and algebra. He also learnt (English, world history, and politics through self study.

Azad was trained and educated to become a clergyman, He wrote many works, reinterpreting the holy Quran. His erudition let him to repudiate Taqliq or the tradition of conformity and accept the principle of Tajdid or innovation. He developed interest in the pan¬ Islamic doctrines of Jamaluddin Afghani and the Aligarh thought of Sir Syed Ahmed Khan.

Imbued with the pan-Islamic spirit, he visited Afghanistan, Iraq, Egypt, Syria and Turkey. In Iraq he met the exiled revolutionaries who were fighting to establish a constitutional government in Iran. In Egypt he met Shaikh Muhammad Abduh and Saeed Pasha and other revolutionary activists of the Arab world. He had a first hand knowledge of the ideals and spirit of the young Turks in Constantinople. All these contacts metamorphosed him into a nationalist revolutionary.

On his return from abroad; Azad met two leading revolutionaries of Bengal- Aurobinto Ghosh and Sri Shyam Shundar Chakravarty,-and joined the revolutionary movement against British rule. Azad found that the revolutionary activities were restricted to Bengal and Bihar. Within two years, Maulana Abul Kalam Azad helped set up secret revolutionary centers all over north India and Bombay. During that time most of his revolutionaries were anti-Muslim because they felt that the British government was using the Muslim community against India's freedom struggle. Maulana Abul Kalam Azad tried to convince his colleagues to shed their hostility towards Muslims.

In 1912, Maulana Abul Kalam Azad started a weekly journal in Urdu called Al-Hilal to increase the revolutionary recruits amongst the Muslims. Al-Hilal played an important role in forging Hindu-Muslim unity after the bad blood created between the two communities in the aftermath of Morley-Minto reforms. Al-Hilal became a revolutionary mouthpiece ventilating extremist views. 'The government regarded Al- Hilal as propagator of secessionist views and banned it in 1914. Maulana Abul Kalam Azad then started another weekly called Al-Balagh with the same mission of propagating Indian nationalism and revolutionary ideas based on Hindu-Muslim unity. In 1916, the government banned this paper too and expelled Maulana Abul Kalam Azad from Calcutta and internet him at Ranchi from where he was released after the First World War 1920.

After his release, Azad roused the Muslim community through the Khilafat Movement. The aim of the movement was to re-instate the Khalifa as the head of British captured Turkey. Maulana Abul Kalam Azad supporded Non-Cooperation Movement started by Gandhiji and entered Indian National Congress in 1920. He was elected as the president of the special session of the Congress in Delhi (1923). Maulana Azad was again arrested in 1930 for violation of the salt laws as part of Gandhiji's Salt Satyagraha. He was put in Meerut jail for a year and a half. Maulana Abul Kalam Azad became the president of Congress in 1940 (Ramgarh) and remained in the post till 1946. He was a staunch opponent of partition and supported a confederation of autonomous provinces with their own constitutions but common defense and economy. Partition hurt him great(y ant shattered his dream of an unified nation where Hindus and Muslims can co-exist and prosper together.

Maulana Abul Kalam Azad served as the Minister of Education (the first education minister in independent India) in Pandit Jawaharlal Nehru's cabinet from 1947 to 1958. He died of a stroke on February 22, 1958. For his invaluable contribution to the nation, Maulana Abul Kalam Azad was posthumously awarded India's highest civilian honour, Bharat Ratna in 1992.

2

Maulana Azad : A Revolutionary Journalist

These were the words of Maulana Abul Kalam Azad at the Presidential Address of the Congress Session in 1923. The analogy and juxtaposition of Swaraj and inter-communal harmony that Maulana Azad emphasized then is equally pertinent today. Maulana Azad, as it can be inferred from his above quoted statement, was a strong campaigner of peace and a vociferous freedom fighter. He used the power of his writings and public orations to create a national awakening among the masses. We shall briefly examine some of his prominent journalistic contributions which served as milestones in the Indian freedom struggle.

Born on November 11, 1888 in a deeply orthodox Muslim family, Maulana Azad had his initial formal education in Arabic, Persian and Urdu with theological orientation. He also learnt English on his own. But Maulana Azad had a natural inclination for writing and this resulted in the miraculous start of the monthly "Nairang-e-Alam" in 1899 at Calcutta when he was hardly eleven years old. The periodical carried the poetical collection of the contemporary poets. This was followed by the launch of the weekly "Al-Misbah" in 1900 which carried articles on contemporary issues.

But the genesis of Maulana Abul Kalam Azad's revolutionary journalism was in 1908. This was the time when he undertook an extensive visit of Egypt, Turkey, Syria and France. In Egypt, Maulana Azad came into contact with the followers of Mustafa Kemal Pasha who were publishing a weekly from Cairo. In Turkey, Maulana Azad met the leaders of the Young Turks Movement. The contacts between Maulana Azad and the leaders of Movement were further cemented by the exchange of letters between them which continued years after his return to India. Maulana Azad also interacted with the Iranian revolutionaries and famous French Orientalist Louis Massignon in Iraq. These contacts reaffirmed Maulana Azad's belief that Muslims in India should join their fellow countrymen against the British in the Freedom Struggle. He was of the view that the Freedom Movement against the British is the combined responsibility of all communities and hence it should be carried unitedly. With these thoughts in his mind, Maulana Azad started the "Al-Hilal" Press and a weekly by the same name.

The "Al-Hilal" weekly was a landmark in the history of the press in India. Its circulation figures rose to 26,000 copies. Further, even back issues of this weekly had to be republished as every new subscriber wanted to hold all copies of "Al-Hilal".

The message of patriotism and nationalism coupled with religious fervor inherent in the weekly gained wide acceptance among the masses. But these developments disturbed the British Government. In 1914, a security of two thousand rupees was imposed on "Al-Hilal" under the Press Act. When Maulana Azad deposited this amount, it was confiscated and a further security of rupees ten thousand was imposed. When these punitive measures failed to tone down the anti-establishment stance of the periodical, the government banned "Al-Hilal" and confiscated its press in 1915. Maulana Azad was not discouraged by this move.

1915, barely five months after the ban on "Al-Hilal", Maulana Azad started the publication of the "Al-Balagh" weekly. It was similar in its content to "Al-Hilal". The British realized that the provisions of the Press Act are not enough to counter the onslaught of Maulana Azad's writings. Hence the Maulana Azad was asked to leave Calcutta after the Defence of India Provisions were invoked against him in 1916. Punjab, U.P., Delhi and Bombay also prohibited his entry under the same law. Bihar was the only state in which he could move without any hindrance. But the moment he reached Ranchi he was kept under house arrest. This detention continued till December 31, 1919. He was released on January 1, 1920.

In 1921 Maulana Azad started a weekly named "Paigham". But it was banned in December 1921 and he arrested. Maulana Azad's detention continued till January 1, 1921. In 1927, Maulana Azad restarted the publication of "Al-Hilal" and this weekly continued to be published till the end of the year.

Apart from these publications, Maulana Azad was in the forefront in all the major movements for the independence like the Khilafat Movement (1919-23), the Non-Cooperation Movement (1920-22) the Civil Disobedience Movement (1930-32) and the Quit India Movement (1942). He was a strong advocate of undivided India and had the foresight to predict that the Urdu-speaking Muslims of India leaving for either East or West Pakistan will be marginalized by the local population. This has come true today when one looks at the plight of the "Mohajirs" in Pakistan and "Biharis" in Bangladesh.

After India became independent in 1947, Prime Minister Pandit Jawaharlal Nehru inducted Maulana Azad as Education Minister in his Cabinet. Under Maulana Azad's tenure, a number of measures were undertaken to promote primary and secondary education, scientific education, establishment of universities and promotion of avenues of research and higher studies.

On February 22, 1958 Maulana Abul Kalam Azad passed away. Pandit Jawaharlal Nehru described Maulana Azad as "a great man ' a man of luminaries, intelligence and intellect with an amazing capacity to pierce through a problem to its cause. The word "luminous" is perhaps the best word I can use about his mind. When we miss and when we part with such a companion, friend, colleague, comrade, leader and teacher, there is inevitably a tremendous void created in our life and activity."

The Government of India celebrates the Birth Anniversary of Maulana Abul Kalam Azad on November 11 every year as Education Day. Maulana Azad National Urdu University was established at Hyderabad by an Act of Parliament in 1998 for the promotion of Higher Education with Urdu as the medium of instruction. These steps can be described as fitting tributes by the nation to a person who had unchallenged credentials as a freedom fighter, revolutionary journalist, social reformer, champion of communal harmony and an unparalleled Education Minister.

MAULANA ABUL KALAM AZAD

Maulana Abul Kalam Azad was one of the most influential independence activists during India's freedom struggle. He was also a noted writer, poet and journalist. He was a prominent political leader of the Indian National Congress and was elected as Congress President in 1923 and 1940. Despite being a Muslim, Azad often stood against the radicalizing policies of other prominent Muslims leaders like Muhammad Ali Jinnah. Azad was the first education minister of independent India. Maulana Abul Kalam Azad was posthumously awarded 'Bharat Ratna', India's highest civilian honor, in 1992.

Early Life and Education

Maulana Abul Kalam Azad was born Abul Kalam Ghulam Muhiyuddin on November 11, 1888 in Mecca, Islam's main center of pilgrimage. His mother was the daughter of a rich Arabian Sheikh and his father, Maulana Khairuddin, was a Bengali Muslim of Afghan origin. His forefathers came to India during the reign of Mughal Emperor Babar, from Heart, Afghanistan. Azads were the descendent of eminent Ulama or scholars of Islam. In 1890, he returned to Calcutta (now Kolkata) along with the family.

Maulana Azad had his initial formal education in Arabic, Persian and Urdu with theological orientation and then philosophy, geometry, mathematics and algebra. He also learnt English language, world history, and politics on his own.

Maulana Azad had a natural inclination towards writing and this resulted in the start of the monthly magazine "Nairang-e-Alam" in 1899. He was eleven years old when his mother passed away. Two years later, at the age of thirteen, Azad was married to young Zuleikha Begum.

Early Revolutionary Activities

In Egypt, Azad came into contact with the followers of Mustafa Kemal Pasha who were publishing a weekly from Cairo. In Turkey, Maulana Azad met the leaders of the Young Turks Movement.

After his return to India from an extensive visit of Egypt, Turkey, Syria and France, Azad met prominent Hindu revolutionaries Sri Aurobindo Ghosh and Shyam Sundar Chakraborty. They helped in developing radical political views and he began to participate in the Indian nationalist movement. Azad fiercely criticized the Muslim politicians who were more inclined towards the communal issues without focusing on the national interest. He also rejected the theories of communal separatism advocated by the All India Muslim League.

Azad, inspired by the passion of Indian as well as foreign revolutionary leaders, started publishing a weekly called "Al-Hilal" in 1912. The weekly was a platform to attack the policies of the British Government and highlight the problems faced by the common Indians. The paper became so popular that its circulation figures went up to 26,000 copies. The unique message of patriotism and nationalism blended with religious commitment gained its acceptance among the masses. But these developments disturbed the British Government and in 1914, the British Government put a ban on the weekly. Unfazed by the move, Maulana Azad, few months later, launched a new weekly, called "Al-Balagh". Failed to put a prohibition on the writings of Maulana Azad, the British Government then finally decided to deport him off Calcutta in 1916. When Maulana Azad reached Bihar, he was arrested and put under house arrest. This detention continued till December 31, 1919. After his release on January 1, 1920, Azad returned to the political atmosphere and actively participated in the movement. In fact, he continued to write provocative articles against the British Government.

Pre-Independence Activities

As an activist demanding the reinstatement of the Caliph in Istanbul, Maulana Abul Kalam Azad came onboard with the Khilafat movement during 1920. He became involved with the Indian freedom struggle through the Non-cooperation movement initiated by Gandhi, of which the Khilafat issue was a big part of. He wholeheartedly advocated the principles of the non-cooperation movement and in the process became drawn to Gandhi and his philosophy. Although initially skeptical of Gandhi's proposal to launch an intensified drive against the British Raj demanding independence, he later joined the efforts. He travelled all over the country giving speeches and leading various programs of the movement.

He worked closely with Vallabhbahi Patel and Dr. Rajendra Prasad. On August 9, 1942, Maulana Azad was arrested along with most of the Congress leadership. Their incarceration lasted for four years and they were released in 1946.

During that time, the idea of an independent India had solidified and Maulana headed the Constituent Assembly Elections within Congress as well as led the negotiations with the British Cabinet mission to discuss the terms of independence. He vehemently opposed the idea of partition based on religion and was deeply hurt when the idea went forward to give rise to Pakistan.

Post-Independence Activities

During the violence that erupted following partition of India, Maulana Azad assured to take up the responsibility for the security of Muslims in India. Towards this, Azad toured the violence-affected regions of borders of Bengal, Assam, Punjab. He helped in establishing the refugee camps and ensured uninterrupted supply of food and other basic materials. It was reported that in the crucial Cabinet meetings both Sardar Vallabhbhai Patel and Maulana Azad clashed over the security measures in Delhi and the Punjab.

The role and contribution of Maulana Abul Kalam Azad could not be overlooked. He was appointed as India's first Minister for Education and inducted in the Constituent Assembly to draft India's constitution. Under Maulana Azad's tenure, a number of measures were undertaken to promote primary and secondary education, scientific education, establishment of universities and promotion of avenues of research and higher studies.

Association with the Indian National Congress

While extending his support to Mahatma Gandhi and non-cooperation movement, Maulana Azad joined the Indian National Congress in January 1920.

He presided over the special session of Congress in September 1923 and was said to be the youngest man elected as the President of the Congress.

Maulana Azad emerged as an important national leader of the Indian National Congress Party. He also served as a member of the Congress Working Committee (CWC) and in the offices of general secretary and president on numerous occasions. In 1928, Maulana Azad endorsed the Nehru Report, formulated by Motilal Nehru. Interestingly, the Motilal Nehru Report was severely criticized by a number of Muslim personalities involved with the freedom movement. As opposed to Muhammad Ali Jinnah, Azad also advocated for the ending of separate electorates based on religion and called for a single nation committed to secularism. In 1930, Maulana Azad was arrested for violation of the salt laws as part of Gandhiji's Salt Satyagraha. He was put in Meerut jail for a year and a half.

OPINION: MAULANA AZAD: AN EMINENT EDUCATIONIST

Maulana Mohiuddin Ahmad Abulkalam Azad was born on 11 November 1888, in Mecca. He was a great scholar, a freedom fighter, a revolutionary journalist, a leader and an advocate of secular and undivided India.

He had gained popularity by his journalism in his early age; however he remained away from active politics till the beginning of the twentieth century. But the partition of Bengal in 1905 compelled him to enter into active politics.

He considered the partition as an attack on the unity of Hindu-Muslim. Thus, he began his political career by opposing the partition of Bengal and ended it by opposing the partition of India. He joined the movement against Bengal partition with Arvind Ghosh and Shyam Sunder Chakarvarti. Since then he remained an active and enthusiastic leader of India till the last breath of his life in 1958.

He became the first education minister of independent India and held the post until his death. From 1952, he also assumed the charge of Ministry of National Resources and Scientific Research. Maulana, an eminent educationist, contributed to the laying of a strong foundation for education in India. He designed the education policy of the country. His firm belief in providing secular, liberal, modern and universal education is apparently relevant even today. It obviously continues to guide us for achieving education for all. The corner stone of his education policy was his conviction that democracy cannot function without the eradication of illiteracy. He realized that the introduction of adult franchise needed a national programme of mass education. He was of the view that citizens of free and independent India had to be different from the colonial subjects of a foreign empire.

So, he immediately set up a section of Social Education in his ministry to conduct the programme of mass education. On January 16, 1948, Maulana Azad, while addressing the conference of 'All India Education', emphasized, "We must not for a moment forget, it is a birth right of every individual to receive at least the basic education without which he cannot fully discharge his duties as a citizen."

In other words, he was convinced that education is a tool of social transformation. As chairman of the Central Advisory Board of Education, he gave thrust to adult literacy, universal primary education, free and compulsory education for all children up to the age of 14 and to girls education. He favored a diversified secondary education.

Here, it is worth noting that India has recently achieved a key vision of Maulana Azad in the name of 'The Right of Children to Free and Compulsory Education Act, 2009'. To fulfill his vision Indian government has also launched the 'Saakshat Bharat Programme' focusing on women's literacy. There is no doubt that he was a great educationist.

It was demonstrated in molding the educational system of the country in the immediate post-independence years. It was he who established the University Grants Commission (UGC), All India Council of Technical Education (AICTE) and the Indian Council for Cultural Relations (ICCR) which are now playing significant role in academics.

For the promotion of art, music and literature he came with the idea to establish three Academies: Sahitya Academy, Lalit Kala Academy and Sangeet Natak Academy. Azad assisted Jawaharlal Nehru in setting up the Indian Council of Scientific and Industrial Research (CSIR) and many a chain of Science Laboratories in India. As the Minister of Education he insisted that both the Union and States must share responsibility in the promotion of education. He appointed University Education Commission in 1948 and Secondary Education Commission in 1952.

It is interesting to know that such an eminent educationist never attended a formal educational institution. He was schooled at home, and was later self-taught. Yet, he is known as a great scholar.

Maulana Azad, first felt that there was a need for careful prioritization in planning. He first emphasized the universal primary education and then set out for secondary education. While Maulana envisioned a modern India built through strengthening higher and technical education, he also held the belief that along with training engineers and technicians for the development of industries, it is equally necessary to spread general education for raising the general level of economic activities in the country.

Maulana Azad was purely a secular leader. However, his definition of secularism was very different. He believed in multiculturalism and interfaith understanding. So, he advocated religious teaching in schools, not from a narrow sense but from a liberal and open perspective. He was of the view that the solution to the problems created by religious fanatics was not in rejecting religious instruction in elementary stages but in imparting sound and healthy religious education so that children in their formative stages would not be misguided to fanaticism and intolerance of other religions.

Text books and reading materials, especially history, geography and civics are very important for the promotion of national unity on the basis of rich diversity of cultures and belief. He advocated that cultural content of education and some knowledge and appreciation of the main tenets of all religions could elevate the mind and enrich the sprit. For him, true secularism calls for tolerance and sympathetic understanding of beliefs and cultures other than one's own.

Immediately after independence, in his speeches, he argued that our Five Year Plans is not for the production of more material wealth and resources but the creation of a new mind and a new character for which right education is more important than the development of agriculture, industries, trade or other projects. According to Maulana, education must contribute to the individual realizing his immense potential. On one occasion, he stressed the importance of seven values which contributed to the making of man and his society in pursuit of excellence. Those are truth, justice, enlightenment, co-operation and unity, courtesy, chivalry and humility.

Having said all, the question still remains unanswered whether we have acknowledged Maulana Azad's contributions to our nation or not. I would like to leave this question to my readers.

Dr. Syeda Hameed says, "It is ironic that the country neither recognizes Maulana Azad's contributions to the nation nor is it willing to work on the values the great leader had stood for."

In 2008, Indian government declared 11 November, the day of his birth, as the National Education Day. He has been posthumously awarded India's highest civilian honor, Bharat Ratna, in 1992. The eminent educationist and first education Minister of independent India died in 1958.

It is disheartening to know that unlike Raj Ghat, Shanti Van and Kisan Ghat, his soul rests in an ordinary place near Jama Masjid in Delhi.

ROLE OF JOURNALISM

Journalism had been the most supportive in coping with the pressures, and helping the community to adapt to emergent challenges. After 1857, it helped the Muslim community launch its campaigns for social reforms, modern education, political awakening, and female freedom, to enlist a few. It was just in around 1857 that some writings appeared about women's actual lives, when the first Urdu newspaper Jam-e-Jahan Numa was published from Calcutta in 1822. Delhi Urdu Akhabr was the first Urdu newspaper from Delhi (1836). In 1858, Muslims had lost all their newspapers except one. Awadh Akhbar came out in 1858, on weekly basis. Akhbar Scientific Society was started in 1866 by Sir Syed Ahmed Khan. Sir Syed in the sixth issue of Tahzib-ul-Akhlaq (the leader of reform journals, started 1870), wrote about the need to reform social customs, improve girls' education, and teach them handicraft. During the decade of 1870s, there emerged an inclination in the print culture to address women's issues along with other topics.

The challenge of educating women was very well taken up by the journals, which created a favourable atmosphere to overcome cultural, psychological and financial obstacles. Shaikh Abdullah before starting a girls' school, started a journal Khatun, edited by him, to mobilize the community resources for the cause of women education. It continued for about ten years (1904-14) and projected women's ideas and writings. It also tried to promote female education. Khatun also published Hali's famous poem Chup ki Dad for the same purpose. The campaign in Khatun resulted in creating Female Education Association, in around 1911. Two years later (1913), it led to the establishment of Ladies Conference in 1913. The Female Education Association promoted girls education by setting up new schools, and supporting needy female students. All this shows how reform and educational activities were realized through journalistic and associational strategies.

As the newly available technology of printing press had given a boost to reform efforts; journalism and publishing enterprise had taken up the cause of women's education on collaborative basis. The same press and group of persons were involved in bringing out journals and books. It was a profitable business as well. Small literate audience and large number of journals created an atmosphere of competition. When female education became a hotly debated topic, journals and publishers, taking benefit of the chance, tried to offer something marketable and appealing to different sections.

These magazines became a powerful mouthpiece of the forces of change, and they enjoyed widespread influence. They carried the reformatory contents in various forms, and their articles covered subjects ranging for politics, economics, culture, and literature. The magazines were mostly literary and reformatory before 1900, like Tahzib-ul-Akhlq and Moallim, but with the turn of century new experiments were made; new forms and new themes invited involvement of the readers in current debates. In 1903, Urdu-e- Mu'alla was started by Hasrat Mohani, which was a literary and political magazine. Some others with similar contents were Alnaazir, Zamana, Ma'araf, and Jamia. Urdu and Humayun were reporting current affairs and literature side by side. Undoubtedly, the social impact of these magazines was mostly because of their knowledge-oriented articles.

The popular journalism has to cater interests of the popular readership. For the just literate women of the 1860s onwards, it was mainly fiction, but due to dearth of printing facilities, journals could not reach many women. Moreover, only a very small number of women were literate, hence the need to present creative writing was intermingled with socio-political issues of the day. Literary magazines then became a mirror of life – engaged in creative, educational, and reformation-oriented writings – giving impetus to the process of consciousness-raising.

ROLE OF MUSLIM LEADERS IN JOURNALISM IN SUBCONTINENT

Sir Syed Ahmad Khan:

Sir Syed Ahmad Khan was a great Muslim reformer, educationists and politician of the Sub-continent. After the revolt against the British, when the position of the Muslims in the Sub-continent was quite pathetic and Muslims were going through a social and financial crisis, Sir Syed Ahmed Khan came to the forefront and created awareness amongst Muslims about the importance of education and a lifestyle which was closer to the British. Sir Syed Ahmed Khan made sure that the Muslims understood the importance of the modern education and science, so that they could compete with the Hindus and could claim their rights for the job opportunities and a better lifestyle.

Sir Syed started Aligarh Movement, which had a motto of promoting education amongst the Muslims after the revolt of 1857. He fought against the Hindu conspiracies against Urdu. Risala-dar-Asbab-i-Bhagawati-i-Hind, Ahkam-i-Ta'am-i-Ahl-i-Kitab and Loyal Mohammadans of India were some of his best works. He started various schools and colleges where English language was taught with Urdu and Persian. He founded a Scientific Society where he started the periodical which was first called Scientific Society Papers and later, the Aligarh Institute Gazette.

Sir Syed Ahmed Khan played a significant role in reshaping the public opinion amongst the Muslims. After 1857, Sir Syed had realized that it is very hard for Muslims to survive with the Hindus but still he was in favour of the

United India until the Urdu-Hindi controversy. Sir Syed Ahmed Khan would always be remembered in the history books as a revolutionary leader who gave a new direction to the Muslims of the Sub-continent which took them to the way of independence. Sir Syed's role can be referred as the root of the making of Pakistan and the separation from the Hindus. For the purpose of creating awareness amongst the Muslim masses in India, Sir Syed used press to great effect during the late 19th century.

Khilafat movement was an effort by the Indian Muslims to save the Ottoman Empire. It was a pan-Islamic movement between 1919 till 1924. Some of the great journalists of that time like Maulana Mohammad Ali Johar and his brother Maulana Shaukat Ali worked very hard for this cause with lots of other important personalities. The Muslim press and newspapers also played an important role amongst the Muslims about the importance of the Khilafat Movement. Initially the movement was quite successful through strikes and protests all over India but this movement could not gain a lot of success in the long run. However, the role of Muslim press during that time would always be remembered in history with golden words.Although the Khilafat Movement was not a success, it united the Muslims of Sub-continent and injected a new spirit amongst them which was the real energy behind the independence movement later on.

Maulana Zafar Ali Khan:

The one who fought for the freedom movement with his pen and used it as a unifier for bringing the required nationalism in the Muslim community will be remembered as the father of Urdu Journalism. January 18, 2013 marks the 140th birth anniversary of Maulana Zafar Ali Khan.

Maulana continued the legacy of his father, after taking charge as the editor of 'Zamindar' by converting it into a revolutionary press (initially the paper was published keeping in view the farmers). This paper started to write articles that were full of political thoughts and Muslim unity. Soon this newspaper earned a great repute among the people. It is said that Zamindar was so popular among the people that even illiterates spent 1 paisa to pay the price of Zamindar and 1 paisa to that person who read that newspaper for them. This popularity was disliked by the English rulers and no of times Zamindar was banned over a specific time period.

With the irrefutably powerful art of rhetoric he also served as an exemplary spokesman for the Muslim community. There is a remarkable contrast in the various phases of Urdu journalism that evolved since 1911, strictly, to preserve the legitimate rights of the Muslims in sub-continent. Regardless of where they stand today, Pakistani journalistic ambitions were based on sincerity, devotion, truth and a visionary mirror for reflecting 'community opinion'.

There was no important incident (involving the Muslisms) that was left unattended by the veteran journalist. All the historical events that brought Muslims as a minority against the ruling British or the majority Indians, before the creation of Pakistan, received Zamindar's glare. Maulana Zafar Ali Khan was part of the formidable chain of 'militant Muslim journalists'. Khanpur mosque agitation in 1935 combined with Maulana's effective persuasion made 'mosque' the symbol of 'community identity'. Khilafat movement also received a wide range of coverage by Zamindar.

His bold stance brings the 'nationalistic flare' that resonated among the literary and poetic circles as well. He championed the cause of Muslims by transforming Urdu poetry into idioms of political expressions. The most interesting aspect of his poetic verses was that they were understood by the unlettered in Punjab province. Moreover, he attracted Muslim youth of the Punjab. In light of Maulana's influential verbal communication, it wasn't a surprise as to how Zamindar's circulation reached 15.000 (unprecedented for an Urdu newspaper at that time) even when it was 'the most' persecuted newspaper of sub-continent.

Undoubtedly, Zamindar, under the editorship of Maulana Zafar Ali Khan remained irresistible and an outlet for the Muslims to vent out their feelings. It reached the zenith of glory for its unique way of reaching the Muslims hearts via doorsteps. The reason. Maulana Zafar Ali Khan is regarded, as the father of Urdu journalism is that he established the traditions of sacrifice, perseverance, boldness and devotion towards social responsibility in journalism. Zamindar knocked at the door of a common man and played a pivotal role to build an enthusiastic lot of newspaper readers among the Muslims. This intrepid journalistic standard helped the Pakistan movement to gain momentum, which thwarted any insurmountable barrier.

During the First World War, Turkey was supporting Germans and people of united India were very eager to know the real situation of war. Maulana often started the paper with the World War news in which the success stories of Germans and Turkish were quoted. This was definitely hated by the English Rulers so they compelled Maulana Zafar Ali not to publish the news from the First World War. However, when Turkey was declared a democracy then all the attention of Muslims of the sub-continent was diverted to the internal politics. Maulana Zafar Ali Khan started to highlight the brutal attitude of the English rulers to the natives. This newspaper reported the incidents of the Muslim League and gained the confidence of the Muslims of the Sub-continent.

Maulana faced punishment and arrested several times by the government but he did not stop his courageous and bold stance and his enthusiasm provoked Muslims and they became aware of their political rights.

The father of Urdu journalism has left an immutable model that was based on the dialectic of nationalism and communitarianism that moulded Muslim mindset. It was rather an intellectually wise way to equip the Muslims with the ability to recast the ideas of 'community' and 'nationalism'. Journalism at that time was a perfect example, proposed by Maulana Zafar Ali Khan, to be emulated.

Maulana Muhammad Ali Jauhar

He possessed remarkable brilliance as a writer and orator, He wrote articles in various newspapers like "The Times", "The Observer" and "The Manchester Guardian" as well as other major English and Indian newspapers, in both English and Urdu. He was man of a versatile genius and played a great part in the actions against the British colonial rule. He was a great orator and still greater Journalist. He became firm opponents of British rule under the combined shock of the Balkan wars and Kanpur Mosque incident in 1913. His relentless determination and ardor in the cause of India's freedom, and his persistence in pursuing the goal most dear to him won him the respect and affection of his numerous countrymen.

Maulana Muhammad ali Jauhar published two newspapers, the Comrade in English and Hamdard in Urdu. The Comrade was started on January 1, 1911, from Calcutta. The Maulana had made thorough preparations for the paper and everything concerned with it was of a high order. He himself was a man of parts about whom H.G. Wells said: "Maulana Muhammad Ali had the pen of Macaulay, the tongue of a Burke and heart of Napolean". Lovat Fraser wrote in an editorial in the Times of India, that Maulana Muhammad Ali had "marvellous command over the English language. No Indian, and perhaps few Englishmen could write better that he did. Thus, Maulana Muhammad ali Jauhar, with the help of a talented band of youngmen, gave Muslim India the best weekly it ever had.

From the date of its first appearance, the Comrade was looked upon as the mouthpiece of the grievances of the Muslims and voice of their ambition. "Throughout its existence The Comrade rendered yeoman service to the cause of socio-economic and political advancement of the Muslims of Indian in particular, and to the cause of India in general, by attacking the anti-Indian attitude both of the bureaucracy and of the British Government." The Comrade played an important role in formulating the political policy of Muslim India.

Maulana Muhammad Ali Jauhar always defended, very valiantely, the Muslim interests through The Comrade about which S.M. Ikram writes: "It was fearless in denouncing discrimination and hardships to which the editor's community was exposed, but it also systematically criticised the Bengalee, the Tribune and other Hindu newspapers, which opposed the newly organized All-India Muslim League, or the efforts of Aligarh leaders to secure suitable safeguards for the Muslim.

The Comrade did not start with any bitterness towards the British Government, but certain event had taken place, to wit, he annulment of the partition of Bengal and political tension generated by the Tripoli and Balkan Wars which affected it attitude. Before long, there were a few other causes which fed the fires of hatred between the rulers and the Indian Muslims. Controversy about the Muslim University was one; and before it died down. There was a serious trouble at Cawnpur after the demolition of the portion of a mosque. These entire events went a long way to change the attitude of The Comrade towards the Government.

When the First World War started, Maulana Muhammad Ali Jauhar in an editorial in The Comrade, under the caption, "Choice of the Turks", supported the cause of Turkey in the Balkan war. The editorial was indigestible to the British rulers and eventually the security of The Comrade and its Urdu counterpart Hamdard was declared forfeited to the Government and Ali Brothers were interned under the Defence of India ordinance. The Comrade once again started its career some time later, and then finally it had to close down. And in his farewell message, Maulana Muhammad Ali wrote, "we have lived because we have dared, and we shall still dare, and we shall still live."

The Hamdard also earned a great reputation in Urdu medium newspapers and had a respectable place in the Indian press, but it could not continue for a long time.

3

Maulana Azad and Education System in India

Maulana Abul Kalam Azad is an icon of Indian Politics as well as Urdu literature. He is popularly called Azad. He was born in Mecca on November 11, 1888 in a wealthy Islamic family and passed away on February 22, 1958 in Delhi. He was a poet, philosopher, writer, educationist, politician, architect of the Indian education system and a specialist on Indian culture too. He was an accomplished scholar in Arabic, Persian, Urdu, English, Hindi, Bengali and a prolific debater. But we are yet to study and understand him properly and thoroughly.

We all know Maulana Azad as a great leader of the Indian freedom movement but very few of us know that Maulana Azad has a prominent place in Urdu literature. He was a great champion of secularism and national integration. He opposed the partition of India because he cherished the opinion that an undivided India would, in no time, emerge as a superpower in the world. Following India's independence, he became the first Minister of Education in the Union Government. He was the chair of the 9th UNESCO session which was held in Delhi. He was the founder of the Indian Council of Cultural Relations, University Grants Commission, Indian Institute of Technology, Sahitya Akademi, Sangeet Natak Akademi and so many organisations.

In 1992 he was posthumously awarded India's highest civilian award, the Bharat Ratna. We celebrate his birthday as the "National Education Day" across India. Maulana Abul Kalam Azad was not only a creative genius but well versed in the Western education system, especially in science and technology. An article on various aspects of his life and work will surely help the new generation to comprehend in full his contributions in post-independence India. It will also focus on the contemporary educational scenario.

He was a rare example of a personality with such multiple qualities. The former Congress President, Acharya Kripalani, had once expressed his views on him in the following words:

"Maulana Azad's personality was great. He was not a historical personality, rather a considerable period of history was inherent in his personality."

Dr Syed Abid Hussain divided Maulana Azad's literary life into three periods—the first period started from the age of 12 years when he began writing articles which continued till 1916. Just thereafter, the second period of his literary writings started and continued till 1936. In this period he launched his famous journal *Al-Hilal*, and wrote his autobiography *Tazkira* and *Tafseer-e-Quran*. The third period started from 1936 and continued till 1945 during which period he wrote *Ghubar-e-Khatir*. It was at this stage that Maulana Azad's literary life ended.

As a journalist Maulana Azad remained associated with a large number of reputed journals/newspapers, like *Vakil,Zamindar,Muslim Gazette, Paisa Akhbar, Mashrique, Halel-al-Matin, Musalmaan, Al-Hakam, Al-Haque, Hamdard* and *Comrade* (an English journal). All these journals were painted with "pan-Islamic" colours.

MAULANA AZAD'S EDUCATIONAL LEADERSHIP

What distinguished Maulana Azad was his association with education. He brought his educational thought to bear on his leadership in the field, spread intermittently over five decades of the last century. The process of his educational leadership may chronologically be split into three broad stages. From 1900 to 1920 his leadership focused attention on the freedom programme in the Islamic system of learning in India. From 1920 to 1946, the process of his leadership was marked by the expansion of its scope to the country as a whole in the most resurgent period of her history. From 1947 to 1958 was the stage of his educational leadership in full bloom, synchronising with his stewardship of the Education Ministry During the period of over a decade, he availed of the unique opportunity of setting new national goals for education in New India.

Much has been written on Maulana Azad's educational ideas, his educational philosophy, his educational planning, and his views on Islamic education. But less stress has been given on his political leadership, his political ideas on patriotism, solidarity and unity and lastly on his involvement in the independence movement. So, it is indispensable to expose our country's public to Maulana Azad's ideas, thoughts and feelings on these aspects.

In the process of Maulana Azad's educational leadership, its culmination lay in his stewardship of the Union Education Ministry. On his assuming charge of the Ministry, the very first public assertion he made was naturally about transforming the system of education as inherited from the British to suit "our national requirements". In his very first official statement at the press conference held on February 18, 1947 Azad, on the one hand, criticised the then prevailing system as one "shaped by non-nationals in the non-national interests", and, on the other, paid a tribute to its service to Indian people in general.

In his statement of policy as the Education Minister before the Constituent Assembly on March 11, 1948, Azad defined the situation in the country that the popular Government was faced with on the eve of independence in the following words:

"It entered into a heritage which was burdened with many encumbrances. There was no clear state to write with but a palimpsest on which was scrawled the marks of generations of scribes who had each his own mode and style."1

Maulana Azad's Ideas on Educational Policies

From the study of Azad's ideas on the educational policies, one is able to comprehend the four important objectives that he promoted as the new goals of education in post-independence India:

1. Democratisation of education;
2. Maintenance of educational standards;
3. Broadening of educational outlook; and
4. Promotion of mutual understanding.

For democratisation of education in India, with a view to liquidating mass illiteracy, Azad strove to introduce two important reform measures in the country—universalising elementary education and launching a nationwide drive for adult education. For the purpose of making education free and universal for the younger generation, he emphasised the implementation of the 40-year Post-War Educational Plan within one-fourth of its time.2 What characterised Maulana Azad's uniqueness of broadening of the educational outlook was his insistence on making education free and compulsory upto the secondary stage.

For promotion of mutual understanding Azad brought his ideology of human fraternity and fellowship to bear on the office of the Education Ministry. Azad was an apostle of international amity and the indivisible unity of man. He had expressed his abiding faith in the essential unity of man holding it above all other objectives of human life, such as religious salvation, economic prosperity, cultural advancement and political emancipation. For this philosophy of universalism, he found support from both the Islamic and Hindu world-views.

Apart from the fact that education is the dynamic side of philosophy, what presently justifies taking up a study like this is Azad's association with education throughout the course of his public life is his involvement with education as a mission of guiding mankind towards higher goals covering more than half-a-century.

On Problem of Language

When the question of replacement of the English language, by another language was under consideration and there ensued intense discussions, Maulana Azad had expressed his opinion against abruptly replacing the English language by any other language to avoid any law and order problem stemming from propular unrest.

He was not opposed to replacing the English language, but what he wanted was to give at least five years time, because at that time there was no language which could be spoken in all the provinces of India and outside India, except the language spoken in the northern part of the country.

At that stage, there were two prominent languages in India—Hindi and Urdu. Maulana Azad, having discussed the matter with Mahatma Gandhi and Motilal Nehru, decided not to chose either Hindi or Urdu, but the word "Hindustani", which has got more elasticity. On this proposal some people thought that the word "Hindustani" was intended to enable the entry of the Urdu language through the backdoor. Ultimately, the proposal of Maulana Azad was not accepted and he expressed his dissatisfaction at this in the speech he delivered in Parliament.

EDUCATIONAL LEADERSHIP OF MAULANA AZAD AS EDUCATION MINISTER

During Maulana Azad's tenure as the Minister of Education, the Union Ministry had attained educational leadership in the country. Before that, until Sir John Seargent was made the Educational Advisor, that is, upto 1937, the Ministry of Education was a dead organisation, which had no function except to form a few committees and present a report on educational activities at the end of the year. After a few years, when the National Government was formed, Pandit Jawaharlal Nehru included the name of Maulana Azad in his Cabinet as the Education Minister. The Departments of Social, Cultural and Scientific Research were also placed under his charge. In such a way the Union Education Ministry, under the guidance of Maulana Azad, for the first time in its history adopted thoughtful and visionary ideas and translated those into reality. Different Commi-tttees and Commissions were comtituted in respect of different levels of education, for example, Primary, Secondary University, Technical, Adult Education, etc. These bodies inspected the different wings, drew up new plans and tried to bring uniformity in national plans.

The following Departments/Organisations/ Commissions/Councils/ Boards/Bureaus were established during Maulana Azad's Ministership:

1. University Commission: This Commission was established in 1948. Most of the recommen-dations of this Commission were accepted by the government. Teaching in many new disciplines was started in the universities due to the efforts of Maulana Azad. The UGC functioned under his leadership.
2. All India Council for Secondary Education: This Council was established with a view to develop mutual relations amongst States.
3. Secondary Education Commission: Maulana Azad felt that the old syllabi of the high schools should be changed to bring new ones. For this purpose, he established the Secondary Education Commission on September 1952 of which Dr A.L. Mudaliar was made the Chairman. On the recommendation of this Commission, the structure of Secondary Education was changed.
4. All India Council for Technical Education: After the All India Council for Technical Educationwas established, on its recommendation a large number of Technical Schools and Colleges were opened.
5. Adult Education: The Board for Adult Education was established with a view to facilitate education amongst the uneducated adults.
6. Rural Higher Education: The Board for Rural Higher Education was established with a view to extend higher education in the villages.
7. Central Social Development Board.
8. Central Education Board.
9. Educational and Vocational Guidance Bureau.
10. National Organisation for Basic Education.
11. Council for Scientific and Technical Research.

Besides the above, Maulana Azad drew up several programmes for development of Hindi and its acceptance as the national language. He launched several schemes for physical education, excursions, betterment of youngsters, social service, education for disabled persons, etc. It is indisputable that the educational development plans were started during Maulana Azad's stewardship of the Union Education Ministry.

Apart from the above development plans, three academies were established, (1) Sahitya Academi, (2) Art Academi and (3) Dance-Drama and

Music Academi. A new Department was opened in the Education Ministry for establishing cultural relations with UNESCO and international cultural organisations. A new organisation was also established for strengthening education through exchange of views between teachers and the taught. All these steps taken by Maulana Azad offer ample testimony to the fact that he was an ardent votary of the theory of united nationalism. The only aims of his life were unity, friendship and love and he put all his endeavours towards reinforcing these.

AZAD'S EFFORTS IN SHAPING THE INDIAN EDUCATION POLICY

Maulana Azad held a position unique in several ways. He was emotionally and intellectually close to both — Mahatma Gandhi and Nehru. He was closely associated with crucial decision making since the twenties. With the dawn of freedom in 1947, his was a natural choice to be in the Cabinet- He was the Minister of Education during 1947-52, and Minister of Education, Natural Resources and Scientific Research from 1952-58. His influence on the process of policy making was immense. He was Nehru's, comrade-in-arms during the days of the freedom movement and was-one of his closest confidante and adviser in the Cabinet.

Maulana Azad was a great educationist too. His standing as an outstanding scholar of Oriental learning was demonstrated in moulding the educational system of the country in the immediate post-independence years. It was he who established the University Grants Commission and launched the Indian Council for Cultural Relations (ICCR) which has now come up to play a significant role in the academic growth of the country. The three Academies-Sahitya Academy, Lalit Kala Academy and SangeetNatak Academy—topromote art, music and literature were his ideas. He assisted Pandit Nehru in setting up the Indian Council of Scientific and Industrial Research (CSIR) and many a chain of Science Laboratories in India.

As the Minister for Education he insisted that both the Union and the States must share responsibility in promotion of education. He appointed the University Education Commission in 1948 and Secondary Education Commission in 1952. Between 1947 and 1958, on his initiative the budgetary allocation for Education was raised fifteen fold.

A leader is defined as a person who knows the way, who shows the way and who goes the way, Azad was one of those who went the way carrying his people with him and thus obtained a legendary fame in his lifetime itself, a feat earned by only a few statesmen. At a time when it was in the understanding of most Muslims of India that it is an offence against religion to be both a nationalist and a Muslim, Maulana Azad showed us how one could be both at one and the same time. His greatest contribution perhaps lies in the fact that he was chief instrumental in converting a passive and sometimes collaborationist section of the Indian society to become a very active and vocal opponent of the British Raj.

Any realist assessment of Maulana Azad's contribution to Modern India will not be complete unless we look into the manner in which he reached out to his co-religionists during the freedom movement and after the advent of freedom and persuaded them to play a constructive role in shaping the destiny of the newly liberated State. It is here that the relevance of his religious philosophy, his standing as an inspiring writer and scholar and the philosophical basis of his nationalist outlook come.

Azad's writings reflect a synthesis of his political nationalist philosophy and his religious philosophy based on secularism. Though they are saturated with a religious fervor it is easy to discern the secular message from between the lines.

He wanted discern the secular message from between the lines. He wanted to act as scholar dissemination ideas through the instrumentality of his writings, among the Muslim religious teachers whom he regarded as natural leaders. He thought that it was the educated class that ought to be educated first so that they could influence the behavior of the general public.

Maulan Azad was a patriot, a leader, a philosopher-statesman and a great scholar. By a profound learning and "luminous intelligence" he did a real good job for Islam, by clearing it of the dust of prejudice and bigotry which had gathered up on it during the eleven hundred years of its history in India.

He was a rightful inheritor of all the thought movements of the past. In the unfolding of his intellectual life and in the evolution of his thought, we find staged the whole history of Islamic thought. He was one of the very few acquainted with the philosophies of India and had deep insight into the various religions of the world and could isolate the real and essential from the spurious.

Reminding of Azad's unique intellectual achievements, Pandit Nehru said, ".....He was great in many ways. He combined in himself the greatness of the past with the greatness of the present. He always reminded me of the great men of several hundred years ago about whom I have read in history, the great men of the Renaissance, or in a later period the encyclopaedists who proceeded the French Revolution, men of intellect and men of action. He remembered also of what might be called the great quality of olden days - the graciousness which we sadly seek in the world today....It was the strange and unique of the good qualities of the past, the graciousness, the deep learning and toleration and the urges of today which made Maulan Azad what he was."

MAULANA ABUL KALAM AZAD AND EDUCATION

Sachar Committee has well documented the educational backwardness among Muslims at all levels – literacy rates are much below the national average, dropout rates are higher among the Muslims and therefore, their numbers in graduation and post graduation are much lower. Various reasons are being attributed for this backwardness, however, the varied analyses emanate from basically two perspectives. The first perspective blames either Islam as a religion which is against secular education or blames Muslims as a community for lack of interest in getting their children to schools. While the second perspective takes a closer look at the structure of the education system that tends to keep the minorities, dalits, adivasis outside the system. The first perspective is pushed by people with communal attitudes or subscribed by those who form quick and lazy opinions. While the second perspective is subscribed to by educationists, or those who are engaged with the problem of educational backwardness.

Reasons for educational backwardness among Muslims

Poverty is the biggest contributing factor behind the educational backwardness among the Muslims. There is great diversity among the Muslim community along linguistic and regional lines, sectarian lines and caste biradaries. Those Muslim biradaries or communities that enjoy higher incomes, are educationally more forward. The Bohras, Khojas and Memons for example, are more forward than, say, mehtars (scavangers), bagwans or telis. Upwardly mobile biradaries like Ansaris and Qureshi have increasingly taken towards educating their children and some of them are doing well and even becoming professionals. The awareness and thirst for education has particularly increased after the demolition of Babri Masjid and the riots that followed the demolition. Education is seen as key to secured jobs and professions that cannot be destroyed during riots. Muslim girls have been topping in SSC and HSC exams. The image of a domestic worker arguing with the principal of a convent school with high fees to admit her child when we had gone for a fact finding mission is still fresh in my mind. She told the principal that she would forgo her meal one time and undertake extra work to pay the fees of the school but not to keep her child out of the school gates.

Poor Muslim families are forced to send their children for earnings or apprenticeship so that s/he can start supporting the family. There is high rate of child labour among Muslims in zardosi, carpet, bangles and other industries. Many Muslim children have high skills, but no formal training and no certificates, which forces them to remain on low survival incomes lifelong. Low income means the next generation too would be labourers. There is no inter-generational asset transfer and the community continues to decline. Communal violence ensures that the meagre assets generated through hard work get destroyed without adequate compensation and without rehabilitation of the victims. Some members of the tiny middle class within the community slip into poverty and doing small odd jobs when their small trade or business is destroyed in violence. About 75-80% of Muslim families live off labouring jobs.

Muslims are forced into ghettos on the outskirts of towns and cities or rural areas. These ghettos have poor infrastructure like approach roads, adequate water, sewerage, electric connections, banking institutions and educational institutions. Lack of schools within ghettos leave the option of seeking admission in schools that are far away increasing the cost of education and in cases of lack of proper approach roads, making it even more difficult. Schools situated far away from Muslim ghettos also increase the security risk, particularly after communal violence and for girl students. Parents in such situations withdraw their children from school leading to high dropout rates. Sachar Committee Report (SCR) finds that higher the proportion of Muslims in a given locality, poorer is the infrastructure in the locality. There is inverse relation between the proportion of Muslims in a given locality and the infrastructure that has been provided by the state.

The fourth reason is discriminatory attitude of school managements towards Muslim children at the time of admission. Ghettos also exist in our minds, which often informs us that Muslims should study in Urdu medium schools, even though Urdu is not their mother tongue. They are less preferred as common attitudes are that they would not be able to so well in their studies or continue. Alien environment in the schools, which include imposition of religious prayers that are against the creed of Islam and rituals like Saraswati Vandana, teaching of Geeta, surya namaskar and other such rituals dissuade Muslim children from continuing their education.

Last but not least, Muslims are less represented in all walks of life, including in political processes. Often they are less than one-third the number warranted by their proportion in population. Needy parents have no one to approach to or seek guidance and testimonies from. Good schools under the Muslim management are too few and far between. Muslim trusts wanting to establish educational institutions are not readily helped by the state by allotting land or coming forth with grant-in-aid or even for granting recognition. The community is least networked and it lacks social capital which is necessary for promotion of education among the community.

The problem lies with the nature of political leadership of the community as well. The political leadership of the community represents the interests of the upper-caste converts, or ashrafs and the tiny section of upper-middle class. It is more engaged on issues of identity and resisting any change in the Shari'a laws even within Quranic framework.

The political leadership find a sympathetic ear within the corridors of power in perpetuating the medieval interpretation of Shari'a laws and Islamic jurisprudence which is discriminatory towards women and against Quranic spirit. Having sympathetic ear on the issue of Muslim Personal Laws helps the political leadership gain legitimacy. The political leadership of the community with honourable exceptions has not emphasised the issue of promotion of education or addressed livelihood issues of the community.

There are too few good primary and secondary educational institutions mostly in urban areas and members of Muslim community are less preferred and not inclusive enough. The Indian state too has realized that India cannot really progress if a large section of its population remains backward and uneducated.

Therefore Sachar Committee was appointed and some half hearted measures have been taken like the PM's New 15 point programme which partly attempts to address only one of the problems listed above – poverty. The programme includes provision of scholarships, hostel facilities, education loans and merit-cum-means scholarships. But the programme faces triple jeopardy – lack of adequate funds, lack of motivation among bureaucracy and lack of proper policy to address real problems of the community. Due to lack of space, we are not going into the details of the causes of failure of the programme to promote education. Poverty is only one small cause that the state however inadequately attempted to address. The net result is low figures in achievement on educational front.

Maulana Azad's vision on education

If Maulana Azad had succeeded in persuading the Indian State to adopt his policies, the scenario would have been different today. For him, appropriate education policy of independent India was even more important than the industrial policy. Maulana Azad, being the first education minister of the independent India wanted to lay a strengthen and democratize our education system. He worked for democratizing of education in order to universalize achievement and thereby break the dominating structure of hegemonic hierarchies of caste and class. Azad viewed "Every individual has a right to an education that will enable him to develop his faculties and live a full human life. Such education is the birth right of every citizen. A state cannot claim to have discharged its duty till it has provided for every single individual the means to the acquisition of knowledge and self-betterment." ... "regardless of the question of employment the state must make available to all citizens the facilities of education up to the secondary stage."

For Maulana Azad, education was a crucial tool to inculcate the citizenship among the people who just emerged from colonial rule and hierarchical structures like caste and gender. Citizens needed to imbibe the values of equality and needed to be sensitized on the religious, ethnic and linguistic diversity of the country. In order to achieve universal primary and secondary education, according to Maulana Azad, India needed to allocate at least 10% of its budget for education.

The allocation for education in budget was at best 6% and often times, merely 2 to 3%. Maulana Azad wanted a substantial portion of the educational budget to be spent on primary and secondary education and adult education, including women. This would mean expanding and strengthening schooling in every village and kasba and equal access to all – Hindus or Christians or Muslims. The schools in India would teach values of equality and justice, and sensitize the younger generation to the diversity. Maulana Azad laid emphasis on teaching of values drawn from all religions.

The Indian state not only gave less importance to education, but substantial portion of its budget on education was allocated to creation of higher institutions like IITs, IIMs, AIIMS, JNU and the rest, mostly based in the four metros and accessible to relatively richer class who could afford costly tuitions in competitive entrance examinations in English language and after schooling in expensive public schools. The doors of these elite institutions were not entirely closed to those from poorer backgrounds and marginalized sections like the SCs, the STs, the OBCs, women and minorities but the barriers were so high that these section entering these institutions was more of an exception rather than rule. Expenditure on these islands for elite education was at the cost of expansion of primary and secondary school networks.

Conclusion

Islam lays much emphasis on education. According to Tirmidhi and Ibn Majah, Ibn Abbas narrated that the Messenger of Allah (SAW) said: "A single scholar of religion is more formidable against shaytaan (the devil) than a thousand devout persons". The first and most crucial obligation on Muslims is to acquire knowledge and secondly to practice, teach and preach this knowledge. No man becomes a true Muslim without knowing the meaning of Islam, because he becomes a Muslim not through birth but through knowledge and deed. Islam lays emphasis on rationality. However, the Muslim religious and political leadership has ignored this obligation. Perhaps Maulana Azad was inspired by his understanding of Islam in spreading knowledge and education.

Education is one instrument that can help members of a community to take part and contribute meaningfully to the collective social life of the community. Education helps imbibe values necessary for harmonious and peaceful collective life, as well as for the environment and nature, for the development of frontiers of knowledge and new understanding. Education can help us to be better informed of our long term and sustainable interests, i.e. enlightened self-interests. Education can also help us build and develop skills that are necessary for livelihood and to contribute to the community.

Education is a continuous process in the life of all individuals. We get educated through our struggles for survival, interaction with other human beings; through interaction with nature and through varied experiences. Some minimum education is acquired by all individuals from the family and the members of extended family and community. However, meaningful education takes place through institutions of learning, like – schools, colleges, research institutes, universities, seminaries, institutions imparting professional and vocational knowledge and skills. Access to quality education, professional courses and higher education is always limited to privileged elite. It is the structure of education system in India that has not included Muslims and at the same time laying the blame on the community. If we do pursue the dreams of Maulana Azad, the whole nation would be benefited. Let us pursue the dream with urgency.

AZAD AND EDUCATION IN INDIA

Education is a magic wand that can help human beings meet any challenge in life. It is essential to sustainable development. Education is as necessary as food for us. It can not only get us jobs and status in the society, but also enables us to shape our future and make the world a sustainable place for everyone.

In India, there's one man who first set a well-thought goal for education after independence from cunning colonial rule: "Free education for all". People remember him as Maulana Abul Kalam Azad.

Every year, Indians celebrate National Education Day on 11 November marking his birth anniversary. He was India's first Education Minister. He earns respect from Indians for laying foundation for India's education future. The Government of India first declared 11 November as "National Education Day in 2008, honoring Maulana Azad.

He was notable among many Muslim freedom fighters who joined hands with Mahatma Gandhi in India's Freedom Movement. Being Education Minister, Maulana Azad dreamt of an India where all Indians would be educated.

He is called Maulana in reverence for his abilities and extensive knowledge, both contemporary and Islam. Perhaps, the very first verse of Holy Qur'an "*Read: In the name of thy Lord...*" has inspired him to study hard and become exemplary figure in Indian history. He receives rich tributes every year from students, teachers, academicians, politicians, and in fact every citizen. His life is a symbol of pluralism and religious tolerance in the country.

In his maiden press conference in independent India, Azad said: "A truly liberal and humanitarian education may transform the outlook of the people and set it on the path of progress and prosperity, while an ill-conceived or unscientific system might destroy all the hopes which have been cherished by generations of pioneers in the cause of national struggle."

Today, India's national education system follows the highest ideal of Mahatma Gandhi: "Education for All", which is further emphasized by eminent educationist Maulana Azad who said that education must be imparted by heart.

In an event at MANUU in 2012, former Union HRD Minister Kapil Sibal praised Maulana Azad and said that the farsightedness of eminent educationist Azad's ideas of human and cultural values of education mirrored in the four clear-cut aims of education identified in an International Commission on Education of UNESCO for the 21st century.

Today, we have right to education (RTE) and free primary education. Thanks to our visionary leaders who foresaw the need for it. The RTE Act was passed in Dr. Manmohan Singh's government.

Right to Education:

Passed in 2009, the RTE Act specify that private schools reserve 25% of seats at the entry level for children belonging to 'weaker sections' and 'disadvantaged groups' of the society. This may not be the best push to ensure educational opportunities for children from weaker sections, but it has come as a major initiative from the government for welfare of downtrodden. This act is a progressive piece of legislation, which could help in taking education to the masses.

Dr. Singh once admitted that elementary education was not free when he was a school kid, and there was no fundamental right to education. Despite those conditions, the education he received being a child helped him realize his aspirations.

He noted: "This is why I believe that education can help us realize our aspirations." Thanks to many education welfare schemes, now we are in a better position to stay competent. There are plenty of opportunities for those who strive for education.

Also, education is magical as it helps us in rediscovering ourselves. Many people have become prominent figures in India after pursuing their education despite unfavorable conditions in their lives. Dr. APJ Abul Kalam, Lal Bahadur Shastri, Dr. Manmohan Singh are a few names. Dr. Singh once confessed: "I owe to education, everything that I have achieved in the journey of my life."

Students Imitate Azad at Insight

Inspired by great leader Abul Kalam Azad, students at Insight International School in Hyderabad dressed like Azad to celebrate his birthday today. They also delivered speeches recalling noble thoughts of Maulana Azad. A Grad VII student, Areeb Hisham muttered: "Education imparted by heart can bring revolution in the society."

Islam inspired Bedouin to learn. These Arab tribals, who were once uncivilized, laid foundations for many fields in education, philosophy, medical science, and other social sciences as well. Talking about it, a Grade VI student Khaja Moin Abdullah spoke in today's speech: "Islam fosters scientific inquiry, open learning circles, use of community resources, peer view, problem solving approaches, storytelling, and free education."

Weaker sections of the society are always at receiving end when it comes to benefits utilization.

In some cases, they are being sidelined or ignored by well-off people and ruling classes. Schools in remote areas, slums, and rural areas are not in good conditions. They are relatively unsafe for children. "It is necessary to build and promote safer schools in disadvantaged communities," says Shaik Sana of Grade VII.

While India is prospering on various fronts, it also has few inherent problems. May it be corruption or system bias, one needs strong will and courage to challenge and change the fate of the nation. For that better education is of paramount importance. "Climbing to the top demands strength, whether it is to the top of the Mount Everest or to the top of your career," opined a tender soul Syed Raaid Azzam Hussaini of Grade IV.

CONSISTS OF REAL EDUCATION

Real education consists in drawing the best out of yourself. What better book can there be than the book of humanity?

I hold that true education of the intellect can only come through a proper exercise and training of the bodily organs, *e.g.*, hands, feet, eyes, ears, nose, etc. In other word an intelligent use of tile bodily organs in a child provides tile best and quickest way of developing his intellect.

But unless the development of the mind and body goes hand in hand with a corresponding awakening of the soul, the former alone would prove to be a poor lopsided affair.

By spiritual training I mean education of the heart. A proper and all round development of the mind, therefore, can take place only when it proceeds pari passu with the education of the physical and spiritual faculties of the child. They constitute an indivisible whole. According to this theory, therefore, it would be a gross fallacy to suppose that they can be developed piecemeal or independently of one another.

By Education I mean an all-round drawing out of the best in child and man-body, mind and spirit. Literacy is not the end of education nor even the beginning. It is only one of the means whereby man and woman can be educated. Literacy in itself is no education would therefore begin the child's education by teaching it a useful handicraft and enabling it to produce from the moment it begins its training. Thus every school can be made self-supporting, the condition being that the State takes over the manufactures of these schools.

I hold that the highest development of the mind and the soul is possible under such a system of education. Only every handicraft has to be taught not merely' mechanically as is done today but scientifically, *i.e.*, the child should know the why and the wherefore of every process. I am not writing this without some confidence, because it has the backing of experience. This method is being adopted more or less completely wherever spinning is being taught to workers. I have myself taught sandal-making and even spinning on these lines with good results. This method does not exclude a knowledge of history and geography. But I find that this is being taught by transmitting such general information by word of mouth. One imparts ten times as much in this manner as by reading and writing.

The signs of the alphabet may be taught later when the pupil has learnt to distinguish wheat from the chaff and when he has somewhat developed his or her tastes. This is a revolutionary proposal, but it saves immense labour and enables a student to acquire in one year what he may take much longer to learn. This means all-round economy. Of course the pupil learns mathematics whilst he is learning his handicraft.

I admit my limitations. I have no university education worth the name. My high school career was never above the average. I was thankful if I could pass my examinations. Distinction in the school was beyond my aspiration. Nevertheless I do hold very strong views on education in general, including what is called higher education. And I owe it to's old be clearly known and taken for what they may be worth. I must shed the timidity that has led almost to self-suppression. I must not fear ridicule, and even loss of popularity or prestige. If I hide my belief, I shall never correct errors of judgement. I am always eager to discover them and more than eager to correct them.

Let me now state my conclusions held for a number of years and enforced wherever I had opportunity of enforcing them:

1. I am not opposed to education even of' the highest type attainable in the world.
2. The State must pay for it wherever it has definite use for it.
3. I am opposed to all higher education being paid for from the general revenue.
4. It is my firm conviction that the vast amount of the so-called education in arts, given in our colleges, is sheer waste and has resulted in unemployment among the educated classes. What is more, it has destroyed the health, both mental and physical, of the boys and girls who have the misfortune to go through tile grind in our colleges.
5. The medium of a foreign language through which higher education has been imparted in India has caused incalculable intellectual and moral injury to the nation. We are too near our own times to judge the enormity of the damage done. And we who have received such education have both to be victims and judges-an almost impossible feat.

I must give my reasons for the conclusions set forth, above. This I can best do, perhaps, by giving a chapter from my own experience. Up to the age of 12 all the knowledge I gained was through Gujarati, my mother tongue. I knew then something of arithmetic, history and geography. Then I entered a High School. For the first three years the mother tongue was still the medium. But the schoolmaster's business was to drive English into the pupil's head. Therefore more than half of our time was given to learning English and mastering its arbitrary spelling and pronunciation. It was a painful discovery to have to learn a language that was not pronounced as it was written. It was a strange experience to have to learn the spelling by heart. But that is by the way, and irrelevant to my argument. However, for the first three years, it was comparatively plain sailing.

The pillory began with the fourth year. Everything had to be learnt through English-geometry, algebra, chemistry, astronomy, history, geography. The tyranny of English was so great that even Sanskrit or Persian had to be learnt through English, not through the mother tongue. If any boy Spoke in Gujarati which he understood, he was punished. It did not matter to the teacher, if a boy spoke bad English which he could neither pronounce correctly or understand fully. Why should tile teacher worry ? His own English was by no means without blemish. It could not be otherwise. English was as much a foreign language to him as to his pupils. The result was chaos. We the boys had to learn many things by heart, though we could not understand them fully and often not at all. My head used to reel as the teacher as struggling to make his exposition on geometry understood by us. I could make neither head nor tail of geometry till we reached the thirteenth theorem of the first book of Euclid. And let me confess to the reader that in spite of all my love for the mother tongue, I do not to this day know the Gujarati equivalents of the technical terms of geometry, algebra and the like.

I know now that what I took four years to learn of arithmetic, geometry, algebra, chemistry and astronomy, I should have learnt easily in one year, if I had not to learn them through English but Gujarati. My grasp of the subjects would have been easier and clearer. My Gujarati vocabulary would have been richer would have made use of such knowledge in my own home. This English medium created an impassable barrier between me and the members of my family, who had not gone through English schools. My father knew nothing of what I was doing. I could not, even if I had wished it, interest my father in what I was learning. For though he had ample intelligence, he knew not a word of English. I was fast becoming a stranger iii my own home. I certainly became a superior person. Even my dress began to undergo imperceptible changes. What happened to me was not an uncommon experience. It was common to the majority.

The first three years in the High School made little addition to my stock of general knowledge. They were a preparation for fitting the boys for teaching them everything through English. High Schools were schools for cultural conquest by the English. The knowledge gained by the three hundred boys of my High School became a circumscribed possession. It was not for transmission to the masses.

A word about literature. We had to learn several books of English prose and English poetry. No doubt all this was nice. But that knowledge has been of no use to me in serving or bringing me in touch with the masses. I am unable to say that if I had not learnt what I did of English prose and poetry, I should have missed a rare treasure. If I had, instead, passed those precious seven years in mastering Gujarati and had learnt mathematics, science, and Sanskrit and other subjects through Gujarati, I could easily have shared the knowledge so gained with my neighbours. I would have enriched Gujarati, and who can say that I would not have with my habit of application and my inordinate love for the country and mother tongue, made a richer and greater contribution to the service of the masses?

I must not be understood to decry English or its noble literature. The columns of the Harijan are sufficient evidence of my love of English. But the nobility of its literature cannot avail the Indian nation any more than the temperate climate or the scenery of England can avail her. India has to flourish in her own climate and scenery and her own literature, even though all the three may be inferior to the English climate, scenery and literature. We and our children must build on our own heritage. If we borrow another, we impoverish our own.

We can never grow on foreign victuals. I want the nation to have the treasures contained in that language, for that matter in other languages of the world, through its own vernaculars do not need to learn Bengali in order to know the beauties of Rabindranath's matchless productions. I get them through good translations. Gujarati boys and girls do not need to learn Russian to appreciate Tolstoy's short stories. They learn them through good translations. It is the boast of Englishmen that the best of the world's literary output is in the hands of that nation in simple English inside of a week of its publication. Why need I learn English to get at the best of what Shakespeare and Milton thought and wrote?

It would be good economy to set apart a class of students whose business would be to learn the best of what is to be learnt in the different languages of the world and give the translation in the vernaculars. Our masters chose the wrong way for us, and habit has made the wrong appear as right....

Universities must be made self supporting. The State should educate those For all other branches of learning it should encourage private effort. The medium of instruction should be altered at once and at any cost, the provincial languages being given their rightful place. I would prefer temporary chaos in higher education to the criminal waste that is daily accumulating....

Thus I claim that I am not an enemy of higher education. But I am an enemy of higher education as it is given in this country. Under my scheme there will be more and better libraries, more and better laboratories, more and better research institutes. Under it we should have an army of chemists, engineers and other experts who will be real servants of the nation, and answer the varied and growing requirements of a people who are becoming increasingly conscious of their rights and wants. And all these experts will speak, not a foreign tongue, but the language of the people. The knowledge gained by them will be the common property of the people. There will be truly original work instead of mere imitation. And the cost will be evenly and justly distributed.

The Indian culture of our times is in the making. Many of us are striving to produce a blend of all the cultures which seem today to be in clash with one another. No culture can live, if it attempts to be exclusive. There is no suck thing as pure Aryan culture in existence today in India. Whether the Aryans were indigenous to India or were unwelcome intruders, does not interest me much. What does interest me is the fact that my remote ancestors blended with one another with the utmost freedom and we of the present generation are a result of that blend. Whether we are doing any good to the country of our birth and tile tiny globe which sustains us or whether we are a burden, the future alone will show.

I do not want my house to be walled in on all sides and my windows to be stuffed. I want the cultures of all lands to be blown about my house as freely as possible. But I refuse to be blown off my feet by any. I would have our young men and women with literary tastes to learn as much of English and other world-languages as they like, and then expect them m give the benefits of their learning to India and to the world like a Bose, a Ray or the Poet himself. (Sir Jagdish Chandra Bose and Sir P. G. Ray were eminent Indian scientists; 'the Poet' refers to Rabindranath Tagore.) But I would not have a single Indian to forget, neglect or be ashamed of his mother tongue, or to feel that he or she cannot think or express the best thoughts in his or her own vernacular. Mine is not a religion of the prison-house.

Music means rhythm, order. Its effect is electrical. It immediately soothes. Unfortunately like our shastras, music has been the prerogative of the few. It has never become nationalized in the modern sense. If I had any influence with volunteer boy scouts and Seva Samiti organizations, I would make compulsory a proper singing in company of national songs. And to that end I should have great musicians attending every Congress or conference and teaching mass music.

In Pandit Khare's opinion, based upon wide experience, music should form part of the syllabus of primary education. I heartily endorse the proposition. The modulation of the voice is as necessary as the training of tile hand. Physical drill, handicrafts, drawing and music should go hand in hand in order to draw the best out of the boys and girls and create in them a real interest in their tuition.

The eyes, the ears and the tongue come before the hand. Reading comes before writing and drawing before tracing the letters of the alphabet. If this natural method is followed, the understanding of the children will have much better opportunity of development than when it is under check by beginning the children's training with the alphabet.

Nothing can be farther from my thought than that we should become exclusive or erect barriers. But I do respectfully contend that an appreciation of other cultures can fitly follow, never precede, an appreciation and assimilation of our own....

An academic grasp without practice behind it is like an embalmed corpse, perhaps lovely to look at but nothing to inspire or ennoble. My religion forbids me to belittle or disregard other cultures, as it insists under pain of civil suicide upon imbibing and living my own.

The utterly false idea that intelligence can be developed only through book-reading should give place to the truth that the quickest development of the mind can be achieved by artisan's work being learnt in a scientific manner.

True development of the mind commences immediately the apprentice is taught at every step why a particular manipulation of the hand or a tool is required. The problem of the unemployment of students can be solved without difficulty, if they will rank themselves among the common labourers.

I am not sure that it is not better for the children to have much of the preliminary instruction imparted to them vocally. To impose on children of tender age a knowledge of the alphabet and the ability to read before they can gain general knowledge is to deprive them, whilst they are fresh, of the power of assimilating instruction by word of mouth.

Literary training by itself adds not an inch to one's moral height and character-building is independent of literary training.

I am a firm believer in the principle of free and compulsory primary education for India. I also hold that we shall realize this only by teaching the children a useful vocation and utilizing it as a means for cultivating their mental, physical and spiritual faculties. Let no one consider these economic calculations in connection with education as sordid or out of place. There is nothing essentially sordid about economic calculations. True economics never militates against the highest ethical standard, just as true ethics to be worth its name must, at the same time, be also good economics. I value education in the different sciences. Our children cannot have too much of chemistry and physics. I would develop in the child his hands, his brain and his soul. The hands have almost atrophied. The soul has been altogether ignored.

As regards children's curiosity about the facts of life, we should tell them if we know, and admit our ignorance if we do not. If it is something that must not be told, we should check them and ask them not to put such questions even to anyone else. We must never put them off. They know more things than we imagine. If they do not know and if we refuse to tell them, they try to acquire the knowledge in a questionable manner. But if it has to be withheld from them, we must take such risk.

A wise parent allows the children to make mistakes. It is good for them once in a while to burn their fingers. We cannot properly control or conquer the sexual passion by turning a blind eye to it. I am, therefore, strongly in favour of teaching young boys and young girls the significance and right use of their generative organs. In my own way I have tried to impart this knowledge to young children of both sexes, for whose training I was responsible. But the sex education that I stand for must have for its object the conquest and sublimation of the sex passion.

Such education should automatically serve to bring home to children the essential distinction between man and brute, to make them realize that it is man's privilege and pride to be gifted with the faculties of head and heart both, that he is a thinking no less than a feeling animal, and to renounce the sovereignty of reason over the blind instinct is, therefore, to renounce a man's estate. In man, reason quickens and guides the feeling, in brute the soul lies ever dormant. To awaken the heart is to awaken the dormant soul, to awaken reason and to inculcate discrimination between good and evil. Today, our entire environment-our reading, our thinking, and our social behaviour-is generally calculated to sub serve and cater for the sex urge. To break through its coils is no easy task. But it is a task worthy of our highest endeavour.

AZAD : EDUCATIONIST & SCHOLAR EXTRAORDINARY

Maulana Abul Kalam Azad is one of those rare personalities through whom the distinctions of the 20th century can be recognized and possibilities of the 21st century determined. He stood for a learning society through liberal, modern and universal education combining the humanism of Indian arts and the rationalism of western sciences, a society where the strong are just and the weak secure, where the youth is disciplined and the women lead a life of dignity – a non-violent, non-exploiting social and economic order. He was free India's first Education Minister and guided the destinies of the Nation for eleven years.

He was the first to raise the issue of the National System of Education which is today the bed-rock of the National Policy on Education (1986) updated in 1992. The concept implies that, upto a given level, all students, irrespective of caste, creed, location or sex have access to education of a comparable quality. All educational programmes, he said, must be carried out in strict conformity with secular values and constitutional framework.

He stood for a common educational structure of 10+2+3 throughout India. If Maulana Azad were alive today he would have been the happiest to see the Right to Free Education Bill getting cabinet approval for the approval of Parliament. The Right to Education Bill seeks to make free and compulsory education a fundamental right. The wealth of the nation, according to Maulana Azad, was not in the country's banks but in primary schools. The Maulana was also a great votary of the concept of Neighbourhood schools and the Common School System.

Born in Mecca on November 11, 1888, his father Maulana Khairuddin was a noted scholar, his mother Alia was an Arab, niece of Shaikh Mohammad Zahir Vatri of Madina. His father gave him the name of Feroze Bakht but he became Abul Kalam and the name stayed. At 10 he was well-versed in Quran. At 17 Abul Kalam was a trained theologian recognized in the Islamic world. His studies at Al Azhar University Cairo further deepened his knowledge. At Calcutta where his family had settled he started a magazine called 'Lisan-ul-Sidq'. His early influences were Maulana Shibli Naomani and Altaf Hussain Haali, the two great Urdu critics.

Azad made a debut in politics when the British Government partitioned Bengal in 1905 on religious grounds. The Muslim middle classes supported the partition but Azad rejected it outright. He took active part in the agitation, joined the secret societies and revolutionary organization, came in contact with Sri Aurobindo Ghosh and Shyam Sundar Chakravarty. He stood for a unified India and never deviated from his stand. He writes in his famous book 'India Wins Freedom' : 'It is one of the greatest frauds on the people to suggest that religious affinity can unite areas which are geographically, economically and culturally different'. It is a fact of history that while other Congress leaders accepted the partition in 1947, Maulana stood steadfast. His famous statement on Hindu-Muslim unity stands out as Magna Carta of his faith : "If an angel were to descend from the heavens and proclaim from the heights of Qutab Minar: Discard Hindu-Muslim unity and within 24 hours Swaraj is yours, I will refuse the preferred Swaraj but shall not budge an inch from my stand. The refusal of Swaraj will affect only India while the end of our unity will be the loss of our entire human world."

At the age of 20 he went on a tour of Iraq, Syria and Egypt and met the young Turks and Arab nationalists including Christians. The tour proved very useful to Azad to crystallize his thoughts on the neo-colonialists who were exploiting those countries and how India could help them. On return he started a journal in Urdu named 'Al Hilal' in 1912. It was this journal where he aired his liberal views, 'Rationalist in outlook and profoundly versed in Islamic lore and history'. Writes Nehru in his 'Discovery of India'. The Maulana interpreted scriptures from the rationalist point of view. Soaked in Islamic tradition and with many personal contacts with prominent Muslim leaders of Egypt, Turkey, Syria, Palestine, Iraq and Iran, he was profoundly affected by political and cultural developments in these countries. He was known in Islamic countries probably more than any other Indian Muslim.

The journal 'Al-Hilal' became extremely popular and in two years its circulation rose to 30,000. The inevitable happened when in 1914 the British Government confiscated the press and banned the journal under the Defence of India Act. Azad was arrested and sent to Ranchi jail where he suffered untold hardships.

Released from jail he resumed his educational writings. He spoke in a new language, writes Nehru. It was not only a new language in thought and approach, even its texture was different, for Azad's style was tense and virile though sometimes a little difficult because of its Persian background. He used new phrases for new ideas and was a definite influence in giving shape to Urdu language as it is today. The older conservative Muslims did not react favourably to all this and criticized Azad's opinion and approach. Yet not even the most learned of them could meet Azad in debate and argument, even on the basis of scriptures and tradition, for Azad's knowledge of these happened to be greater than theirs. He was a strange mixture of medieval scholasticism, eighteenth century rationalism and modern outlook. There were a few among the older generation who approved of Azad's writings, among them being Shibli and Sir Sayyaid of Aligarh University.

After the confiscation of 'Al-Hilal' Azad brought out a new weekly called 'Al Balagh' but this too came to an end when Azad was interned in 1916. He remained in jail for four years. When he came out he was an acknowledged leader and took his seat with the great might of the Indian National Congress. In 1920 he met Tilak and Gandhi which was the turning point of his life. Gandhi had launched the 'Khilafat Movement' under the Deoband School and Firanghi Mahal where Gandhi and Azad were frequent visitors. But when Muslim League denounced Gandhiji's Satyagraha, Azad who had enrolled himself in the League when a boy, left the Muslim League forever. His popularity was so high that at 35 he became the President of the Indian National Congress, the youngest ever to hold that office. In 1942 during the Quit India Movement he was elected as the Chief spokesman of the Congress. This distinction he also had during the negotiations with the Cabinet Mission in 1946 at Simla.

As Education Minister (15.08.47 to 22.02.1958)

In 1947 when the Interim Government was formed Maulana Azad was included as Member for Education and Arts. On August 15, 1947 when India attained Independence he became Free India's first Education Minister with a cabinet rank where he achieved a number of distinctions and established institutions of excellence to promote education and culture.

Among the new institutions he established were the three National Academies viz the Sangeet Natak Academy (1953), Sahitya Academy (1954) and Lalit Kala Academy (1954), the Indian Council for Cultural Relations having been established by him earlier in 1950. The Maulana felt that the cultural content in Indian Education was very low during the British rule and needs to be strengthened through curriculum. As Chairman of the Central Advisory Board of Education, an apex body to recommend to the Government educational reform both at the center and the states including universities, he advocated, in particular, universal primary education, free and compulsory for all children upto the age of 14, girls education, vocational training, agricultural education and technical education. He established University Grants Commission (UGC) in 1956 by an Act of Parliament for disbursement of grants and maintainence of standards in Indian universities. He firmly believed with Nehru that if the universities discharged their functions well, all will be well with the Nation. According to him the universities have not only academic functions, they have social responsibilities as well. He was pioneer in the field of adult education. His greatest contribution, however, is that in spite of being an eminent scholar of Urdu, Persian and Arabic he stood for the retention of English language for educational advantages and national and international needs. However primary education should be imparted in the mother-tongue. On the technical education side he strengthened All Indian Council for Technical Education. The Indian Institute of Technology, Kharagpur was established in 1951 followed by a chain of IIT's at Bombay, Madras and Kanpur and Delhi. School of Planning and Architecture came into existence at Delhi in 1955.

Student Unrest

Secular to the marrow of his bones Maulana's advice to students was: 'Bury communalism once for all.' Student indiscipline, however, continued to worry him. Presiding over the meeting of the Central Advisory Board of Education (CABE) on February 7, 1954 he said: "What worries me most is that the extent and magnitude of the student's unrest is very often without any relation whatsoever to the supposed cause. Such unrest among the students strikes at the root of our national culture. The student of today is the potential leader of tomorrow. He will have to sustain the social, political and economic activities. If he is not properly trained and does not develop the necessary resources of character and knowledge he cannot supply the leadership which the national will need".

As an Author

Maulana Azad was a prolific writer with books in Urdu, Persian and Arabic notably amongst which is 'India Wins Freedom', his political biography, translated from Urdu to English. Maulana's translation of Quran from Arabic into Urdu in six volumes published by Sahitya Akademy in 1977 is indeed his 'Magnum Opus". Since then several editions of 'Tarjaman-e-Quran' have come out. His other books include 'Gubar-e-Khatir', 'Hijr-o-Vasal', 'Khatbat-I-Azad', 'Hamari Azadi', 'Tazkara'. He gave a new life to Anjamane-Tarrqui-e-Urdu-e-Hind'. During the partition riots when the 'Anjamane-Tarrqui-Urdu suffered, its Secretary Maulvi Abdul Haqq decided to leave for Pakistan alongwith the books of the Anjaman. Abdul Haqq had packed the books but Maulana Azad got them retrieved and thus saved a national treasure being lost to Pakistan. He also helped the Anjaman to revive by sanctioning a grant of Rs. 48,000 per month from the Ministry of Education. Likewise he increased the grants of Jamia Millia Islamia, Aligarh Muslim University in their days of financial crisis. He paid particular attention to the Archaeological Survey of India's efforts to repair and maintain the protected monuments.

Throughout his life he stood for the chords of cordiality between Hindus and Muslims and the composite culture of India. He stood for modern India with secular credentials, a cosmopolitan character and international outlook.

Orator

As an orator Azad had no equal among his contemporaries. When he spoke the audience listened to him spell-bound. Recalling the memories of the Roman and the Greek orators, there was magic in his words, his language was chaste, civilized, his speech was dramatic. In October 1947 when the Delhi Muslims were leaving for Pakistan tens of thousands of them, he spoke from the ramparts of Jama Masjid, like an ancient oracle: "Behold, the high towers of Jama Masjid are asking you: where have you lost the pages of your history. Only yesterday your caravans had performed 'Wazu; (Ablutions) on the banks of Jamuna. And today you are afraid to live here. Remember that you have nourished Delhi with your blood. You are afraid of tremors, time was when you yourself were an earthquake. You fear darkness when you yourself symbolized light only recently. The clouds have only poured dirty water and you have raised your trousers for fear of being drenched. They were your forefathers who had dived deep into the seas, cut across the mighty mountains, laughed away the lightnings, answered the thunder of the skies with the velocity of your laughter, changed the direction of the winds and turned the typhoons that they have been misled to a wrong destination. It is an irony of faith that those who played with the destinies of the kings are victims of their own destiny today. And in doing so they have become so forgetful of their God as if it never existed. Go back it is your home, your country...."

The effect of his speech was dramatic. Those who packed up their baggages to migrate to Pakistan returned home filled with a new sense of freedom and patriotism. There was no mass migration thereafter. In the history of international oratory Maulana Azad's Jama Masjid speech can only be compared with the Gettysburg address of Abraham Lincoln, Birla House speech of Nehru on Gandhi's assassination and recently of Martin Luther's speech: 'I have a dream'.

As a man Maulana was even greater, he led an austere life. He had the madness of a Spinoza, the courage of Prometheus Unbound, the humility of a Dervesh. At the time of his death he had neither any property nor any bank account. In his personal almirah were found some cotton 'Achkans'. A dozen 'Khadi Kurtas' and 'pyjama', two pairs of sandals, an old dressing gown and a used brush. But there were lots of rare books which are now a property of the Nation.

A man like Maulana Azad is born rarely. Throughout his life he stood for the unity of India and its composite culture. His opposition to partition of India has created a niche in the hearts of all patriotic Indians.There he stands with Khan Abdul Ghaffar Khan, his senior an Ashfaqullah his junior. In the words of Iqbal : Hazaron sall Nargis apni benoori par roti hai, Bari Mushkil sey hota hai chaman mein deeda var paida. (For a thousand years the Narcissus weeps for her blindness, With great difficulty is born in the garden a man with vision). Maulana Abul Kalam Azad's Birthday 11th November has been declared as National Education Day .

4

Maulana Azad and Role in National Movement

Maulana Abul Kalam Azad played, with great dedication and distinction, the roles of a leader of the Indian Muslim community and the Indian national movement. If, on the one hand, Azad firmly maintained that the *Quran* was the true guide for religion and politics, on the other he described himself as "...a reformer, guide, of the Caravan of the Quam, the Muslims".

This great reformist Muslim leader and scholar of Islamic holy texts and traditions comfortably merged his Islamic loyalties with secular Indian nationalism and, as a committed Muslim believer and a nationalist, he unhesitatingly - and unambiguously - fought for Hindu-Muslim unity. Syeda Saiyidain Hameed deserves to be congratulated for writing an extremely competent biography of the scholarly nationalist leader who remains an unquestioned symbol of India's "composite culture".

The first six chapters are devoted to the development of Azad's personality and ideology, and the remaining four narrate his role in the freedom struggle.

Although Azad's world view was rooted in the *Quran*, he took a firm stand against the *ulemas*, or Muslim legal scholars, who interpreted the texts. To quote Ms Hameed, "The perpetrators of oppression, Azad says, have always availed of the services of the *ulema* who are more than willing to serve the state." According to Azad, the ulemas are "...worse than snakes and scorpions" and, as a reformist, Azad told his community that "Man's ultimate guidance is therefore to be derived not from these ulema-e-duniya paras ... but from the word of the Koran and the Sunnat of the Prophet".

Azad himself wrote and translated the Holy Quran into Urdu. In Chapter 8, titled "Tarjuman-ul-quran", the author clearly shows that Azad wanted to educate Muslims in the doctrines of Islam and liberate believers from the misrepresentation of Quranic injunctions by motivated and political time servers, whether they were *ulemas* or self-appointed Muslim leaders of the community.

Azad believed it was every Muslim's religious duty to participate in politics against "oppressors" and colonialists. Therefore, the Khilafat movement, which was launched in India against the enemies of Islam, was naturally aligned with Mahatma Gandhi's non-cooperation movement and the first five years of the 1920s witnessed a unity in struggle against both the destroyers of Muslim holy places and the struggle for India's independence.

Chapter 5, "Muslim politics: Khilafat", focuses on Azad's efforts to educate Indians about the "natural bond between India and Islamic nations" so that the Khilafat movement was not launched for a cause that was "external" to India but was an integral part of Indian struggle for causes dear to Arab friends. This philosophy can be best summed up in his own words: "Because I am an Indian, I am a Muslim, I am a human being."

Is this effort to base politics on religion inherently flawed and contradictory? Azad and many others like him think religion, as understood by them, cannot be divorced from politics because religious spirituality is a moral guide for the lofty goals of the politics of freedom. But the facts are contrary to the belief in religion-based politics, because while talking of Hindu-Muslim unity it is often forgotten that people remain separate entities, as Hindus and Muslims.

In fact, the last four chapters concretely show that not everyone involved in the freedom struggle shared the hefty ideal of Hindu-Muslim unity at any cost that Azad held dear. This divergence of views was not limited to purely religion-based parties such as the All-India Muslim League and the Hindu Mahasabha; Azad himself had to sit in the company of protectors of Hindu interests in the Indian National Congress.

Chapter 11, titled "President and negotiator", bears enough testimony to the fact that in crucial negotiations with British Prime Minister Clement Attlee or his viceroy in India, Lord Louis Mountbatten, several Hindu leaders took positions that could only be described as communal. Azad's experience as Congress president and Congress Working Committee member should have made him realise that it was quite another thing to make everyone believe in real secularism.

Azad's tragedy was that full-fledged Muslim communalists described him, in the words of Muhammad Ali Jinnah, as the "Showboy of Indian National Congress", and he had to negotiate his way in the Gandhi-Nehru Congress in which practitioners of realpolitik also played the Hindu card. He was deeply uneasy when K F Nariman, a Parsi, and Syed Mahmud, a Muslim, were not made leaders of the Congress party in Bombay and Bihar, respectively, after the 1937 elections. "Congress did not come out fully successful in its test of nationalism," he wrote at the time.

The description of 20th-century India till Azad's death in 1958 has considerable relevance for 21st-century India; the most important lesson is that without the separation of religion from politics, democracy in the country - formally or informally - remains involved in the struggle for claims like first-class Hindu citizens versus second-class Muslim citizens. This Amir of the Quam's Caravan could neither liberate his community from the control of the fanatics nor leave a strong legacy of Hindu-Muslim unity in post-Independence India.

Ms Hameed's rich and well-researched biography is, however, incomplete because it does not analyse the basic contradiction in Azad's beliefs, personal practices and politics. Religion in politics pollutes politics and is a divider of society. Azad never reflected on this side of his belief in "religion-based politics". This criticism is not intended to denigrate his immense contributions, but not analysing the fundamental weaknesses in the philosophy of a leader like Azad does disservice to the hero of the many battles he fought.

ABOUT MAULANA ABUL KALAM

Maulana Abul Kalam Azad was born on 11 November, 1888 in Mecca, Saudi Arabia. He was a leading figure in India's struggle for freedom and a noted writer, poet and journalist. He adopted the pen name Azad (Free). In his childhood, Azad had a traditional Islamic education, along with training in subjects like mathematics, philosophy, world history and science by tutors at his home. Through his own efforts, he learnt English, along with Western philosophy, history and contemporary politics. He visited countries like Afghanistan, Iraq, Egypt, Syria and Turkey. He opposed the partition of Bengal in 1905.

Azad established the Indian Institute of Technology and also contributed in the foundation of the University Grant Commission.

Personal Life

His real name was Abul Kalam Ghulam Muhiyuddin, but became known as Maulana Azad. He was born to father Bengali Maulana Muhammad Khairuddin and mother Arab. He was born in Mecca, but the family relocated to Calcutta in 1890. He married Zulaikha Begum when he was thirteen years old.

Literary Work

He established an Urdu weekly newspaper in 1912 named Al-Hilal. It was consequently banned in 1914, following which he started a new journal, the Al-Balagh.

'Ghubar-e-Khatir' is one of his most noted works which he wrote between 1942 and 1946.

He published many works criticising the British rule and advocating self-rule for India. His exhaustive book on India's freedom struggle titled 'India Wins Freedom' was published in 1957.

Political Career

It was as a leader of the Khilafat movement that he became close to Mahatma Gandhi. He became the youngest President of the Indian National Congress in 1923.He always supported the cause of Hindu-Muslim unity and opposed the demand for a separate Muslim state of Pakistan. He was one of the most important leaders behind the Dharasana Satyagraha in 1931. He became the Congress president in 1940 and continued till 1945 and during that time, the Quit India rebellion also came up.

He served in the Constituent Assembly formed to draft India's constitution and was elected to the Lok Sabha in 1952 and in 1957. In 1956, he served as president of the UNESCO General Conference in Delhi.

MAULANA AZAD IN *INDIA WINS FREEDOM*

On 15 April 1946, I issued a statement dealing with the demands of Muslims and other minorities. Now that the division of India is a fact and ten years have passed, I again look at the statement and find that everything I had then said has come to happen. As this statement contains my considered views on the solution of the Indian problem, I feel I should quote it in full. This is what I then said, and would still say:

I have considered from every possible point of view the scheme of Pakistan as formulated by the Muslim League. As an Indian I have examined its implications for the future of India as a whole. As a Muslim I have examined its likely effects upon the fortunes of Muslims of India.

Considering the scheme in all its aspects I have come to the conclusion that it is harmful not only for India as a whole but for Muslims in particular. And in fact it creates more problems than it solves.

I must confess that the very term Pakistan goes against my grain. It suggests that some portions of the world are pure while others are impure. Such a division of territories into pure and impure is un-Islamic and is more in keeping with orthodox Brahmanism which divides men and countries into holy and unholy- a division which is a repudiation of the very spirit of Islam. Islam recognizes no such division and the prophet says, 'God has made the whole world a mosque for me.'

Further, it seems that the scheme of Pakistan is a symbol of defeatism and has been built up on the analogy of the Jewish demand for a national home. It is a confession that Indian Muslims cannot hold their own in India as a whole and would be content to withdraw to a corner specially reserved for them.

One can sympathize with the aspiration of the Jews for such a national home, as they are scattered all over the world and cannot in any region have any effective voice in the administration. The conditions of Indian Muslims is quite otherwise. Over 90 million in number, they are in quantity and quality a sufficiently important element in Indian life to Influence decisively all questions of administration and policy. Nature has further helped them by concentrating them in certain areas.

In such a context, the demand for Pakistan loses all force. As a Muslim, I for one am not prepared for a moment to give up my right to treat the whole of India as my domain and to share in the shaping of its political and economic life. To me it seems a sure sign of cowardice to give up what is my patrimony and content myself with a mere fragment of it.

As is well known, Mr. Jinnah's Pakistan scheme is based on his two nation theory. His thesis is that India contains many nationalities based on religious differences. Of them the two major nations, the Hindus and Muslims, must as separate nations have separate states. When Dr. Edward Thompson once pointed out to Mr. Jinnah that Hindus and Muslims live side by side in thousands of Indian towns, villages and hamlets, Mr. Jinnah replied that this in no way affected their separate nationality. Two nations according to Mr. Jinnah confront one another in every hamlet, village and town, and he, therefore, desires that they should be separated into two states.

I am prepared to overlook all other aspects of the problem and judge it from the point of view of Muslim interests alone. I shall go still further and say that if it can be shown that the scheme of Pakistan can in any way benefit Muslims I would be prepared to accept it myself and also to work for its acceptance by others. But the truth is that even if I examine the scheme from the point of view of the communal interests of the Muslims themselves, I am forced to the conclusion that it can in no way benefit them or allay their legitimate fears.

Let us consider dispassionately the consequences which will follow if we give effect to the Pakistan scheme. India will be divided into two States, one with a majority of Muslims and the other of Hindus.

In the Hindustan State there will remain three and a half crores of Muslims scattered in small minorities all over the land. With 17 per cent in U.P, 12 per cent in Bihar and 9 per cent in Madras, they will be weaker than they are today in the Hindu majority provinces. They have had their homelands in these regions for almost a thousand years and built up well known centres of Muslim culture and civilization there. They will awaken overnight and discover that they have become alien and foreigners. Backward industrially, educationally and economically, they will be left to the mercies to what would become an unadulterated Hindu raj.

On the other hand, their position within the Pakistan State will be vulnerable and weak. Nowhere in Pakistan will their majority be comparable to the Hindu majority in the Hindustan States. In fact, their majority will be so slight that it will be offset by the economical, educational and political lead enjoyed by non Muslims in these areas. Even if this were not so and Pakistan were overwhelmingly Muslim in population, it still could hardly solve the problem of Muslims in Hindustan.

Two states confronting one another, offer no solution of the problem of one another's minorities, but only lead to retribution and reprisals by introducing a system of mutual hostages. The scheme of Pakistan therefore solves no problem for the Muslims. It cannot safeguard their rights where they are in a minority nor as citizens of Pakistan secure them a position in Indian or world affairs which they would enjoy as citizens of a major State like the Indian Union.

It may be argued that if Pakistan is so much against the interests of the Muslims themselves, why should such a large section of Muslims be swept away by its lure? The answer is to be found in the attitude of certain communal extremists among the Hindus. When the Muslim League began to speak of Pakistan, they read into the scheme a sinister pan-Islamic conspiracy and began to oppose it out of fear that it foreshadowed a combination of Indian Muslim with trans-Indian Muslims States.

The opposition acted as an incentive to the adherents of the League. With simple though untenable logic they argued that if Hindus were so opposed to Pakistan, surely it must be of benefit to Muslims. An atmosphere of emotional frenzy was created which made reasonable appraisement impossible and swept away, especially the younger and more impressionable among the Muslims. I have, however, no doubt that when the present frenzy has died down and the question can be considered dispassionately, those who now support Pakistan will themselves repudiate it as harmful for Muslim Interests.

The formula which I have succeeded in making the Congress accept secures whatever merit the Pakistan scheme contains while all its defects and drawbacks are avoided. The basis of Pakistan is the fear of interference by the Centre in Muslim majority areas as the Hindus will be in a majority in the Centre. The Congress meets this fear by granting full autonomy to the provincial units and vesting all residuary power in the provinces. It also has provided for two lists of Central subjects, one compulsory and one optional, so that if any provincial unit so wants, it can administer all subjects itself except a minimum delegated to the Centre. The Congress scheme therefore ensures that Muslim majority provinces are internally free to develop as they will, but can at the same time influence the Centre on all issues which affect India as a whole.

The situation in India is such that all attempts to establish a centralized and unitary government are bound to fail. Equally doomed to failure is the attempt to divide India into two States. After considering all aspects of the question, I have come to the conclusion that the only solution can be on the lines embodied in the Congress formula which allows room for development both to the provinces and to India as a whole. The Congress formula meets the fear of the Muslim majority areas to allay which the scheme of Pakistan was formed. On the other hand, it avoids the defects of the Pakistan scheme which would bring the Muslims where they are in a minority under a purely Hindu government.

I am one of those who considers the present chapter of communal bitterness and differences as a transient phase in Indian life. I firmly hold that they will disappear when India assumes the responsibility of her own destiny. I am reminded of a saying of Mr. Gladstone that the best cure for a man's fear of the water was to throw him into it. Similarly India must assume responsibilities and administer her own affairs before fears and suspicions can be fully allayed.

When India attains her destiny, she will forget the chapter of communal suspicion and conflict and face the problems of modern life from a modern point of view. Differences will no doubt persist, but they will be economic, not communal. Opposition among political parties will continue, but it will be based, not on religion but on economic and political issues. Class and not community will be the basis of future alignments, and policies will be shaped accordingly. If it be argued that this is only a faith which events may not justify I would say that in any case the nine crores of Muslims constitute a factor which nobody can ignore and whatever the circumstances they are strong enough to safeguard their own destiny.

Comment

Viceroy Wavell and Stafford Cripps dismissed the implications of Jinnah's advocacy of the two nation theory, Wavell terming it 'some rather foolish remark about separate nationalities'.

Viceroy Wavell's Journal Wntry, April 3, 1946 (excerpt)

Maulana Azad was less suave and well-mannered than on the other occasions I have met him, and frequently walked up and down the room in obvious tension. Asaf Ali interpreted.

Azad put out a scheme for Indian Federation, in which there were two lists of Federal subjects-compulsory and optional. He also admitted the right of a Province or Area to stand out altogether under certain conditions. He produced a novel theory that if there were a division, Muslims domiciled in Hindustan and Hindus in Pakistan would be 'aliens', which Cripps said was juridically impossible. I am sure Azad only meant it as a debating point against Jinnah-towards whom he showed great animosity-because Jinnah had made some rather foolish remark about separate nationalities.

MAULANA AZAD AS FREEDOM FIGHTER

The first major turning point for Azad came after the partition of Bengal, when he rejected the mainstream of the Muslim middle class, which wanted partition and considered the colonial government as its benefactor. Repudiating it, he associated himself with the anti British Movement.

In 1908, after his father's death, his visits to France and some Islamic countries, Iraq, Syria, Egypt, and Turkey had a profound and decisive influence on Azad's political thinking. While abroad, he met a number of groups, the young Turks, the Arab Nationalists and the prominent leaders of the pan-Islamic Movement who wanted to throw away the yoke of imperialism to free the Arab countries.

He was influenced by the writing of Jamaluddin Afghani (l 837_97), a pan–Islamist modern reformer who regarded European countries as enemies of Islam. He also met the Iranian revolutionaries fighting against the Qajar autocracy and the followers of Sheikh Muhammad Abduhu and Saeed Pasha and supporters of Mustafa Kamal Pasha. He was apprised of the programmes of the young Turks. These Indian, Arab, Turkish, Irani and Afghani revolutionaries vividly demonstrated their anti-imperial attitude to Azad. They lamented over Indian indifference to their struggle for freedom. All these experiences also motivated him in plunging into the political arena. He found a new world astir with ideas of liberty, progress and revolutionary Islam. He noticed that the Muslim world was facing various kinds of threats. Italy had conquered the provision of Tripoli in 1911. The Balkan states were determined to dismember Turkey. Morocco had yielded to French yoke and Russia threatened Iran. Turkey was encircled by Russia, England and France. These events deeply affected Azad.

In India too, the Muslim Community was going through a serious ideological crisis at the turn of the century. Earlier, during the last quarter of the 19th century, Sir Syed Ahmad Khan tried to persuade the Muslim elite that its political future laid in adopting a liberal outlook at the same time as it adopted a cooperative attitude towards British Imperialism in the subcontinent. However this call for an alliance with imperialism was totally unacceptable to large sections of the Muslim community in India, particularly among the elite and the popular classes. Young Maulana Azad, in common with leaders like Muhammad Ali and Shaukat Ali, Wazir Hasan and others represented those within the Muslim community who challenged this concept of Islamic modernism in alliance with Imperialism, propounded by Sir Syed. These leaders looked upon Great Britain as an alien power bent upon humiliating Islam in Asia at the same time as it sought to undermine the spiritual and secular status of Islam within the Indian sub-continent.

It was at this juncture that Azad launched his Urdu weekly Al-Hilal on June, 1912 when he was only 24. He believed that only by educating the 'Ulama, the learned in Law and in theology, there would emerge a nucleus of dedicated and idealistic elite which can act as a lever for the moral and intellectual regeneration of the Muslim community. With the launching of Al-Hilal, Azad shot into the National Movement. He gave fearless and powerful expression to his nationalist ideas through the journal. The basic intent of Al-Hilal was to launch a vigorous attack not only on the colonial distortions of our history but more on the pro-colonial modernism of the Aligarh School, which had poisoned the minds of the Modernist Muslim intelligentsia. Al-Hilal held out the message of nationalism to the Muslim elites as well as the popular classes and urged them to join other communities in the struggle for the liberation of the country.

Al-Hilal became immensely popular among the Muslim intelligentsia within a short period.

Its circulation had reached 2, 90,000 by 1914, when the Government confiscated the Al-Hilal Press after two years of continuous publication. Azad took the view that by their crafty policy of divide and rule, the British had made Hindus and Muslims antagonistic to each other. Azad suggested to his people that the right course for both the communities was to fight the British to prevent them from bringing ruination to their country. Al-Hial was also critical of the Muslim League, its aristocratic leadership and its style of functioning. The journal inspired the educated Muslim to awaken to a new political sense.

It is significant that all these moves and various political activities of Azad were initiated before the emergence of Gandhiji on the political horizon. Advent of Gandhiji into the National Movement and Azad's meeting with him had crucial bearing on the future course of the movement. Azad met Gandhiji on 18 January 1920 at the residence of Hakim Ajmal Khan in the presence of Lokmanya Tilak and Ali brothers.

Before his meeting with Gandhiji, he defined collective identity of the Muslim Community in terms of Islam and denned and visualized a safe and legitimate place for the Muslims within the sub-continent. In Gandhiji, he found institutional support for his political stand. The Khilafat Movement and later the non-cooperation Movement was to provide a broader platform and offer more serious challenges to Azad's budding political career.

Yet another turning point in Azad's political career was marked by the Non-Cooperation Movement launched under the leadership of Gandhiji. It was during the Non-Cooperation Movement that he began to think of Hindus and Muslims of forming nation. Until this time Azad was a member of both Congress and the Muslim League. But after the league at its session of 1921, denounced the Civil Disobedience Movement, Azad along with several other prominent Muslim leaders, left the league for good.

He exhorted the Muslim masses to join the freedom struggle by giving a religious justification for the Movement. For the Hindus working for independence might be a patriotic gesture. But for the Muslims it is a religious duty. In the 1920s, Azad was, to a large extent, responsible in sanctifying the Hindu-Muslim partnership and in drawing more and more Muslims to the folds of the Congress, thus enhancing the momentum of the Freedom movement.

In 1923, at its Delhi session, he was elected President of the Indian National Congress at the age of 35, becoming the youngest Congress President to date. He was an ardent protagonist of Hindu-Muslim unity. On his election, he said, "If an angel were to descent from the high heavens and proclaim from the heights of the Qutab Minar, discard Hindu-Muslim unity and within 24 hours, Swaraj is yours, I will refuse swaraj but will not budge an inch from my stand. If Swaraj is delayed it will affect only India while the end of our unity will be the loss of our entire human world."

At a time when many Indian Muslims led by the Muslim league were crying for partition, Azad stood up in defence of the unity of the sub-continent. When the Congress launched the Satyagraha Movement in 1930, Azad was arrested. He was a party to every direct action launched by the Congress during the course of the freedom struggle and spent 11 years of his life in British jails. He accepted the most challenging assignment of his life when he took over the presidentship of the Indian National Congress at its Ramgarh session in 1940.

Shortly before Azad presided over the Ramgarh Session of the Congress in 1940, Nehru said of him, "...he is not the type of man who likes the rough and tumble of politics. He is very sensitive and rather avoids crowds and publicity. He lacks a certain vital energy. In a wider world he is rather out of place as he thinks on political lines and hardly at all on social or economic lines... In the Muslim world of India he is tremendously very advance. Probably he is the ablest among the Muslim divines. Most of them are afraid of him because he can floor them in any argument. His knowledge even of the scriptures and traditions is very great,"

Maulana Azad's tenure as Congress President was longest in its pre-independence history. He presided over the Congress during the most crucial phase of the struggle. It was under his presidentship that All India Congress Committee passed the famous Quit India Resolution and gave the call of "Do or Die". The Movement was ruthlessly suppressed by the British Government and Maulana Azad, along with the rest of the Congress leaders, was arrested and put behind the bars.

On his release in 1945, he was entrusted with the most delicate task of negotiating with the British and the Muslim League for transfer of power to Indians. He negotiated with Lord Wavell, the Viceroy of India later at Shimla. He led the Congress delegation in talk with the Cabinet Mission headed by Sir Pethwick Lawrence, the Secretary of State for India. He wanted to have a dialogue with Mohammad Ali Jinnah who brushed him away and refused to talk to one he considered as the Congress' Show-boy.

However, he pulled through these turbulent times. He had to face the might of the apologists of the British Raj as well as the proponents of the vivisection of the sub-continent. He did it with equanimity and stoicism and without losing poise or dignity. Maulana Azad carried the Congress with him through these historic six years with matchless grace and distinction. He also consistently tried to heal the rift-between the Congress and the League.

Maulana was an intellectual par excellence and a political giant. Above all he was an uncompromising patriot. Though he had to suffer incarceration in British Jails, his spirit remained unbowed. He had to move from jail to jail from Alipur in Calcutta to Naini in Allahabad, Meerut, Gonda, Moradabad, Ahmed Nagar and Delhi but the sensitivity of his intellect remained intact. He did most of his writings during those jail days. Azad lost his wife Zuleikha Begum when he was detained in the Ahmednagar fort in the wake of the Quit India Movement.

When partition came about, Maulana Azad and his nationalist Muslim followers were heartbroken. Azad's dream of a United India was shattered and he was a broken man. But he kept a brave face and in his loyalty to his political colleagues, he never lamented in public.

However, he took pride in identifying himself as an Indian as well as a Muslim. For him there was no dichotomy between the two. When the Pakistan Resolution was passed at Lahore under the leadership of Jinnah, Azad said, "I am part of the indivisible unity that is Indian nationality. I am indispensable to this noble edifice and without me this splendid structure of India is incomplete. I am an essential element which has gone to build India. I can never surrender this claim."

Indeed he was an indispensable part of this noble edifice, namely India. When the Muslims of India were deeply worried about their future within the country after the partition of the subcontinent Maulana Azad, in his characteristic statesman-like manner, reached out to them and helped in infusing confidence and faith in being Indians, reminding his co-religionists of the disastrous role played by fanatic leaders who propounded the two-nation theory and thus betrayed the cause of composite nationalism. He urged them to address themselves anew to the task of creating for the

Islamic world a "place of dignity" in the new order of things. In an inspiring address to the Muslims in 1948 he said, "I am not asking you to seek certificates of loyalty out of the fear of the ruling power or to live as camp followers, as you did during the days of foreign domination. Let me remind you that some of the bright signs and symbols that you discern today in India, as a heritage of the past, were contributed by our own forefathers. Don't forget them. Don't forsake them. Live like their worthy inheritors. Realise that if you yourself are not willing to run away no power on earth could make you do so."

Maulana Azad held a position unique in several ways. He was emotionally and intellectually close to both — Mahatma Gandhi and Nehru. He was closely associated with crucial decision making since the twenties. With the dawn of freedom in 1947, his was a natural choice to be in the Cabinet- He was the Minister of Education during 1947-52, and Minister of Education, Natural Resources and Scientific Research from 1952-58. His influence on the process of policy making was immense. He was Nehru's, comrade-in-arms during the days of the freedom movement and was-one of his closest confidante and adviser in the Cabinet.

THE SWARAJIST STRATEGY

The return of elite politics to its old constitutional track was both a consequence and a cause of the underclass retreat. As the promise of *swaraj* faded and as it became clear that the Surtis were gradually dissociating themselves from noncooperation, many of the Congress leaders began to reconsider their political options. Often they felt the need to resume bargaining with their rulers too compelling to continue their efforts to undermine the institutions of local self-government. And as they reentered the politics of legislative councils and municipalities, they often pursued their claims to justice through the idiom of public politics, reproducing conventional civic discourse through their political practice. They now became only representatives of the people, losing their identities as *chelas* and *sannyasis.* Abandoning the hard line of noncooperation in turn indicated clearly to the larger population that the achievement of some alternative to the colonial order was unlikely in the near future and that continued participation in the most conspicuous forms of nationalist resistance would probably not bear much more fruit.

The emergence of the Swarajya party during early 1923 opened the first cracks in the Gandhian strategy of noncooperation. Led in the Bombay Presidency by Vithalbhai Patel and M. R. Jayakar, the Swarajists proposed entering the reformed legislative council to pursue a policy of obstructing government from within. When Patel visited Surat from Bombay in early May to solicit support for his party, a number of local politicians, including some who had been the staunchest supporters of noncooperation only two years earlier, quickly jumped on board. Surat suddenly became the centre of Swarajist activity in Gujarat. Dr. Dixit, Dr. Mehta, and Maganlal Vidyarthi, all local noncooperators with sufficient education and professional training to make the shift to a politics based upon the idiom of constitutionalism and progress, assumed important positions in the Gujarat Provincial Swarajya party. All three planned campaigns to run for provincial office. Opposition to the Swarajya program came largely from activists who had been arrested and their supporters. In Surat, however, this opposition was muted owing to the intervention of Dayalji Desai, now president of the District Congress Committee. Fearing the potential for a major rupture between local nationalists, Dayalji attempted to cultivate mutual respect among the two factions. With his encouragement, "NoChangers" and Swarajists both appeared in the same public meetings to present their views on entry into the councils while confirming their shared commitment to Gandhi's constructive program, to agitation against the local municipality, and to the national schools. Dayalji even encouraged Vithalbhai Patel to address Surat's citizens from a Congress platform just before the elections.

In recent years, historians have tended to view the willingness of Congress politicians to back the Swarajya party after 1923 as evidence of a materialistic concern with gaining access to networks of patronage controlled by the provincial legislatures. Evidence from Surat certainly indicates that an interest in personal political influence was important, but it also suggests that scholars might need to probe further into the question of why this influence was sought. In Surat local Gandhians of all stripes were genuinely flustered by the ability of Liberal politicians to frustrate the Congress cause.

Many felt that Chunilal Gandhi, the city's representative in the Bombay council, was partly responsible for the suspension of the noncooperating municipality, the appointment of the Committee of Management, and a variety of other government efforts to suppress the cause of *swaraj*. As long as persons with little commitment to the Congress program remained in control of the legislatures, they reasoned, government could easily thwart their activities. In entering the Bombay legislature, Dixit, Mehta, and Vidyarthi sought not only to paralyze the colonial government of the province but also to restore the municipality to Congress hands.

By gaining control of the council, they believed that they could reinvigorate such efforts essential to attaining independence as nationalizing local schools. They by no means wished to abandon other aspects of the Congress constructive program such as the promotion of *khadi* and of Hindu-Muslim unity.

But once they decided to reenter legislative politics, the Swarajists found themselves compelled to adhere to political conventions quite different from those that had governed noncooperation.

They defended their actions largely in terms of the principles of public discourse, in part because these principles allowed them best to dismiss the claims of their opponents. In the election campaign of September and October 1923, none of the Swarajya party's candidates used Gandhian rhetoric extensively. Each stressed the violations of citizen rights that had occurred under their opposition's tenure of office. According to their arguments, a coterie of Liberals such as Chunilal Gandhi, voted in by tiny minorities of the population during the boycotted elections of 1920, had frustrated the true will of the people. M. M. Mehta, running for Surat's single urban seat, contended that as a result of moderate cooperation with the British in the legislative councils, "the whole country has had to accept increases in the salt tax; citizens in the municipalities of Surat, Ahmedabad and Nadiad have had their rights of self-government taken from them; the birthright of mothers and fathers to educate their children as they wish has been trampled upon; reputable householders have been prosecuted and fined under the compulsory education law; and national schools have been locked up under various government schemes."

"It is a duty of the representatives of the people," he insisted, "... to attempt to prevent such disastrous developments," thus criticizing the moderates for failing to perform their responsibilities as legislators while claiming that he, if elected, would certainly fulfill his obligations to his voters. Dixit, running in the rural constituency of South Gujarat, promised in his speeches that the Swarajists would try to regain popular control over municipalities, to free Mahatma Gandhi and other political prisoners from jail, and to fight for independence and other political rights. For the most part, the rhetoric of both candidates was devoid of the religious allusions they had employed just a year or so earlier. The language of representative government was clearly beginning to reestablish its preeminence in the civic arena.

Such appeals, however, were by themselves hardly sufficient to ensure election Vietories. After all, the public meetings of the Swarajist candidates, often attended by no more than fifty people, could not hope to reach the entire urban electorate of Surat, now more than seven thousand voters, or the even larger rural constituency.

To a great extent the election of 1923 relied on techniques that had often been used in the campaigns of prewar Surat but that had been abandoned during the noncooperation years. Candidates again secured the support of agents—that is, men of local influence—to canvass neighborhoods of the city and persuade voters to attend the polls. On the day of the election, these agents intensified their personal methods of contacting citizens. With a number of private motor cars and carriages at their disposal, the Swarajists ferried many voters to the polling station at the city castle individually. The district magistrate's remarks that there had been "a great deal of improper influence used in the town," while obviously reflecting a heavy bias against the Congress, confirmed the existence of a second, more personal, idiom of politics operating alongside and supplementing civic discourse, one that the Swarajists used more effectively than the Liberals. During the next provincial campaign, in 1926, the *Gujarat Mitra* would remark that these electoral practices had become so engrained that even "a voter only a hundred yards away from the polling station... expects a car to be near his door before he thinks of leaving his place for the purpose of voting." English-educated politicians of every party tended to agree that these methods were necessitated by an electorate "ignorant of the value of the vote" which required further "training" in the proper exercise of democratic government. No doubt the inaccessibility of constitutional rhetoric for the local population inhibited plebeian participation in the exercise of public power. But no one gave voice to the possibility that the language of liberal representative politics could be as responsible for that as any deficiency in the political education of the Surtis.

As a result of their effective use of this bilingual campaign, the Swarajists won a resounding success in the 1923 election. In Surat City, Dr. Mehta won easily, with 2,433 votes to Chunilal Gandhi's 407 and Jamshedji Antia's 302. Dr. Dixit won one of the two rural seats. Vidyarthi finished far down in the polling, but H. B. Shivdasani, a former assistant collector who had recently resigned his post and who had won the tacit backing of Dayaiji when he signed up as a Congress member, was the leading vote getter in the countryside. Shivdasani immediately became one of the most vocal and effective members of the Bombay Swarajists in the legislature. Even the old home ruler Kanaiyalal Desai, who finished third in the rural voting, signed the Congress pledge just before the election.

Once in the councils, Mehta, Dixit, and Shivdasani found themselves bound by severe constraints, some of which they had never anticipated. Within the Bombay council, colonial authority was still strong. Under the system of dyarchy that had been created by the Montagu Chelmsford reforms of 1919, wide areas of policy were entirely excluded from discussion by the elected legislators. But even in those spheres of policy designated as appropriately within the council's domain, government and its Indian allies retained considerable informal influence. Owing to unevenness in support for the Swarajists elsewhere in the Bombay Presidency and to the abundance of separate electorates and reserved seats for Muslims, non-Brahmans, and a variety of special interests, the nationalists captured only a minority of the positions on the council.

Only persons with "loyal" inclinations—including one Britisher and two Muslims—were selected as ministers. Of course, Dixit, Mehta, and Shivdasani could have chosen—as the all-India program of their party suggested—to resign from the council, but this would again leave them with no influence in such matters as the restoration of Surat Municipality. On issues that concerned them most, their best option seemed to lie in alliance with Bombay Independents and, on occasion, the Moderates. Any partnership in the council, however, required at the very least a relatively civil demeanor, that is, a renewed adherence to the conventions and idiom of parliamentary politics. In the end, to paraphrase David Arnold's work on Madras politics, it was not the Swarajists who captured the legislature but the legislature which captured the Swarajists.

Members of the new party continued to espouse the ideal of obstruction in principle. Dixit and particularly Shivdasani pestered the governor's ministers with endless questions, which usually had to be sent off to the departments of government for answers; they made long tirades on the budget and on other issues that came before the legislature, whether or not these issues genuinely engaged their interest.

And, for a brief period in 1926, they joined the other Swarajists in boycotting the council. But when matters they considered to be vital arose, such as municipal affairs, they made sure their voices were heard. In March 1924, only a few months after the council began its sessions, Dixit petitioned Gulam Hussein Hidayatullah, the minister of local selfgovernment, to allow new municipal elections in Surat and to bring the Committee of Management's administration to an end.

In July he fought a municipal bill giving government the power to dissolve municipalities and call new elections in addition to the powers of supercession it already possessed. In both cases, he reminded government of its own avowed commitments to the devolution of power. In the July debates, for instance, he argued: "We are now working the new reforms; the ultimate aim of the British government is to give self-government to India, and if you go on adding further powers to the power already possessed by government in dealing with the municipalities which they consider as defaulting, I do not think it will be consistent in spirit so far as the present reforms are concerned."

This sort of constitutional argument was obviously a major departure from the rhetoric noncooperators had used three years earlier when they had claimed that it was a sinful or *adharmik* act to participate in the legislature and that boycott of the councils embodied the Hindu ideal of renunciation and self-sacrifice.

But now the Congress leaders were addressing a different audience and with different purposes. The need to influence provincial ministers and to win the support of Independents and Moderates required use of an idiom more at home in the halls of the legislature than on the streets of Surat. Ironically, representation of the people now involved using symbolic skills that uneducated citizens could not hope to master: knowledge of legislative rituals and procedures, familiarity with parliamentary traditions, the ability to speak and think quickly in English and to manipulate legal rules and statistics in debate. In following the conventions of public debate, even for the purpose of contesting colonial policy, the Swarajists in essence conceded that the major issues of provincial politics were going to be fought on the terrain of constitutional and devolutionary principle. At a more implicit level, they agreed to strive for the same kind of polity that their British overlords were now themselves attempting to forge: a liberal, representative order that would pursue the objective of political and economic progress.

MAULANA ABUL KALAM AZAD , INDIAN FREEDOM FIGHTER

Maulana Abul Kalam Azad was born on November 11, 1888 in Mecca. He belonged to an orthodox Muslim scholar family. The original name of Maulana Abul Kalam Azad was Abul Kalam Ghulam Muhiyuddin. His ancestors came to India from Afghanistan. His mother was an Arab and his father Maulana Khairuddin, was a Bengali Muslim of Afghan origin. Maulana Khairuddin shifted to Mecca in 1857. He returned to India in 1890 and started living in Calcutta. His mother died when he was only 11 years old. Initially Maulana Abul Kalam Azad received the traditional Islamic education at home. After that he was taught Arabic, Persian, philosophy, geometry, mathematics and algebra by some great teachers. He also acquired huge knowledge in English, history, politics and general science.

After completing education, Maulana Abul Kalam Azad started writing new articles reinterpreting and analyzing the Qur'an, the Hadith, and the rules of Fiqh and Kalam. He rejected the orthodoxy of Taqliq and accepted the modern principles of Tajdid. At that time he was influenced by Pan- Islamic views of Jamaluddin Afghani and the Aligarh thought of Sir Syed Ahmed Khan. Maulana Abul Kalam Azad was also deeply inspired by modernism and Western philosophy. He visited Iraq and met the revolutionary nationalist who opposed the imperialism. He also went to Egypt and met Shaikh Muhammad Abduh ,Saeed Pasha and other revolutionary leaders of the Arab world. Maulana Abul Kalam Azad was moved by the idea of anti-imperialism.

He came back to India and joined the Indian freedom movement.He protested against the racial discrimination of the British Government and opposed the views of Muslim politicians who were more interested in the communal issues than national interest. Maulana Abul Kalam Azad also opposed the communal separatism of All India Muslim League. In 1905 he criticised the partition of Bengal.During that time Maulana Abul Kalam Azad met revolutionary leader Sri Aurobindo and Shyam Sundar Chakravarthy and started working with them. He established many secret revolutionary centers all over north India and Bombay. He persuaded the Muslim leaders to join the revolutionary activities.

In 1912 Maulana Abul Kalam Azad started publishing a weekly journal in Urdu named Al Hilal to propagate revolutionary ideas amongst the Muslims. He also wrote many articles in this journal to promote communal harmony. In

1914 British Government banned Azad's Al-Hilal for spreading extremist views. After that he started a new journal, the Al-Balagh. Maulana Abul Kalam Azad again srarted propagating revolutionary ideas and nationalism through this paper. During that time he supported the Khilafat movement. In 1916 The government banned Al-Balagh under Defence of India Regulations Act. He was arrested and imprisoned in Ranchi.In 1920 he was released from the jail. After that he joined the National congress and played a crucial role in Non-Cooperation Movement. In 1923 Maulana Abul Kalam Azad was nominated as the President of the special session of the Congress in Delhi. In 1930 participated in Gandhiji's Salt Satyagraha. He was again arrested and sent to the Meerut jail. He was released after a year. Maulana Abul Kalam Azad was selected as the president of Congress in Ramgarh session. In his presidential speech he clearly stated that ignoring the idea of religious separatism is very important. His speech thus still stands as the insignia of communal harmony. He held this post till the year 1946. He wanted unified nation and opposed the partition as well as Jinnah's Two-Nation Theory.

After independence Maulana Abul Kalam Azad became Minister of Education in Pandit Jawaharlal Nehru's cabinet. He was the member of Constituent Assembly, which was responsible for drafting the constitution of India. Maulana Abul Kalam Azad wanted to spread education among the common people of the country. In 1956 he was selected as the President of the UNESCO General Conference in Delhi. In 1957 his famous book India Wins Freedom was published.

He left the mortal coil on February 22nd, 1958. Maulana Abul Kalam Azad was posthumously awarded India's highest civilian honour, Bharat Ratna in 1992.

MAULANA ABUL KALAM AZAD THE FREEDOM FIGHTER

Maulana Abul Kalam Azad The Freedom Fighter:

Maulana Abul Kalam Azad was one of the famous Indian freedom fighters and later became Union educational Minister for Independent India. He was born on November 11, 1888. His father Maulana Khairuddin and his mother Zaher Watri. His forefathers came from Afghanistan during the Mughal emperor Babar. Abul Kalam Azad family belonged to an orthodox Muslim family. He educated in Arabic, Persian and Urdu with theological orientation. Hence Maulana Abul Kalam Azad had very passion in English language learning, on his own, he learned English also. Since his childhood days, he interested in writing poetry.

Maulana Abul Kalam Azad Influence As a Journalist:

Abul Kalam Azad traveled to Egypt, Turkey, Syria, and France and wrote so many articles on various issues. These made him build up the friendship with 'Mustafa Kemal Pasha' the publisher and the Young Turks Movement leaders in Turkey. However their interaction and ideas made Maulana to the belief that Indian Muslims should join with fellow countrymen to fight against British to get India free. With these thoughts, he started a press and weekly by 'Al-Hilal' to bring awareness among the Indians about the Independence. The weekly was very famous in those days and circulation figure rose to 26,000 copies. The ideas of the magazine distributed British Government and subsequent events the government banned 'Al-Hilal' magazine named 'Al-Balagh' weekly.

Maulana Abul Kalam Azad As a Freedom Fighter:

Apart from this publication he also participated in the Freedom movements like Khilafat Movement, Non-Cooperation Movement, The Civil Disobedience Movement and the Quit India Movement. Abul Kalam Azad had very far sight about the future of India. So that he was very against of undivided India. The division of India and Pakistan made him very disappointment. Maulana Abul Kalam Azad strongly emphasized the internal communal harmony. He campaigns about the importance of Peace and need of Freedom. He used the power of writing and speeches to awaken the masses towards the freedom fight.

Here we need to recall a piece of speech, which needed to follow still by the Indians...........

"If an angel were to descend from the clouds today, settle on the Qutub Minar of Delhi and proclaim from there that India will attain Swaraj provided Hindu-Muslim Unity is renounced, then I would renounce Swaraj and not sacrifice Hindu-Muslim Unity, because if Swaraj is delayed, it is the loss to India, but if Hindu-Muslim Unity is lost, it is the loss to Humanity."

Maulana Abul Kalam Azad As an Educational Minister:

After India got Independence in 1947, Abul Kalam Azad worked as the Education Minister in Nehru Cabinet. He established many universities and promoted the scientific and research education. He brought many reforms among the primary and secondary education.

On February 22, 1958, Maulana Abdul Kalam Azad passed away. His Birth Anniversary of Maulana Abul Kalam Azad on November 11 celebrates as National Educational Day.

5

Azad on Nehru's 'Blunders' Leading to the Partition of India

As we all appreciate, food together with smells, faded photographs and half-remembered tunes are all highly evocative of distant places and earlier times. Drawing directly on our most intimate senses, they resurrect forgotten memories and transport us back, in an instant, to worlds that may no longer exist; whether to our childhoods or other nostalgic moments in our lives. Of late, elderly Pakistanis who migrated during Partition have become more willing to reminisce – whether in the form of oral testimonies and traditions, published biographies, newspaper articles or simply what they tell their grandchildren – about the homes that they left behind. Among other memories, they recall the juiciness of the enormous lychees that grew plentifully in western Uttar Pradesh, and fondly savour recollections of the splendid vegetable dishes cooked by their former Hindu neighbours (they claim to have tasted nothing like it since they arrived in Pakistan).

Such nostalgia is symptomatic of Partition's main impact — a sense of loss. Just because we may choose to forget (or suppress) particular aspects of the past does not mean what we later remember did not exist. For much of the period since 1947, however, a collective amnesia has operated on both sides of the border created by Partition when it comes to reminding ourselves of what people living in Pakistan and India have in common, rather than what separates them. That amnesia has informed perceptions and policies in both the countries.

As with many aspects of Pakistan-India relations, events in the years before, during and immediately after Partition in 1947 have tended to frame how individuals as well as institutions on both sides of the border have engaged with each other ever since. As is well known, by the 1940s, the Indian National Congress was seeking the creation of a unitary and centralised independent India. This was a prospect that the All-India Muslim League challenged in an effort to defend what its high command believed were the best interests of Indian Muslims, regardless of whether or not all of the Muslims of the subcontinent accepted the League's championing of their collective cause. The political stalemate of the post-Second World War years eventually made compromise unachievable and, with Britain determined to relinquish control over its South Asian holdings as quickly and conveniently possible, the stage was set for the bloody end of an empire, which changed the lives of millions on both sides of the hastily drawn up Radcliffe Line.

It may be stating the obvious but Partition has clearly meant different things to the different interests involved. For many people in India the division came to represent loss not just of territory but also of key aspects of the country's core identity — the infamous vivisection of 'Mother India' on the one hand, and the defeat of the Congress's secular vision on the other. For those in what became Pakistan, Partition constituted a proud (though not universally expected) founding moment, albeit secured at great human cost (for Pakistanis and Indians alike).

As I argue in my own contribution to Roger D Long's edited volume *A History of Pakistan* (2015), "Partition, marred by the extreme communal violence that characterised it, represented a tragic experience for hundreds and thousands of ordinary South Asian people [...] who died and millions more who were uprooted and made refugees thanks to the passions and uncertainties that it unleashed. Thus, rather than an unabashedly triumphal moment, independence in general and the creating of a new state of Pakistan in particular [were] threaded through with loss and human suffering on a massive subcontinental scale. Yet for many of those who became Pakistani citizens in the years after 1947 [...] the detail of what actually happened became less important than the fact that it represented a defining episode in the collective past. Without it, Pakistanis would not be who they are today."

In retrospect, however, Partition seems to have happened in quite a distant past. On the 68th anniversary of its creation, Pakistan has reached, as it used to be politely said, 'a certain age'. No longer in the first flush of youth, nor – as it once was – a relative newcomer on the world stage, the focus of much discussion nowadays tends not to be why it came into existence, all those years ago, but how it has managed to survive for so long, bearing in mind the myriad challenges that the state has faced since 1947, among which we must include losing more than half of its population when Bangladesh broke away in 1971. One of the most enduring of these trials and tribulations has been the country's dismal relationship with its eastern neighbour. Pakistan has fought a series of hot and cold wars with India and, in the process, usually emerged second best.

It can be argued, however, that this state of perpetual strife is also a legacy of Partition, which ended one story – that of empire in South Asia – but marked the beginning of another — that of a subcontinent dangerously divided and poised for war. With the status of disputed territories such as the princely state of Jammu and Kashmir still unsettled, the future of Pakistan-India relations after August 14 - August 15, 1947, was left hanging in the balance, unresolved. And while the first India-Pakistan war (in 1947 - 1948) resulted in another (UN-sponsored) "Line of Control" being superimposed on maps of the region, this early conflict only further frayed the loose ends produced by decolonisation, instead of tying them up. Indeed, Kashmir has remained an open sore, epitomising joint failure of Pakistan and India to find a way of getting along with each other.

The territorial contours of the Muslim homeland

Under these circumstances, it is not surprising that most efforts to communicate the broad sweep of Pakistan's post-1947 history find themselves grappling at some point in their narrative with how far Partition has shaped subsequent relations between the two neighbours. This is certainly the case in the publications under review here, which all adopt the long view when it comes to assessing the connections between earlier events and the present.

That Partition still casts a lengthy shadow over how Pakistan and India engage with each other is the central premise in Dilip Hiro's *The Longest August: The Unflinching Rivalry Between India and Pakistan* (2015). Around a quarter of the chapters in this book are dedicated to explaining the mounting communal rivalries that produced the division of the subcontinent on August 14 - August 15, 1947. Such an approach inevitably reinforces a commonly shared belief that relations between the two South Asian 'siblings' were 'blighted' from birth. In other words, it offers the reader a scenario in which Partition forms the crucial opening episode in an epic family saga (or, alternatively, a particularly nightmarish soap opera). *The Longest August* (unlike other recent publications discussed here) focuses very specifically on how Pakistan and India have engaged with each other over the last seven decades.

Hiro's initiative represents a rare attempt to throw light on an understudied topic (there have been surprisingly few studies that concentrate specifically on explaining Pakistan-India relations). The scope of the book's starting ambition, however, is hard to sustain, which allows for factual inaccuracies as well as irritating idiosyncrasies to feature in its coverage of events. Some of these are more annoying than serious: Hiro insists on calling Gandhi as "Mahatma Mohandas Gandhi"; first Pakistani Prime Minister Liaquat Ali Khan's name gets abbreviated to "Ali Khan"; and senior Congress politician and independent India's first education minister Maulana Abul Kalam Azad is repeatedly referenced as "Maulana Abul Kalam Mohiyuddin Ahmed Azad". More worrying in its coverage of the build-up to Partition is the absence of any discussion regarding the March 1940 Lahore Resolution's reference to Muslim states (in the plural). By glossing over this important point, Hiro reinforces assumptions that the 'Pakistan' which emerged in 1947 was precisely what had always been on the League's 'wish list'. As other historians have demonstrated, this was not necessarily the case.

Similarly, Hiro's study fails to reflect sufficiently on where South Asian independence fitted into the bigger processes of decolonisation at work, nor does it engage with vitally important geo-political developments such as the Cold War (which had important repercussions for the region over a 50-year period).

And, although *The Longest August* concludes with Narendra Modi's recent inauguration as Indian Prime Minister in 2014 – arguably the latest challenge to India and Pakistan reconciling their long-standing differences – the book struggles to substantiate its basic premise regarding the direct connection between Partition and subsequent Pakistan-India relations.

The impact of Partition also forms the starting point for Ayesha Jalal's latest exploration of Pakistan's chequered history since 1947, which includes consideration of ups and (mostly) downs in its interaction with neighbouring India. But Jalal, unlike Hiro, highlights why the wider geo-political context of the subcontinent's early post-independence years hardened enmities here. Drawing on analysis that underpinned her earlier studies of the decades before and after 1947, she pulls no punches with respect to the negative fallout of Partition while also highlighting just how far Pakistan's foreign relations – and hence, its interaction with India – have been shaped by regional and global political developments.

Accordingly, in *The Struggle for Pakistan: A Muslim Homeland and Global Politics* (2014), Jalal argues that "the crystallisation of Muslim hopes and distinctive culture, reconciling the claims of nationhood with the winning of sovereign statehood proved impossible. The territorial contours of the Muslim homeland [Pakistan] ensured that there were nearly as many Muslim non-citizens outside as there were Muslim citizens within. The contradiction was not addressed, far less resolved, and has been one of the principal fault lines in Pakistan's quest for an identity that is Islamic yet also national." From the outset, she says, "an anti-Indian and anti-Hindu stance in state-supported historical reconstructions was considered necessary for national self-preservation".

But the irony of this negative approach, as Jalal explains, was that it made friction with India more rather than less likely, in turn raising the real risk of confrontation and potential defeat: in the aftermath of Partition and the war over Kashmir, "paranoia about Pakistan's ability to survive fanned a state-sponsored narrative of security that painted Hindu India as the archenemy acting in utter disregard of its [own] large Muslim population. Kashmir and fears of India manipulating the flow of river waters to Pakistan's disadvantage [rivers having also been 'divided' somewhat arbitrarily between the two new states] provided a popular rallying cry against Hindu conspiracies [...] An acute sense of threat from India melded critical policy decisions, including on Kashmir, and saw the army become a key player in shaping the destiny of the country. There was nothing inevitable about this outcome even if the odds were heavily stacked against the votaries of a democratic Pakistan".

Like others who have written about the idea and reality of Pakistan in order to plot a convincing 'history of the present', Jalal points to many instances when distrust of India has affected decisions that Pakistani governments have made in terms of both domestic and foreign policy. Equally important, however, she avoids the temptation to trace everything negative in this relationship back to the events of 1947, whether implicitly or explicitly. When the spectre of Partition came back to haunt Pakistan again during the bloody civil war fought over East Bengal, which once more saw borders being crossed by refugees escaping violence, she makes it clear that India's intervention on the side of the nascent Bangladesh had much more to do with contemporary regional power struggles than simply with settling old Partition-related scores. For Jalal, while Pakistan's failure to establish its democratic credentials can certainly be linked to the political consequences of Partition, the main problems in 1970-1972 – and the principal lessons to be learned from them – stemmed from "the wilful manipulation of centre-province in the 1950s and 1960s by a military-dominated state" that was only partly the product of Partition.

In the final analysis, Partition may not be the only, or even the central, factor in determining how Pakistan's history has panned out since 1947

Similar essential connections are made in *The Pakistan Paradox: Instability and Resilience* (2015) by Christophe Jaffrelot, who, like Jalal, has already written a great deal on Pakistan. He devotes 700 pages to explaining the resilience of the Pakistani state and its people, and how both persist against the odds. Combining a guide to the cultural and social roots of the Pakistan Movement with a historical 'road map' for making sense of contemporary Pakistan, he highlights ways in which the country's history has been shaped by tensions "rooted in contradictions that were already apparent by the 1940s". However, while Jaffrelot refers only very occasionally to Pakistan's direct encounters with India (the entry 'India' cannot be found in the index, but then 'Partition' is not included there either), his study reinforces the argument that Pakistan was born of a process of political division (Partition) that, in many ways, has (over)determined the state's subsequent trajectory. In other words, the 'fear factor' regarding India's ambitions was put in place in the immediate post-independence period and has never gone away.

As *The Pakistan Paradox* explains, "Even if Partition in 1947 had finally given the Muslim minority in the Raj its own state, the Pakistani elites continued to act under the sway of a strong sense of vulnerability towards India. Not only did Pakistan not carry the same weight as India in demographic, economic and military terms, but neither was the sharing of resources of the defunct Raj devoid of complications [...] In this context Pakistani leaders were even more prepared to believe (or at least to argue in public) that India did not want their country to survive.

This sentiment of vulnerability (which helped them to rally 'their' people behind them and justified their rapprochement with the US in the 1950s) was fostered by statements by Hindu nationalists in favour of '*Akhand Bharat*' (Undivided India) and the words of Congress leaders [...] Whether these Congressmen actually meant what they said (and whether they actually uttered these words) is uncertain, but apparently Jinnah himself took them at face value".

Pakistan Prime Minister Nawaz Sharif and Indian Prime Minister Narendra Modi shake hands at the BRIC/SCO Summits in Ufa, Russia on July 10, 2015

In a nutshell, anxiety revolving around India spawned a security imperative that was bolstered by the perception – as articulated later by General Ayub Khan – that India had tried to cripple Pakistan at birth by depriving it of its share of resources, which in turn aggravated centralising and non-democratic tendencies within the new state. All the same, as Jaffrelot is careful to emphasise, "if the bureaucrats seized power in the mid-1950s, it was less in the name of national defence in face of the threat of India than due to two other factors", namely the ambitions of West Pakistani elites anxious not to lose out to the Bengali strength in numbers, and the failings or failures of political parties during this crucial transition era. Hence, "it was easy for the bureaucrats and the military to criticize politicians for negligence while the 'Indian threat' required the Pakistani elite to develop a keen sense of responsibility".

With the passage of time, Partition as a first-hand experience has receded into the distant past, literally and metaphorically as far as the vast majority of today's third- or fourth-generation Pakistanis are concerned

Like many ruling groups elsewhere in the world, those in charge of Pakistan have rarely flinched from deploying the 'country-at-risk' card as and when they have wanted to rally domestic support or silence political opponents. As C Christine Fair in *Fighting to the End: The Pakistani Army's Way of War* (2014) has pointed out, the Pakistan Army "has long justified its dominant role in running the state by arguing that it is uniquely positioned to protect not just Pakistani territorial integrity but also the very ideology of Pakistan, which centres on protecting Pakistan's Muslim identity from India's supposed Hindu identity". In the same way, The Pakistan Paradox points the finger at Partition's dangerous military inheritance. After all, "the threat of India partly explained Jinnah's viceregal style [...] this threat had even more implications for the military: the country needed a powerful army, all the more since the troops Pakistan inherited at the moment of Partition in 1947 represented only 36 per cent of the British Indian Army (140,000 out of 410,000 men) giving New Delhi a considerable military advantage, as the Land of the Pure soon realised with the first war in Kashmir in 1947-1948".

So while Jaffrelot does not prioritise Pakistan-India relations, nonetheless the aftershocks of Partition are firmly integrated into his analysis. Despite the international environment representing a "full-fledged component of [Pakistan's] domestic policy", he links the influence of global politics with the vulnerability that Pakistani elites have felt in relation to India — quoting Khalid bin Sayeed's remark that "almost every action of Pakistan can be interpreted as being motivated by fear of India".

In the final analysis, Partition may not be the only, or even the central, factor in determining how Pakistan's history has panned out since 1947; yet it is hard for historians and political scientists to deny that the circumstances involved in Partition badly destabilised Pakistan-India relations. All the publications reviewed above collectively testify to this outcome, irrespective of differences in their focus and conclusions.

That bilateral relations between the two countries were destined to be fraught became very clear soon after Partition. In the months and years immediately following independence, Delhi and Karachi found it extremely hard to agree on the logistics of refugee rehabilitation (though they did not encounter the same problem when it came to dealing with the problem of abducted women; both agreed in late 1947 to return any such women to the side of the border that religion dictated they now belonged to, irrespective of what these women themselves wanted and where their children were to remain). In the longer term, despite managing to reach an agreement in 1960 over the Indus Basin dispute, the two sides have found the process of learning to live peacefully with one another, messily and frustratingly, unsuccessful. India's 1.3 million-strong armed forces (the third largest military in the world), and Pakistan's 650,000 active military personnel (ranked seventh globally), both backed up with nuclear weaponry at their disposal, pose a formidable combined military presence that simultaneously reflects and contributes to the insecurity of the region.

All the same, I would suggest that Partition's most damaging bequest (at least for Pakistan) has been in the realm of domestic politics. Decolonisation happened in such a rush – decisions about the subcontinent's future were made so quickly – that after August 14, 1947, in the wake of immense dislocation, uncertainty and human suffering, Pakistan found itself with a set of underprepared federal and provincial authorities, whose links with each other and with the people were both fragile and fraught (despite the stirring nation-building rhetoric of the period). Irrespective of how well or poorly Pakistan has coexisted with India since 1947 – and it has been more the latter than the former – Pakistan has also been grappling with huge internal problems stemming from the circumstances of its creation. These domestic challenges include, among others, how to affect a state in which all those within it feel equally committed to what it represents, how to balance the needs and aspirations of different sections of its citizens, and how to find a space for religion within the contours of the state that does not marginalise or exclude significant sections of the population.

With the passage of time, Partition as a first-hand experience has receded into the distant past, literally and metaphorically as far as the vast majority of today's third- or fourth-generation Pakistanis are concerned. But it is worth remembering that – like Pakistan and India – France and Germany fought three wars (arguably more blood-stained than the ones between the two states in the subcontinent) in the 70 years between the 1870s and the 1940s. Much like Kashmir, a disputed territory (in the shape of Alsace-Lorraine region) came into the equation, as part of their competition for regional dominance. Today these two neighbouring countries lead the European Union, having invested heavily in a common political and economic cause that strengthens their international authority as well as their domestic position. Perhaps, with the 70th anniversary of Independence and Partition fast approaching (in 2017), the moment has finally come for Pakistan and India to learn to live with Partition, to put aside post-1947 differences and to remember their overlapping pre-1947 history with pride. Surely, improvements in regional cooperation would enable Pakistan to take its place beside India at the 'top table' of 21st-century nations, strategically placed to defend South Asia's common concerns vis-à-vis the rest of the world.

ABUL KALAM AZAD

Though he remains an icon of secular nationalism in modern-day India, Azad was actually born in Mecca in 1888 and lived there till he was about seven. His father Khairuddin, a scholar-sufi originally from Calcutta, was persuaded by his Calcuttan disciples to return back to that city. Under the strict tutelage of his father, Azad continued his Islamic studies, though the young prodigy resented the restrictive and authoritarian manner in which this syllabus was taught; therefore, on his own, Azad secretly cultivated a taste for Urdu books and Persian poetry and even learnt to play the sitar. Around this time he also experienced a revulsion against the *pir*-worship of his father's disciples and a diminished desire to succeed his father as pir.

By the time he was thirteen, Azad had become totally disillusioned with his Islamic training and found solace in the modernist writings of Sir Syed Ahmed Khan. However, the rationalism of Sir Syed only ended up reinforcing the boy's earlier doubts about religion and Azad fell into a period of atheism which, according to him, lasted from the age of 14 to 22. During his later teenage years he seems to have come into close contact with the Hindu revolutionaries of Bengal. A combination of brief travel to the Middle East and his Arabic reading also exposed him more deeply to the reformist ideas of Sheikh Abduh of Egypt and the uncompromising nationalism and anti-imperialism of Mustafa Kamil.

After this period of spiritual homelessness, Azad, by the end of 1909, had an emotional/mystical experience that renewed his faith in religion and galvanised his personality in a dramatic way. Following this 'conversion,' Azad's career really began to take-off in 1912 with the appearance of his Urdu journal *Al-Hilal*. Using breathtaking language, the journal simultaneously preached 'pure' Islam and Indian independence. Through his particular interpretation of Islam, Azad sought to bring Indian Muslims onto the platform of the freedom movement and to work in cooperation with Hindus who were already there. Despite his earlier admiration for Sir Syed, Azad was a harsh critic of the loyalist politics of Aligarh University.

Contrary to what is stated in certain types of historiography in India and Pakistan, Hindu-Muslim cooperation was not something that the Maulana adopted out of expediency or after his eventual meeting with Gandhi. Though the journal was ambiguous about specific methods of cooperation and post-Independence political arrangements, Hindu-Muslim unity was a sentiment he had been partial to from very early on in his life. This is evident in his poignant 1910 essay on the broad-minded Sufi saint Sarmad. However, there was a revivalist tone to Al-Hilal which critics would later say inadvertently reinforced communal consciousness among certain Muslims, even though the rhetorical devices had been used to arouse Muslims out of political lethargy.

When World War I broke out in Europe, the British government, viewing the journal as seditious, expelled Azad from Bengal and placed him under internment in Ranchi for three and a half years. A few weeks after his release, he met Mahatma Gandhi in Delhi for the first time; he accepted Gandhi's program of non-cooperation and became the first prominent Muslim in India to declare himself an ally of the Mahatma.

The massacres at Jallianwala Bagh had set all Indians afire, but Indian Muslims too in 1920 were greatly perturbed by the British government's handling of the Turkish empire and the *Khilafat* during the War. In consultation with Azad, Gandhi persuaded the Congress to make the demand for the protection of the Khilafat a part of the national demand for freedom. The overlapping relationship between the Congress and the Khilafat Conference ended up bringing Muslims in large numbers to the freedom movement.

By 1921 Hindu-Muslim unity in the country seemed to be at an all-time high, and Azad was soon arrested.

Yet this solidarity, while impressively achieved, proved to be a short-lived; upon his release in 1923, the country was passing through a particularly strong wave of communal rioting. In addition to other important factors, Muslims were shocked out of their reverie because of the Turkish government's move to abolish the Khilafat.

The ambiguous results of the Khilafat Movement has provoked criticism from some latter-day historians over Azad's attempts at 'fusing' religion with politics. By unsystematically using Quranic arguments to support the Khilafat Movement and Hindu-Muslim cooperation, it has been suggested that Azad inadvertently cultivated identity politics among Muslims and allowed some of his ideas to be misconstrued by more communal interests.

Azad came to realize that in politics he could only be guided by the general principles of his religion and his knowledge of Indian Muslim history, rather than through invoking specific textual injunctions. By this time, he was also increasingly becoming an active member on the Congress stage, and his mediating skills largely prevented a split in the party between constitutionalists like Motilal Nehru and non-cooperatists like Vallabhai Patel. Though he continued his efforts to bring various Muslim organizations in line with Congress and involved in the freedom movement, in 1928 serious differences arose between the Congress and organizations like the Muslim League and the Khilafat Conference over the Nehru report. Azad was forced to break ties with the latter two organizations.

In 1930, the Congress declared complete independence as the goal of the national movement, and civil disobedience continued in vigour following Gandhi's famous Salt March. Azad was imprisoned twice in a row during this period, and then released in 1936 along with the other Congress leaders. It was during these periods of imprisonment that the Maulana was able to complete the first edition of his famous *Tarjuman al-Quran*, his Urdu translation and commentary on the Quran. A second expanded edition was published during the 1940s. This incomplete translation and commentary would end up being his most definitive, though controversial, theological statement on how Indian Muslims could live out their religion in a religiously pluralist and politically secular environment. Hence, he articulated an Islam that was hospitable towards other forms of monotheism, especially Hinduism, and which placed emphasis on commonly held rules of righteous conduct. Though it was a landmark effort to inject a liberal ethos into Islam, the Tarjuman, unfortunately, did not have the overwhelming impact he hoped it would. The controversies that sprung up around this work, particularly from members of the *ulema* that were supporting him politically, dried up any inspiration in him to carry out the larger task of comprehensive religious reform and reinterpretation.

Following the passing away of M.A. Ansari in 1936, Azad became the most prominent Muslim in the Congress. By 1939 he was elected President of the party, though he was not the first Muslim to occupy that position. During the thirties the Muslim League had been gaining steam under Jinnah, and given special impetus because of grievances against certain Congress elected provincial governments. Azad's presidential address at the Ramgarh session of the Congress in 1940 occurred just a few days before Jinnah's historic Pakistan Resolution, and, in addition to articulating the point of view of the nationalist Muslims, became a classic statement on Indian secularism and a refutation of the two-nations theory.

Unfortunately, in addition to being caught in the cross-fire between Hindu and Muslim communalists, Azad by then had become subject to a trenchant campaign of criticism by influential Muslim political opponents. Many members of the religious and modern educated classes who earlier in his career had respected him and his religious ideas eventually turned against him because of this vilifying propaganda. Though he was capable of stirring large crowds with his brilliant oratory when called upon to do so, Azad's pride and good manners kept him from publicly countering his detractors, and his intellectual and aristocratic nature kept him from reaching out directly to the Muslim masses when such an intervention was needed.

Azad was imprisoned for a fifth time in 1940, following a limited campaign of civil disobedience, and released a year later. By 1942, and following the more comprehensive Quit India Movement, he, along with the other Congress leaders, was imprisoned again. Upon his release in 1946, Azad remained Congress President throughout the War years. During his presidency, he tried to encourage Congress to come to terms with certain Muslim fears and to make some concessions with the League to avoid splitting the country; but both Jinnah's single-mindedness and certain Congress mistakes prevented any settlement from occurring.

The Maulana reluctantly relinquished the Congress presidency in 1946, hoping that this would open an avenue between the Congress and the League; the latter party had refused to acknowledge a Muslim presence within the former one. He kept out of the coalition government formed that year, but in 1947, at Gandhi's urging, he became Minister of Education. Azad had been totally opposed to Mountbatten's plan for dividing the country, but by March of that year, Partition had become an inevitability; the polarization within the interim government, formed between the Congress and the League, and the rising communal violence throughout India had become too much. Though, like Gandhi, he was forced to accept Partition, he could never reconcile himself to it and was totally heartbroken by the event and its bloody aftermath.

Following Independence, he would hold the post of Minister of Education for ten years. Though he was not a particularly effective administrator, he did perform some important services such as cultivating technical, adult, and women's education, and an academy of literature, as well as opposing the ejection of English as a national language. As in earlier years, he could not project the mystical piety of, say, a Baba Farid needed to draw the Muslim and Hindu masses to him; but his belief in religious pluralism and the need for a humanistic outlook broadened even further, and he openly identified parallels between Vedantic and Sufi thought in some of his addresses. His last years were marked by sadness and loneliness, a consequence of a life lived so individualistically. Abul Kalam Azad died in 1958 of a stroke and was buried in a dignified corner in Old Delhi near the Jama Masjid. It is a great irony that, while possessing a thorough Islamic training, Azad ended up espousing a secular nationalism informed by personal religious sensibilities, while his opponent Jinnah, a modernist with a minimal religious upbringing, ended up vying for a separate Muslim state informed by purely political considerations.

PAKISTAN WITHOUT PARTITION: LET'S REVIVE THE BURIED IDEA OF INDO-PAK CONFEDERATION

L K Advani, senior leader of the Bharatiya Janata Party, likes to recount an important conversation he had in 2011 with India's then Prime Minister Dr

Manmohan Singh. The occasion was the birth anniversary of Dr Ram Manohar Lohia a great personality of India's freedom struggle and a prominent socialist leader. They had come to the Central Hall of Parliament to offer floral tribute at Dr Lohia's portrait. Dr Singh casually asked Advani, who was then the Leader of the Opposition, "How well had you known Dr. Lohia?" The BJP leader replied, "Quite well."

His interaction with Lohia had begun in the early 1960s when he was a journalist with the RSS weekly *Organiser*. One day Lohia shared with Advani his concern over the belief of the Jana Sangh (previous avatar of the BJP) and the RSS in the concept of "Akhand Bharat" (India Undivided). Advani told him: "I would like you to meet Pandit Deendayal Upadhyaya (philosopher-leader of the Jana Sangh) and hear him explain the Jana Sangh's interpretation of Akhand Bharat."

Advani arranged a meeting between Lohia and Upadhyaya, who had a candid and intensive discussion on the relations between India and Pakistan relations, as well as between Hindus and Muslims in India. Lohia told Upadhyaya that the concept of Akhand Bharat had put Muslims in Pakistan at unease and posed a hurdle in the progress of Indo-Pak relations. "Many Pakistanis believe that if the Jana Sangh came to power in New Delhi, it would forcibly reunify Pakistan with India." Upadhyaya replied: "We have no such intentions. We are willing to put to rest Pakistani people's concerns on this score."

"In the end, the violent vivisection of united India was not inevitable, but a tragic accident of history that could have been avoided."

At the end of the dialogue, and in a remarkable demonstration of consensus-building among leaders with different ideologies, Lohia and Upadhyaya signed a historic joint statement on 12 April, 1964. Apart from appealing for equal protection for Hindus and Muslims in the subcontinent, the two leaders urged the governments of India and Pakistan to hold frank, and not "piecemeal", talks to create mutual goodwill and make a "beginning towards the formation of some sort of Indo-Pak Confederation."

Jinnah and the idea of a confederation

The idea of an India-Pakistan Confederation (which in today's context should also include Bangladesh) may seem far-fetched, even thoroughly impractical given the unremitting mistrust and hostility between our two countries. However, as the two South Asian neighbours celebrate the 68th anniversary of their independence from British rule — a joyous occasion that was accompanied by the horrific Partition-induced communal bloodbath — it is useful to remember that some sort of India-Pakistan federation or confederation was a distinct possibility when the British left our subcontinent.

Jinnah's Lahore Resolution (1940) had the seed of a confederation.

In other words, the blood-soaked Partition of August 1947 could have been avoided, while, at the same time, fulfilling the Muslim League's core demand, as stated in its Lahore Resolution of 1940, for a separate state or states in Muslim-majority areas in British India. It was a win-win opportunity for all the diverse communities to whom India was the common motherland.

Sadly, Congress and Muslim League leaders buried the opportunity due to their series of blunders and misjudgements. In the end, the violent vivisection of united India was not inevitable, but a tragic accident of history that could have been avoided.

It is instructive to briefly revisit the chequered pre-1947 debate to know how Pakistan could have been created without Partition peacefully, within a mutually agreed federal or confederal framework.

The idea propounded by the Muslim League that ultimately led to the partition of India — namely, that India is not one nation but two nations, Hindu India and Muslim India— did not originate with Mohammed Ali Jinnah, the architect of Pakistan. Before him, several Muslim and even Hindu leaders (Sir Syed Ahmed Khan, Sir Mohammed Iqbal, Lala Lajpat Rai, Vinayak Damodar Savarkar) propounded it in their own ways. However, none of them (not even Jinnah initially) advocated the division of India.

"[T]he famous Lahore Resolution, which most Pakistanis regard as the basis of the creation of Pakistan, neither mentioned "Pakistan" nor had any reference to the Two Nations theory."

Iqbal, in his presidential speech at the Muslim League session in Allahabad in 1930 had called for the merger of the four Muslim-majority provinces in the north-west, with the exception of some non-Muslim districts, into "a Muslim India within India". Ironically, Iqbal, whom Pakistanis regard as their national poet, had in 1904 written "*Saare jahaan se achchaa, Hindustan hamara...*", which is still one of the most popular patriotic songs in India.

It would surprise many to know that the famous Lahore Resolution, which most Pakistanis regard as the basis of the creation of Pakistan, neither mentioned "Pakistan" nor had any reference to the Two Nations theory. In fact, the resolution was kept so deliberately vague that it called for the creation of "independent (Muslim) States", and not one State, "in the North-Western and Eastern zones of India". Just two months before the adoption of the Lahore Resolution, Jinnah was still talking of India as the "common motherland" of

Muslims and Hindus. In his article in *Time and Tide* of London, on January 19, 1940, he wrote:

"A constitution must be evolved that recognises that there are in India two nations who both must share the governance of their common motherland. In evolving such a Constitution, the Muslims are ready to co-operate with the British Government, the Congress or any other party so that the present enmities may cease and India may make its place amongst the great countries of the world."

Pakistan-born historian Ayesha Jalal, in her widely acclaimed book *The Sole Spokesman - Jinnah, the Muslim League and the Demand for Pakistan*, tells us some revealing things about the thought process of Jinnah and other Muslim leaders at the time of the Lahore Resolution. For example, H V Hodson, a British officer who was the Reforms Commissioner in India in 1941, reported after speaking to many League leaders that they "interpreted Pakistan as consistent with a confederation". Ismail Ibrahim Chundrigar, a Muslim League leader and trusted follower of Jinnah who went on to become Pakistan's prime minister in 1957, said that the object of the Lahore Resolution was not to create "Ulsters" (a reference to the violent separatist movement aimed at Northern Ireland's independence from the United Kingdom), not to "destroy the unity of India", but to get the "two nations (Pakistan and Hindustan)... welded into united India on the basis of equality".

What Jalal writes further is even more powerful. "That Chundrigar's interpretation was on the right tracks is suggested by the fact that Jinnah himself, Chundrigar's neighbour in Bombay, often stated that 'Pakistan', with its connotation of partition, was not the League's idea but a caricature thrust upon it by the Hindu press: 'They fathered this word upon us,' Jinnah complained at Delhi in 1943. As he told Nawab Ismail (a pioneer of the Pakistan movement who stayed back in India) in November 1941, he could not openly and forcibly come out with these truths 'because it is likely to be misunderstood especially at present'. In a line which reveals more than a thousand pages of research and propaganda, Jinnah admitted: 'I think Mr. Hodson finally understands as to what our demand is'."

All available evidence shows Jinnah's true intention was not to have the kind of Pakistan that was ultimately founded — "a shadow and a husk, a maimed, mutilated and moth-eaten Pakistan" he called it in dejection — but a kind of Hindustan-Pakistan Confederation. Remarkably, all through the partition debate, he always used the word "Hindustan" to refer to what was not Pakistan, and "India" to refer to what he often described as the "motherland" of both.

Even after Jinnah promised, and demanded, Pakistan as a separate and sovereign "Muslim Nation", the absurdity of a separate "Nation" or "Homeland" for Muslims who live in all parts of the subcontinent was as apparent then as it is now. He was also prepared to accept, at different points of time between 1940 and 1947, different kinds of federal or confederal constitutional arrangements that would keep Pakistan within India. For instance, in June 1946, he accepted the Cabinet Mission Plan proposed by the British which specifically ruled out the partition of India. The plan proposed independence for India as a federation comprising three largely autonomous groups or sections, with a Central government, located in Delhi, empowered to handle national affairs such as defence, currency, foreign affairs, etc. In June 1947, Jinnah proposed that the constituent assemblies of India and Pakistan should meet in New Delhi.

Partition: A tragedy written by the Muslim League, Congress and British

It is only after the Congress (rather, Jawaharlal Nehru, without consulting Mahatma Gandhi) rejected this plan that the Muslim League also withdrew its acceptance. The Congress had also passed a resolution in March 1947 demanding division of the Punjab and Bengal, which was its tacit acceptance of the division of India. This too was done without Gandhiji's concurrence.

In Maulana Abul Kalam Azad's book *India Wins Freedom*, parts of which were released 30 years later in 1988, he clearly blamed Nehru for his role in the partition. Azad, who remained the staunchest opponent of Partition till the very end, writes: "I warned Jawaharlal that history would not forgive us if we agreed to Partition. The verdict would be that India was not divided by the Muslim League, but by the Congress."

"All available evidence shows Jinnah's true intention was not to have the kind of Pakistan that was ultimately founded... but a kind of Hindustan-Pakistan Confederation."

Jaswant Singh, in his widely debated book *Jinnah: India - Partition - Independence*, endorses this view: "It has to be said, and with great sadness, that despite some early indications to the contrary, the leaders of the Indian National Congress, in the period between the outbreak of war in 1939 and the country's partition in 1947, showed in general, a sad lack of realism, of foresight, of purpose and of will."

In a similar vein, Jalal persuasively demonstrates that the 1947 partition of India was an accident, "a colossal miscalculation", and that Jinnah initially did not want a separate Muslim Nation. Rather, he was using the threat of

Pakistan as a bargaining point to strengthen the voice and stake of the Muslim minority within a united India. Sadly, this truth is not accepted either by most Pakistanis (for whom Jinnah is a blemish-free hero) or by most Indians (for whom he is an unpardonable villain).

This incontrovertible truth drills holes in the entrenched belief both in India and Pakistan that the Muslim League was solely responsible for Partition, whereas the Congress always stood for a united India. History's verdict casts the responsibility for India's Partition on both the parties, although the Muslim League's guilt is decidedly greater on account of the fact that it anchored its demand for Pakistan on the hollow, dubious and extremely dangerous Two Nations theory.

A still greater share of the guilt lies at the feet of the British government for the needlessly hurried, and wholly insensitive, manner in which it executed the Partition without either anticipating, or making necessary security provisions. It was the duty, primarily, of the British rulers to ensure a smooth and peaceful transfer of power. Their failure to discharge this duty was principally responsible for the killing of more than 2,50,000 Hindus, Sikhs and Muslims (other estimates put the figure at 5,00,000) and for the uprooting of 14 million people from their homes and their migration across the borders that divided India and created Pakistan.

In his admirable book *Shameful Flight*, Stanley Wolpert has chronicled how Britain, and especially Lord Mountbatten, the last viceroy of India, were guilty of ill-planned, sudden and insensitive disengagement from India in 1947. The British government's previous self-declared deadline to exit from India was January 1948. By needlessly advancing it to August 1947, and by drawing the boundaries separating India and Pakistan in an extremely hurried manner — the Radcliffe Commission appointed by Mountbatten completed its job of demarcating a vast territory of 450,000 sq km with 88 million people in just three months — the British created avoidable chaos and panic. This greatly exacerbated the killings and forced displacement of people on both sides of the border. Had this tragedy been avoided - and it was indeed avoidable " the relations between India and Pakistan would not have been as bitter and hostile as now.

This British culpability made Gandhiji rue: "Partition has come in spite of me. It has hurt me. *But it is the way in which Partition has come that has hurt me more."*

Mahatma Gandhi's vision: two States, not two nations

The one man who did his utmost to prevent India's Partition, while granting the Muslim League's core demand for Pakistan as a separate State, was Mahatma

Gandhi. Between 9 and 27 September in 1944, Gandhiji met Jinnah as many as 14 times at the latter's residence in Bombay. The Mahatma stated that the purpose of these talks, which were held at his request, was to understand Jinnah's mind and to make him rethink the demand for Pakistan on the basis of the Two Nations theory. Simultaneously with these meetings, the two leaders also exchanged 24 letters, which are of immense educative value for both Indians and Pakistanis.

In his very first letter to Jinnah on 11 September, 1944, Gandhiji stated: "My life mission has been Hindu-Muslim unity, which I want for its own sake but which is not to be achieved without the foreign ruling Power being ousted."

Jinnah was unimpressed. He wrote back: "The only solution of India's problem is to accept the division of India as Pakistan and Hindustan...In order to achieve the freedom and independence of the people of India, it is essential, in the first instance, that there should be a Hindu-Muslim settlement."

Jinnah's stand was thoroughly untenable, insofar as he equated the creation of Pakistan as a separate and sovereign nation with a settlement of the Hindu-Muslim relations. In doing so, he simply took it for granted that the Muslims in Muslim-minority provinces also constituted the "Muslim Nation", without explaining that his absurd formula would leave this part of the "Muslim Nation" behind in Hindustan.

Similarly, if, according to him, the Hindus constituted a separate nation, he did not care to explain how the Hindus in Hindu-minority provinces in the northwestern and eastern zones of India would cease to be a "Hindu Nation" once they became a part of his "Muslim Nation".

Jinnah's assertion that Hindus and Muslims have nothing in common, and hence constitute two separate nations, was a complete and uncharacteristic U-turn on all that he had said and passionately striven for in the first 25 years of his life. Once hailed as an "Ambassador of Hindu-Muslim Unity", this secular Indian nationalist leader was now championing a hazardous theory which was bound to ignite combustible communal hostility between Hindus and Muslims.

Therefore, four days later, Gandhiji wrote in a tone of dismay:

"You must admit that the (Lahore) Resolution itself makes no reference to the Two-Nations theory. In the course of our discussions, you have passionately pleaded that India contains two nations, i.e., Hindus and Muslims, and that the latter have their homelands in India and as the former have theirs. The more our argument progresses, the more alarming your picture appears to me. It would be alluring if it were true. But my fear is growing that it is wholly unreal. I find no parallel in history for a body of converts and their descendants claiming to be a nation apart from the parent stock. If India was one nation before the advent of Islam, it must remain one in spite of the change of faith of a very large body of her children."

Gandhiji endorsed the principle of sovereign states, on the basis of self-determination, in areas predominantly inhabited by Muslims in the northwestern and eastern parts of India. "You can call it Pakistan if you like," he told Jinnah. To this extent, he accepted the kernel of the Lahore Resolution. He even admitted that he was deviating from the All India Congress Committee's resolution in Bombay in August 1942, which he had himself endorsed in his famous "Quit India" speech. He was doing so in order to ensure that free India remained united India.

In other words, Gandhiji accepted the Muslim League's demand for Pakistan as an independent state, with four crucial caveats. Firstly, Pakistan would be formed not on the basis of the Two Nations theory, but the two States theory. Secondly, the formation of the new State "should be accompanied by bonds of friendship and alliance between Hindustan and Pakistan... there should be a common policy and a working arrangement on foreign affairs, defence, communications and similar matters, since this is manifestly vital to the welfare of both parts of India." Thirdly, the treaty of separation "shall also contain terms for safeguarding the rights of minorities in the two States". Fourthly, before the formation of Pakistan and the simultaneous alliance (a form of confederation) between Pakistan and Hindustan, the first condition is to gain independence for the whole of India "by the joint action of all the parties and groups composing India".

In his letter of 19 September, 1944, Gandhiji asked Jinnah a pertinent question: "Can we not agree to differ on the question of 'two nations', and yet solve the problem on the basis of self-determination? It is this basis that has brought me to you."

On 22 September, 1944, Gandhiji made his opposition to the Two Nations theory even more emphatic, while at the same time offering a practical and reasonable basis for a solution based on the Lahore Resolution.

"The more I think about the two-nations theory, the more alarming it appears to be... I am unable to accept the proposition that the Muslims of India are a nation distinct from the rest of the inhabitants of India. Mere assertion is no proof. The consequences of accepting such a proposition are dangerous in the extreme. Once the principle is admitted, there would be no limit to the claims for cutting up India into numerous divisions which would spell India's ruin. *I have therefore suggested a way out. Let there be a partition as between two brothers, if a division there must be.*" (Emphasis added)

On 24 September, 1944, Gandhi wrote to Jinnah: "I proceed on the assumption that India is not to be regarded as two or more nations but as one family consisting of many members, of whom the Muslims living in the north-west zones i.e., Baluchistan, Sind, North-West Frontier Province and that part of the Punjab where they are in absolute majority over all the other elements and in parts of Bengal and Assam where they are in absolute majority, desire to live in separation from the rest of India."

The talks broke down because Jinnah was unwilling to yield even an inch, in spite of Gandhiji showing utmost flexibility and patience. Had Jinnah shown the kind of flexibility that he showed later, the history of 1947 would have been different. Similarly, history would have been different if the Congress leaders, especially Nehru and Sardar Patel, had not been dismissive about the Muslim League, arrogantly regarding it as a "headache" and a "nuisance", and had the Congress offered to have talks with the League on the future constitutional arrangement for post-British India. The Congress did offer such talks in early 1947, but it was too late.

After the breakdown of talks, Gandhiji said in a press interview to Stuart Gelder of *News Chronicle* on 29 September, 1944: "I want to make it clear that I believe Mr. Jinnah is sincere, but I think he is suffering from hallucination when he imagines that an unnatural division of India could bring either happiness or prosperity to the people concerned."

We should be truly grateful to C Rajagopalachari, who was not only instrumental in facilitating the Gandhi-Jinnah talks, but also devised a formula, which came to be known as the "Rajaji Formula", aimed at securing "the largest quantum of acceptance on both sides" (the Congress and the Muslim League). After the talks failed, Rajaji wrote in the preface to the collection of the letters exchanged between the two leaders during the course of their meetings: "Gandhi has gone to the farthest limit by way of modifying the national aspiration in order to accommodate the League." He showed how Gandhiji had endorsed his formula and, in the course of his talks with Jinnah, further amplified it. It hence came to be known as the Gandhi-Rajaji Formula.

Rajaji's farsightedness can be gauged from the following summation of his preface.

"I do not think that there is any real difficulty in the way of a courageous acceptance by the Muslims of the responsibilities of a separate State as envisaged in the Lahore resolution and in conformity with the reasonable conditions under which it can be given effect to, namely, those set out in my formula. But if there should be any nervousness or unwillingness to take the grave step of separation, there is nothing to prevent the following of a middle course. *Alternative plans could be devised, and confederation could be one, whereby sovereign status could be secured without the disadvantages of outright partition."* (Emphasis added)

Ironically, even Nehru, one of *The Guilty Men of Partition* (which is the title of an incisive book by Dr. Ram Manohar Lohia) expressed contrition over Partition after it had happened. He also favoured a federation between India and Pakistan. In his reply to Nawab Sahib of Bhopal, who had questioned him on the division of India, Prime Minister Nehru wrote on July 9, 1948: "...perhaps we acted wrongly. It is difficult to judge now. And yet, the consequences of that Partition have been so terrible that one is inclined to think that anything else would have been preferable...*Ultimately, I have no doubt that India and Pakistan will come close together....some kind of federal link....There is no other way to peace. The alternative is ...war."*

vIt may not be too late: Kashmir is the key

We have seen that India and what later became Pakistan missed many opportunities to simultaneously achieve three inter-related goals in 1947: freedom from the British rule, unity of India, and a confederal constitutional set-up with two largely independent and autonomous States.

Now, nearly 70 years later, is an India-Pakistan Confederation (with the inclusion of Bangladesh) still possible? Is it necessary?

The necessity is beyond doubt. Together, our three countries account for a population of over 1.6 billion, the largest segment of global population with a common civilisational ancestry and socio-religious-racial-cultural complexion. The problems of poverty, socio-economic backwardness, protection of the environment, guarantee of equal rights and security to all sections of the plural societies in the three countries, safeguarding and strengthening of inter-religious harmony, development of robust democracy and institutions of good governance, peace within and along the borders - these too are common. It is delusional to think that any of the three countries can fully surmount these challenges on its own.

On the contrary, their ability to overcome these challenges will be greatly enhanced by maximising cooperation in a confederal framework. Indeed, the failure of the South Asian Association of Regional Cooperation (SAARC) to realise its vision and potential, even 30 years after its inception, clearly shows that what is lacking is cooperation between India and Pakistan. If Europe has become a zone of peace, after fighting two horrific World Wars in the last century, it is principally because most European countries have come together in a cooperative, confederal framework called the European Union.

There are of course large and dark clouds of doubt over the possibility of an India-Pakistan Confederation, given the enormous trust deficit between our two countries. Nevertheless, these clouds can be dispelled if we rediscover and strengthen the unifying examples in our shared history.

It is a supreme irony that one of these examples was provided by Jinnah himself when he addressed the inaugural session of the Constituent Assembly of Pakistan in Karachi on August 11, 1947. Speaking extempore, the soon-to-become Governor General of Pakistan sketched a highly appealing vision of Pakistan based on religious tolerance and national unity. In other words, soon after he created Pakistan, he jettisoned the divisive Two Nations theory!

Let's hear Jinnah speak: "I cannot emphasise it too much. We should begin to work in that spirit, and in course of time all these angularities of the majority and minority communities, the Hindu community and the Muslim community — because even as regards Muslims you have Pathans, Punjabis, Shias, Sunnis and so on, and among the Hindus you have Brahmins, Vashnavas, Khatris, also Bengalees, Madrasis and so on — will vanish.

Indeed if you ask me, this has been the biggest hindrance in the way of India to attain the freedom and independence, and but for this we would have been free people long long ago. No power can hold another nation, and specially a nation of 400 million souls, in subjection; nobody could have conquered you, and even if it had happened, nobody could have continued its hold on you for any length of time, but for this. Therefore, we must learn a lesson from this.

"You are free; you are free to go to your temples, you are free to go to your mosques or to any other place or worship in this State of Pakistan. You may belong to any religion or caste or creed — that has nothing to do with the business of the State.

As you know, history shows that in England conditions, some time ago, were much worse than those prevailing in India today. The Roman Catholics and the Protestants persecuted each other. Even now there are some States in existence where there are discriminations made and bars imposed against a particular class. Thank God, we are not starting in those days. We are starting in the days where there is no discrimination, no distinction between one community and another, no discrimination between one caste or creed and another. We are starting with this fundamental principle: that we are all citizens, and equal citizens, of one State. The people of England in [the] course of time had to face the realities of the situation, and had to discharge the responsibilities and burdens placed upon them by the government of their country; and they went through that fire step by step. Today, you might say with justice that Roman Catholics and Protestants do not exist; what exists now is that every man is a citizen, an equal citizen of Great Britain, and they are all members of the Nation.

"Now I think we should keep that in front of us as our ideal, and you will find that in course of time Hindus would cease to be Hindus, and Muslims would cease to be Muslims, not in the religious sense, because that is the personal faith of each individual, but in the political sense as citizens of the State."

This speech is iconoclastic in many ways; here Jinnah breaks his own "icon", deliberately sculpted during the days of the Pakistan movement. What is most remarkable is that he still seemed to refer to India ("a nation of 400 million") as his own motherland.

If today's, and tomorrow's, Pakistan returns to embrace this inclusive and tolerant vision of its own Father of the Nation, the doors of rapprochement with India will surely open. It goes without saying that there can be absolutely no place for religious bigotry, extremism, exclusivism and terrorism if Pakistan's rulers and people wish to faithfully follow this founding vision of Jinnah. Pakistan. For its own survival as a nation at peace with itself, and also for wiping out the image in the international community of a nation that harbours terrorists who kill innocent people both at home and in countries near and far, Pakistan must adopt and implement a policy of zero tolerance towards "Islamist terrorism". The term "Islamist terrorism" is indeed self-contradictory in its essence because Islam was founded by a prophet who was a messenger of peace and universal brotherhood.

Happily, an urge to abjure the entrenched anti-India sentiment is currently growing in Pakistan. Here is an example. Farzana Shaikh, a renowned Pakistani historian based in London, writes in her book *Making Sense of Pakistan*:

"There is a strong pressure on Pakistan to re-orient itself away from its perennial stance of confrontation with India. The aim is not only to ease relations with New Delhi, but to distance Pakistan from the appeal of a type of militant Islam that is at odds with Islamic traditions indigenous to South Asia. Historically, these traditions, characterised by their strong syncretistic bias in favour of exploring common ground between Islam and India's indigenous religious, have been judged to be especially responsive to the region's culturally plural character....Reviving these traditions, with their strong syncretistic foundations, could alleviate the pressures on Pakistan. By recasting its enduring quest for religious consensus in terms of a cultural heritage rooted in the discourse of Indian Islam, Pakistan may yet salvage a pluralistic alternative consistent with democratic citizenship. Though any such endeavour will be forced to confront (and adapt to) the challenge of orthodoxy in Pakistan, it remains the only meaningful model for a country that seeks still to project an identity founded on reconciling Islam's universalist message with respect for the rich diversity of its peoples." What enlightened scholars like Farzana Shaikh are proposing is a recognition of the "cultural and spiritual confederation", based on the values of tolerance, acceptance of diversity and social harmony, which are the bedrock of Indian Islam. Surely, this is consistent with Jinnah's own vision for Pakistan, as articulated in his 11 August, 1947 speech, and it is inconsistent with much of what has happened in Pakistan's history thereafter.

However, alleviating the trust deficit is not the responsibility of Pakistan alone. India too must play its constructive role — in three ways. First of all, it must bury the divisive and hegemonic concept of "Hindu Rashtra". India never was, and never will be, a Hindu Nation. By continuing to espouse it, the RSS and BJP give legitimacy to Jinnah's flawed and toxic Two Nations theory. The "Hindu Rashtra" concept played no insignificant role in India's partition in 1947. Its continued espousal will not only raise the spectre of India's future division, but it will also further antagonise Pakistan and Bangladesh. Therefore, if the RSS-BJP are still dreaming of "Akhand Bharat", they need to renounce the idea of "Hindu Rashtra" — India cannot be reunited by making Pakistan and Bangladesh extinct, but a tri-nation confederation is still possible.

Secondly, the people and government of India must accept, without any hesitation, the reality of Pakistan as a separate, independent and sovereign nation, and also sincerely wish for Pakistan to remain united, stable, peaceful and to become prosperous. India must consistently convey a credible message to its estranged neighbour that it poses no threat to Pakistan's security and unity. This is especially important due to Pakistan's concerns after the secession of Bangladesh, in which India played a role. Even though the liberation of East Pakistan and creation of Bangladesh was inevitable, and even though India was forced to intervene on the side of the liberation forces, the fact remains that this has made Pakistan worry that India remains inimical to its existence. New Delhi must address Islamabad's concerns, real or imaginary, on this score.

Thirdly, India - and Pakistan too — must realise that an early and amicable solution to the dispute over Jammu & Kashmir is a precondition for any genuine reconciliation and abiding peace between our two countries. The two governments must stare at, and accept, the reality: neither can India ever recapture the Pakistan-held part of Kashmir, nor can Pakistan hope to get the part of Kashmir that is with India. No military solution can secure this goal in favour of India or Pakistan.

The only viable and workable solution to the Kashmir dispute, therefore, is for India and Pakistan to merge the two sides of Jammu & Kashmir, and co-administer its affairs with a large degree of autonomy for the people of the merged state. Indeed, this is what the interlocutors of Dr Manmohan Singh and his Pakistani counterparts were negotiating, with a fair degree of progress, a few years ago.

Dr Singh had said in 2008: "While we cannot change borders, we can make them irrelevant... I invite Pakistan to work with us to usher in a new era of sub-continental cooperation." This was a wise and innovative stance. Prime Ministers Narendra Modi and Nawaz Sharif (with the cooperation of the Pakistani army and Pakistan's opposition parties) should pursue this approach vigorously, especially since there is simply no other solution to the Kashmir problem. This will surely be welcomed by a large majority of Kashmiris too, since it meets their aspiration to be reunited. Moreover, this solution will lead to large-scale demilitarisation of Kashmir by both India and Pakistan, thus making it possible for Kashmiris to live in peace and security.

If the people of Jammu and Ladakh wish to stay out of this arrangement, their wish should be respected through a suitable democratic mechanism.

The governments of India and Bangladesh recently adopted a creative approach of mutual accommodation by implementing the "land-swap" deal, which has been welcomed by the people in both countries. Why can't the governments of India and Pakistan adopt a similar out-of-the-box approach to solve the Kashmir problem? Yes, then can. They must.

Here, both India and Pakistan should learn a few lessons in pragmatism from China. When Hong Kong ceased to be a colony of Britain in 1997, Beijing adopted a scheme of "One country, two systems", allowing Hong Kong to have its own economic system. In the case of Taiwan, too, it is following this principle. It has even tolerated, to a large extent, Taiwan's existence as a separate country with its own independent government, while promoting rapid economic integration between Taiwan and mainland China.

After making the border in Kashmir irrelevant, the remaining stretches of the Indo-Pak border can also be made porous (making them irrelevant will take time) through modern transport and trade connectivities, both land- and sea-based, linking Punjab, Rajasthan, Gujarat, Sindh and Maharashtra. Today the China-Pakistan Economic Corridor (CPEC) has created concerns in India because parts of it go through PoK. Once PoK and Indian J&K are brought together, and once we create new and smooth connectivities elsewhere between India and Pakistan, we can envision CPEC extending into India and becoming CPIEC. On the eastern side, India and China are already having talks on the BMIC (Bangladesh-Myanmar-India-China) project that plans to build modern infrastructure linkage connecting the four countries. It is clear that China stands to benefit from closer integration between countries of South Asia and South-East Asia. The benefit for Bangladesh is even more self-evident because it is landlocked on three sides by India. If India and Pakistan can make this creative solution work in Jammu & Kashmir, it will immediately open up tantalising possibilities of moving towards a confederation, as envisioned in the Gandhi-Rajaji Formula in 1944.

In 2015, "Confederation" does not mean undoing the Partition of 1947; rather, it means creatively re-defining and recasting Partition. If we are wise enough to do so, before the dawn of August 15, 2047, hundred years after India's bloody division, our subcontinent will have seen three independent and sovereign countries coming together and pursuing a common policy on defence, trade, environment, infrastructure linkages, religious tourism, cultural cooperation and people-to-people contacts. India, Pakistan and Bangladesh would be free to exist as separate entities. However, they will be, as they have always been for thousands of years, "one (South Asian) family consisting of many members", to recall the words of Mahatma Gandhi, the wisest man produced by our common motherland, in his letter to Jinnah seven decades ago.

THE AGE OF UNMIXING

The practice of territorial and demographic rearrangements arose in the context of the early-to-mid-20th-century era of world wars and decolonisation in Asia and Africa. As territorial boundaries in Europe were challenged and peoples in other continents began to break free from the European colonial stranglehold, the political map of the world unravelled. In either case, political elites discovered a new solution: amid flux, fix. the best solution found was to fix territorial boundaries of a changing world. Thus the borders of old and new nation-states in Europe were dug deeper, while fresh borders for the emerging nation-states in Asia and Africa were invented to accommodate expressions of national will and demands for self-determination.

Territories had always changed hands, but what was new was the wholesale transfer of populations inhabiting those territories. A growing idea after the "great war" of 1914-18 was that conflicts arise among ethnically heterogeneous populations, and that the best way of resolving and preventing ethnic conflicts was to engineer the "unmixing of populations". The desired unmixing was achieved (for example) in the exchange of population between Greeks and Turks in 1923, and the expulsion of ethnic Germans from east-central Europe in 1944-49.

Behind the aim of achieving an internally homogenous population in a given nation-state was a view of peoples as a national collective whose membership was defined by ethnic-religious affiliation. This implied less tolerance to ethnic-religious groups that did not fit easily into the national imaginary: only when the defined communities could be fixed in their own territories would violence cease.

The fruit of division

It was against this background, when international opinion was already in favour of territorial rearrangements and population transfers, that the partition of British India took place in 1947. As the tripartite negotiations over power- sharing between the Indian National Congress, the Muslim League and the British colonial government began to fail, partition came to be seen as the most realistic option. At the same time, outside leading circles "partition" was little more than a vague, unfathomable - even harmless - word that cropped up occasionally in the speeches of political leadership. That they would be forced one day to leave their homes and livelihoods amidst raging violence, was yet inconceivable to millions of ordinary people.

This feeling of disbelief is best summarised in the words of an officer in charge of refugee rehabilitation in Punjab, who said: "we in India were only vaguely familiar with the word 'refugee' and used to wonder why people should be compelled to leave homes. Even *our* refugees [my italics] expressed surprise at the strange phenomenon of exchange of population and were heard saying we used to hear about the change of rulers but for the first time the ruled are also changing places".

The partition of 1947 was far more than an abstract line across administrative maps; it sought to create separate enclaves for different religious communities. In August 1947, when the "Radcliffe award" partitioning Punjab and Bengal was announced, millions of Hindus, Muslims and Sikhs now found that they no longer "belonged" to the place they were born in and had lived in forever. The advocates of territorial separation (most prominently according to the "two-nation theory" of Pakistan's founder, Muhammad Ali Jinnah) saw borders as the natural, physical expression of communal differences: that the new borders would exacerbate and reinforce these perceived differences was not considered.

Since the early summer of 1947, the abstract notion of "not-belonging" had become real when private armies belonging to the Muslim League's national guard), the Sikh *Akal Fauj* and the Hindu-nationalist *Rashtriya Swayamsevak Sangh* (RSS) began orchestrating major attacks on minority groups in their area of influence. The formal creation of borders in August meant that what was considered a temporary movement by many people to avoid violence months before had now became absolute and permanent.

From that point, the trickle of refugee movement turned into a deluge as millions began seeking safety in areas across the border where their community was in a majority. Hindus and Sikhs now "belonged" to India, and Muslims to Pakistan. The chaos of the early days abated as the two states began a planned exchange of population amidst continuing violence.

This period in Indian-Pakistani history is often visualised through archival photos of packed "refugee special" trains with people clambered on the rooftops, epic refugee walking-caravans, and women and children in bullock-carts escaping to safety with their meagre belongings. The personal memories of those affected, especially those who witnessed mass violence, are often saturated by scattered limbs, the inescapable stench of dead bodies, extreme sexual violence against women, and of people who took their own lives amid unbearable grief.

Such heartbreaking memories and images are testimony to the unconsolable pain of partition. They also contrast vividly with the single most striking image I encountered during six years of research into violence and identity in the region for my book *Since 1947: Partition Narratives among Punjabi Migrants of Delhi* (Oxford University Press, 2007). It was a photo published in several Delhi newspapers during the nuclear stand-off of 1998, when popular media discourse was spiced with comment about how the Indian nuclear-tipped warheads could reach all the way to Lahore and Islamabad.

The photo showed a crowd of Hindus and Sikhs dancing in patriotic celebration of India's momentary advantage over Pakistan in the race for regional military supremacy. What intrigued me was that the revellers were the descendants of Hindu and Sikh refugees from Pakistan; in hard logic, they were cheering the capacity to annihilate the land of their parents and grandparents. Such nationalist intoxication too is the fruit of partition.

The echo of history

The enduring hostility between India and Pakistan at official level - notwithstanding the efforts of many to seek to cross the divide - is at the very least a warning to those who argue for territorial partition as a solvent of violent antagonism.

Iraq is the foremost contemporary example. Since 2005, the idea of partitioning Iraq into three regions - *Shi'a*, *Sunni* and Kurdish - has gained momentum in direct proportion to the intensification of sectarian violence. A number of policy-makers and commentators in the United States and Britain - among them Peter Galbraith, Joseph Biden, Leslie H Gelb, Richard Betts and Simon Jenkins - have endorsed this idea in one form or another (other analysts, such as openDemocracy authors Zaid Al-Ali and Reidar Visser, have argued powerfully against it). The general notion is that the internecine violence between *Shi'a*, *Sunni* and Kurds would cease once each group has gained political control and territorial sovereignty in a tripartite Iraq; partition is regrettable but inevitable, and the earlier the world accepts it, the better.

The idea of partition may in large part emanate from the good intention of seeking to end violence and chaos in Iraq - though in some cases, a post-imperial "divide and rule" instinct may also be at work. But what is more important than the motive is the logic and the human implications of the proposal to divide people according to an accident of birth. The lesson of India-Pakistan in 1947 for the world is: don't make new borders between people, but work to make borders irrelevant.

PANDIT JAWAHARLAL NEHRU

Nehru's career may be divided into two parts- pre-independence and post-independence periods. In the pre-independence period he started his public life with all the advantages that one could imagine-a rich father, a carefree economic prospect, an English Public School and Cambridge education, a zest for life and a special appeal to the youth as a radical intellectual.

For about a decade, however, since his return to India, he made very little impression in public life. He first took an active part in the non-cooperation movement and that also as an ordinary soldier and not as a leader.

He did not come into the limelight for leadership in any campaign like Sardar Vallabhbhai Patel with the halo of success of the Bardoli Campaign. In the Congress he was a backbencher for many years, being more known to others as the son of Pandit Motilal Nehru. No doubt, he slowly veered to the group of young radicals, critical of the hesitancy of the senior leadership of the Congress. Like Subhas Chandra Bose, he was one of the young radicals who clamoured for complete independence in 1928 and would not settle for anything less.

In the mid-thirties Nehru's socialistic zeal led him to be one of the founders of the left wing of the Congress, known as the Congress Socialist Party. The rise of the left wing was not viewed with favour by either Gandhiji or the other senior leaders of the organisation. Nehru, however, with all his socialist zeal, never had the courage to go against the wishes of the Mahatma. Unlike the other radical young men, Jai Prakash Narain, Ram Manohar Lohia and others who stuck to the socialist principles even at the risk of the displeasure of Gandhiji and the Gandhian wing, Nehru was always careful to avoid any open clash.

He was essentially 'Bapuji's obedient boy' first and a socialist and radical later. Even during the hectic days of 1938-39 when there was an open split in the Congress, following Subhas Chandra Bose's difference with Gandhiji and Gandhian methods, between the radicals and the old guards, Nehru fully supported Gandhiji and the Gandhian wing.

This was not because he was genuinely convinced of the soundness of Gandhian principles, as he himself on many occasions made sarcastic comments on Gandhian ways of thinking as medieval, etc., but because of a blind personal attachment to Gandhiji even at the risk of a sacrifice of his radical and socialist leanings. Thus it was that he was more with the Gandhian wing of the Congress than with the Congress Socialist group after his initial days with that left-wing group.

In the next phase of his career after the Government of India Act of 1935, it was mainly Nehru's indiscretion and lack of political foresight which shaped the future course of events and led ultimately to the partition of India. In 1937, when the Congress was flushed with victory in the majority of Provinces, it was mainly because of Nehru that a chance of communal harmony was spoiled by his idealistic and doctrinaire intransigence.

The Muslim League had proposed a Coalition Government with the Congress in the Provinces under the Provincial Autonomy scheme, but it was Nehru as President of the Congress who thoughtlessly spurned that offer and demanded the virtual liquidation of the Muslim League. As Maulana Abul Kalam Azad, one of Nehru's closest Muslim associates, remarked in his memories that it was a grave political blunder which eventually strengthened the Muslim League and encouraged it to demand a partition of the country.

The political destiny of India would have been shaped in an entirely different way if Nehru had shown more political maturity and accommodating spirit, hoping for a real rapprochement between the two major communities in India. But Nehru could not rise up to the occasion. It was again because of Nehru's opposition that the proposal for a Coalition Government in Bengal between the Congress Party and Fazlul Haque's Krishak Praja Party was turned down unceremoniously.

The blunder of the Congress was fully exploited by the Muslim League, which immediately formed a Coalition Government with the Krishak Praja Party. It is significant to note that in order to exclude any Muslim political influence in the U. P., Nehru deliberately threw away the two Muslim majority Provinces-Bengal and the Punjab-into the arms of the Muslim League. It was from this time onwards that the communal forces in Bengal and the Punjab became more and more strengthened, ultimately leading to the demand for

Pakistan in 1940. History can hardly spare the man who played with a nation's destiny in such a thoughtless and indiscreet manner.

Nehru had never any softness for Subhas Chandra Bose either before or during or after the Second World War. Before the British Victory and particularly before the coming to power of the Labour Party in England, he hardly ever appreciated the venture of Subhas Chandra Bose or the exploits and sacrifices of the INA. Yet, when all was over and the INA trial started in the Red Fort of Delhi, he took the leadership on behalf of the Congress (and indeed of the whole country) in organising the legal defence of the INA accused.

He donned the Barrister's gown after nearly three decades, but that was more a political gesture. Nehru, after all, was not even a second-rank lawyer and the main brunt of the defence fell on Bhulabhai Desai whom the Congress had maligned because of the Desai Liaqat Pact. The INA Trial was used by the Congress as a booster to its morale in the ensuing General Elections in 1946, and Nehru very tactfully adopted Netaji's slogan 'Jai Hind' from this time onwards.

During the Constitutional negotiations which preceded the transfer of power in 1947, Nehru had a prominent hand. But on this occasion again, it was Nehru's indiscretion which ruined all chances of a settlement between the Congress and the Muslim League and the preservation of India's political unity under the Cabinet Mission Plan.

When the Cabinet Mission Plan of preservating India's political unity and at the same time granting some concession to the Muslim League demand for Pakistan in the shape of grouping of Provinces had been accepted, either willingly or grudingly, by both the political parties, Nehru as the newly elected President of the Congress made a most injudicious speech, holding out a threat that once the Constituent Assembly was convened, the Congress would be free to choose any particular part of the Cabinet Mission Plan and reject any other part. Even Azad was aghast at this sort of pronouncement.

The effect of this injudicious pronouncement may best be described in the words of Leonard Mosley : "And on 10 July (1946), after he (Nehru) had been elected President, he called the press together for a Conference to discuss his policy as the new head of the Congress. It was a moment in history when circumspection should have been the order of the day. There was much to be gained by silence. The fortunes of India were in the balance and one false move could upset them.

Nehru chose this moment to launch into what his biographer, Michael Brecher, has described as 'one of the most fiery and provocative statements in his forty years of public life'.... Did Nehru realise what he was saying ? He was telling the world that once in power, the Congress would use its strength at the center to alter the Cabinet Mission Plan as it thought fit. But the Muslim League (as had the Congress) had accepted the Plan as a cut and dried scheme to meet the objections from both sides.

It was a compromise plan which obviously could not afterwards be altered in favour of one side or another. In the circumstances, Nehru's remarks were a direct act of sabotage. Whether he meant them to be so, in the mistaken belief that Jinnah and the Muslim League were not really a force to be reckoned with, or whether they were the ham-handed remarks of a politician who did not know when to keep his mouth shut will never be known."

Even Abul Kalam Azad commented on Nehru's Press Conference as "one of those unfortunate events which change the course of history." The immediate effect was the refusal of Jinnah to accept the Cabinet Mission Plan, as he feared that he could never trust the Congress to give a fair deal to the Muslims once the transfer of power was effected. There are moments when it is best to keep one's mouth shut, but Nehru obviously did not subscribe to that view.

In the final phase of the Constitutional negotiations after the arrival of Lord Mountbatten, Nehru all on a sudden turned a complete volte-face for which no rational explanation can be found. He had all along been opposed to the Muslim League and its Pakistan demand. From 1937 onwards it cannot be said that Nehru did all that was possible to accept the reality of the situation and to try to conciliate Jinnah and his Muslim League.

He hardly considered this aspect of political strategy to be deserving of any serious attention. He always laboured under the delusion that in the constitutional struggle there were only two parties, the British Government and the Congress. He maintained that view even after the general elections of 1946 in which the Muslim League captured practically all the Muslim seats in the Legislature.

He was encouraged in this feeling when he was called upon by the Governor-General, Lord Wavell, to form the Interim Government and to go ahead with preparations for a Constituent Assembly in spite of the fact that the Muslim League refused to join either. Nehru, possibly, felt convinced that the British were so eager to quit India immediately that they would not hesitate to throw the Muslim League overboard and hand over power to the Congress alone. He hardly knew Jinnah and his political potentiality.

The Congress accepted office in the Interim Government, and Jinnah in reply gave the call for Direct Action on 16 August 1946. We need not go into the details of the events that followed. Suffice it to note that when the orgy of mob violence spread in different parts of the country and particularly in the

Punjab, Nehru, the head of the Interim Government, was completely unnerved, and far from facing the situation boldly, he was panicked into an immediate acceptance of the Pakistan demand.

From the evidence available till now, it is difficult to say with certainty why this change came over Nehru
so suddenly and so mysteriously. Different sources have given different explanations, but perhaps the truth is yet to be revealed. One thing is certain, that he was completely unnerved by the orgy of communal violence in the Punjab and came to an immediate decision to accept a division of the country to avoid further bloodshed and brutality. He hardly knew that the division was to be followed by much more violence and brutality than before.

There was possibly some other reason also, namely, the unwillingness of Nehru to go into political wilderness again. He was anxious to get independence immediately and refused to wait heading the government of a freed though truncated India immediately. To quote Leonard Mosley again: "But perhaps Pandit Nehru came nearer the truth in a conversation with the author in 1960 when he said, `the truth is that we were tired men, and we were getting on in years too. Few of us could stand the prospect of going to prison again-and if we had stood out for a United India as we wished it, prison obviously awaited us. We saw the fires burning in the Punjab and heard every day of the killings. The plan for partition offered a way out and we took it.'"

It is difficult to say how far this was the correct version of the motives of Nehru in accepting partition. It is sad to reflect, however, that the earlier champion of the Nationalist Muslims had no scruple now to throw to the wolves the Nationalist Muslims in the NWFP and Sind, not to speak of the minorities in Pakistan, who had done so much to contribute to India's freedom struggle and whose sufferings and sacrifices for more than half a century had enabled Pandit Nehru to become the first Prime Minister of a Free India.

Sardar Patel and Pandit Nehru were the earliest two converts to the Pakistan proposal in the Congress leadership. Both in the Working Committee meeting and in the AICC meeting there were loud protests against the acceptance of partition, but such was the lure of the Mountbatten plan of immediate independence among the higher ranks in the Congress that all protests against acceptance of partition were of no avail. History offers few parallels to such a complete volte-face in political strategy.

In the post-independence period Nehru's record can hardly be regarded as successful or remarkable. His choice as the first head of the Government of Free India was 'Bapuji's' gift to his 'obedient boy' rather than to any tangible contributions made by Nehru in the freedom struggle or his unquestioned pre-eminence among others who belonged to his rank of the Congress leadership. Rajogapalachari, Rajendra Prasad, Sardar Vallabhbhai Patel or Abul Kalam Azad had at least equal claim to head the Government of a Free India.

Nehru's choice as the first Prime Minister, however, did not surprise the public in general, who knew that he was Gandhiji's special favourite, and all high positions in Congress or in the Government were taken for granted to be for 'Bapuji' to bestow. Nehru unfortunately, had no parliamentary, administrative or even legal experience. Hence it was that as Prime Minister his relations were not happy and cordial either with the first President, Dr. Rajendra Prasad, or with the Deputy Prime Minister, Sardar Vallabhbhai Patel.

In fact not only Ambedkar but almost everybody who resigned from his Cabinet later resented his dictatorial methods and his way of dealing with his Cabinet colleagues. Nehru never subscribed to the view that the Prime Minister was only a primus-inter-pares in the Cabinet.

Nor did Nehru show much ability as an administrator or a Parliamentarian. Most of his Parliamentary speeches (he spoke extempore even on very important issues) were dull, stale and verbose. As a Parliamentarian, he cannot be compared to Gladstone or Disraeli, nor even to Bhulabhai Desai or Shyamaprasad Mookerjee. As an administrator he relied more on his personal friends than those who were really responsible for running the machinery of the Government.

The best concrete illustration was his handling of the situation when the three Service chiefs resigned at the same time in protest against the policy of V. K. Krishna Menon, the Defence Minister and Nehru's closest personal friend. Nehru went all out in defence of his personal friend and publicly snubbed the three Service Chiefs, and this was the friend who was mainly responsible for India's debacle in the war with China in 1962.

Nehru was one of those who believed in speeches and not in action. Whenever there was crisis to be faced and a firm decision had to be taken, he faltered and vacillated. Again the best concrete illustration was his handling of the Kashmir Question and his reference of the dispute to the UN. He committed another grave blunder in making a gratuitous offer of holding a plebiscite in Kashmir, for which there was no provision either in the Cabinet Mission Plan or in the Indian Independence Act of 1947.

His later falling back from that position was easily exploited by the Pakistan Government in influencing world opinion. Nehru's vacillation is again evident from the very widely known story that when Sardar Patel had secured his consent to the Hyderabad action, Patel left Delhi, instructing his Ministry officials that he could not be contacted for twenty-four hours, mainly out of a fear that at the last moment Nehru would vacillate and order a stoppage of the action against Hyderabad. While the integration of States in a record time stands to the eternal glory of Sardar Patel as an administrator and a statesman, Nehru's record can show hardly anything equal to it.

In internal matters Nehru believed in planning and the system of Five Year Plans was adopted under his guidance and sponsorship. But before he died, both he and the people of India must have realised that all the three Five Year Plans under his regime had failed miserably. The fault lay no doubt with bad planning by economists, but that again was due to the defective guidance given by Nehru and to his wrong emphasis on certain aspects of economic development.

Instead of looking to the food production problem he started on grandiose plans of large scale industrialisation, which in the course of the first three Plans completely upset the assumptions and calculations of the planners about the development of Indian economy.

In foreign policy again, which was supposed to be Nehru's forte, Nehru's policy proved as much a dismal failure as his Planning policy. His policy of non-alignment might have been right up to a certain point, but not as a fixed permanent principle of foreign policy. Nor did he have the courage or determination to remain strictly non-aligned, e.g., his varying statements during the Soviet invasion of Hungary or his blind espousal of the cause of the Arabs against Israel or his sponsorship of China's application for U. N. membership even after the Chinese invasion of India.

It was Nehru's relations with China that bring out most conclusively the failure of his foreign policy. For the Indian debacle in the War with China in 1962 a large part of the responsibility lay with Nehru. It was his obsession about British imperialism and the wrongs it had done to States on India's frontiers which led him to sacrifice the Tibetan buffer so easily. It was his blind faith in Sino-Indian friendship which made him close his eyes to the realities of the situation till he was rudely disillusioned in 1962.

It was his ambition to play the role of a World statesman and make India's voice heard in all international issues that made him neglect issues which concerned India more directly. It was his unrealistic conviction that if India remained peaceful no other power would drag her into war which made him concentrate on economic development to the extent of totally neglecting defence preparedness.

It was again his fond hope that the justice of India's stand in any dispute would be readily accepted by all non-aligned powers, specially the Afro-Asian powers, which made him neglect timely diplomatic moves to show up China's real intentions and to form an organised Asian opinion against China. In short, both in foreign affairs and in defence, India's policy, during the first decade after independence was wrong, unreal and weak, and India had to pay a heavy price for it in 1962.

What made matters even worse after 1959 was the incredible muddle-headedness in deciding to confront the Chinese in the disputed areas along the border and yet refusing to admit the necessity of making suitable defence preparations for the showdown which, it was apparent by 1959-60, was inevitable. The 1962 debacle had one historical lesson-it is not enough to have the right on one's side, one must also have the strength to assert it. It appears that the lesson has gone home and India's policy has undergone the needed change in the decade following 1962.

Nobody was more conscious of the failure of his foreign policy vis-a-vis China than Nehru himself, as the following broadcast to the nation on 22 October 1962 would clearly show: "I do not propose to give you the long history of continuous aggression by the Chinese during the last five years and how they have tried to justify it by speeches, agreements and repeated assertions of untruths and a campaign of calumny and vituperation against our country. Perhaps, there are not many instances in history where one country, that is India, has gone out of her way to be friendly and co-operative with the Chinese Government and people to plead their cause in the councils of the world, and therefore, it is shocking for the Chinese Government to return evil for good, and even go to the extent of aggression and invade our sacred land. No self-respecting country, and certainly not India with her love of freedom, can submit to this, whatever the consequences may be."

This Editorial Addendum should not be misunderstood as an attempt to belittle the greatness of Jawaharlal Nehru but should be read in the spirit in which it has been written. History is a hard taksmaster and is no respecter of persons. For a historian, the only ideal is to find out the truth about any personality or event, irrespective of current sentimentalism or theory considerations. In an authoritative work like the Dictionary of National Biography we have tried to give an impartial assessment of Nehru's life and career in the true spirit of a devotee of Clio and in total disregard of present-day sentimental or political considerations.

MAULANA AZAD AND PARTITION

IN the debate on partition started by Jaswant Singh's book every one has been talking about the role of Jinnah, Nehru and Sardar Patel in the divide of India but hardly anyone mentioned what Maulana Abul Kalam Azad, an eminent scholar of Islam and president of the Congress party for six long years before partition, had to say and did to avert partition.

It is true that the Maulana was also a party to the Congress Working Committee (CWC) resolution accepting partition but he had never accepted partition. He had warned Jawaharlal Nehru that some of his acts were politically not wise and mighty result in alienation of Jinnah or in partition. Pandit Nehru was not ready to accept a weak centre and hence he consciously contributed to partition but Azad had no such interest in partition and wanted to prevent it. He supported it only as something inevitable.

To understand Maulana Azad's viewpoint one has to go through his book India Wins Freedom and the 30 pages which were published 30 years after his death. About partition Maulana had a definite point of view that cannot be ignored if we have to understand the genesis and causes of partition. Maulana Azad was an important leader of both the Congress as well as of Muslims.

Maulana Azad had a passionate commitment to freedom of India and as the youngest president of the Congress in Ramgarh session he said, in his presidential address, that "if an angel descends from heaven with the gift of freedom of India and declares from Qutub Minar that India is a free country I would not accept it unless Hindus and Muslims were united. If India does not get freedom it would be India's loss but if Hindus and Muslims do not unite it would be entire humanity's loss."

The Maulana writes in India Wins Freedom that "as a Muslim, I for one am not prepared for a moment to give up my right to treat the whole of India as my domain and share in the shaping of its political and economic life. To me it seems a sure sign of cowardice to give up what is my patrimony and content myself with a mere fragment of it."

About possible consequences of the partition, he says if India was divided into two states, "there would remain three and half crores of Muslims scattered in small minorities all over the land. With 17 per cent in UP, 12 per cent in Bihar and 9 per cent in Madras, they will be weaker than they are today in the Hindu majority provinces. They have had their homelands in these regions for almost a thousand years and built up well known centres of Muslim culture and civilisation there."

The Muslims who would be left behind, he said, would discover that they have become alien and foreigners. Backward industrially, educationally and economically, they would be left at the mercy of what would become 'an unadulterated Hindu raj.' On the other hand, their position within the Pakistan state will be vulnerable and weak. Nowhere in Pakistan will their majority be comparable to the Hindu majority in the Hindustan States. "In fact their majority will be so slight that it will be offset by the economical, educational and political lead enjoyed by non-Muslims in these areas. Even if this were not so and Pakistan were overwhelmingly Muslim in population, it still could hardly solve the problem of Muslims in Hindustan."

About the fear that if partition did not take place the Centre with a Hindu majority will interfere in Muslim majority provinces, the Maulana counters by the argument (which was what the Cabinet Mission Plan was about) "the Congress meets this fear by granting full autonomy to the provinces. It has also provided for two lists of central subjects, one compulsory and the other optional so that if any provincial unit so wants, it can administer all subjects itself except a minimum delegated to the Centre.

The Congress scheme, therefore, ensures that Muslim majority provinces are internally free to develop as they will, but can at the same time influence the Centre on all issues which affect India as a whole."

Thus Maulana was not opposing partition only as a Congress leader but also as a learned Muslim who could foresee far reaching consequences. Maulana Azad, unlike other politicians, was a far-sighted leader both of the Muslims and of whole India as well.

The fact remains that if India had not been divided, today there would have been more than 33 per cent Muslims, a huge number in any democracy. In any case they would have formed their own governments in the Muslim majority provinces and would have had stake in the whole of India.

Several Muslim leaders could have become prime minister of India. Today there are about 15 crores of Muslims but are still a minority and face several problems as a minority and also have to carry the guilt — wrongly of course — of having partitioned the country. Ironically there are more Muslims in India than in Pakistan and yet they constitute only 14 per cent minority.

Maulana Azad, in the thirty pages published thirty years after his death blames both Nehru and Sardar Patel. According to him, Nehru made a mistake by refusing to take two Muslim League members as cabinet ministers after provincial elections in 1937 in UP. It made Jinnah distrustful of the Congress leaders whom he began to describe as 'Hindu' leaders.

Second mistake committed by Jawaharlal Nehru was his statement to the press in July 1946 after taking over as president of the Congress in which he said Cabinet Mission Plan could be changed. The Muslim League and Congress both had accepted the Plan and to give such a statement in an atmosphere of mistrust and suspicion was certainly a mistake. That finally drove Jinnah to insist on partition.

PARTITION AND DISLOCATION IN THE EAST INDIA

The uprooted and displaced Hindus who were termed as refugees came phase by phase from East Pakistan to West Bengal. The first batch of refugees arrived after the riot in Noakhali and Tippera in 1946. The shelter-seekers continued to trickle in till the end of 1949. Those, who came during this phase, mostly belonged to the upper and upper middle strata like the landowning, merchant and professional classes.

The after that major influx took place following the massacre in several districts of East Bengal, particularly in the village called Kalshira in the Bagerhat subdivision of Khulna district on December 20, 1949 and then Rajshahi, Faridpur and Barisal in February 1950. This time, those who crossed the border were very poor, mostly agricultural labourers.

It is value mentioning that, the Nehru-Liaquat Pact, signed in April 1950, failed to provide the way for the return of the refugees to their homeland. Later on, when the 'passport system' was introduced for travel from Pakistan to India on 15 October 1952, more people started to arrive. It was a "now or never kind of situation", which scared many people during this phase. Influx again began after 1960-61, and reached a crescendo during 1964-65. Finally, came the massive exodus, when the West Pakistani rulers took the route of genocide to silence the Bengalis in East Pakistan.

While the discourse of partition victim-hood of the East Bengali Hindus reflected their acute sense of insecurity with regard to *dhon*, (wealth), *pran* (life) and *maan* (honour), the reason for the exodus of *bhadralok*, immediately after the partition, was largely due to a fear of losing *dhon* and *maan* rather than *pran* in a numerically and politically subordinate group in a Muslim-majority nation. A small section of these people was able to sell their property in East Bengal or exchanged property to acquire capital to reinvest the same in private industries. Within a short period, they integrated with the local population. There was also a large educated middle class, who, though, did not have enough money with them but had 'social capital' for their survival. Some of them found jobs, or could restart their medical or legal practice again. Almost all the Hindu government servants serving in East Bengal gave an "option" for India.

In the 1950s, also came millions of displaced peasants and agricultural labourers who possessed almost nothing but their manual labour. The threat of their *pran* forced them to leave their *desh*. Most of them were from the so-called lower castes, like Namasudra, Mahisya and Sadgop communities. Initially they hesitated to leave East Bengal because of two reasons. First, being agricultural labourers they did not want to be detached from their traditional cultivable land, and second, due to the influence of their leader Jogen Mondal, who held a cabinet post in Pakistan at that time, they decided to stay back.

But, it is quite known now that, the people, who finally took the hard decision to leave *desh* and to cross over to the other side of the border for safety and security, contributed a lot to the progress and prosperity of their adopted land. The refugees definitely felt some kind of detachment from their new place of residence, but that detachment did not come in their way to make the adopted land more liveable.

Introduction to Refugee

Immediately after the partition, when the mass exodus was going on in full swing in the eastern part of India, the Government of India defined the term 'displaced' in the following words: "A displace person is one who had entered India (who left or who was compelled to leave his home in East Pakistan on or after October 15, 1947) for disturbances or fear of such disturbances or on account of setting up of the two dominions of India and Pakistan."

Those Hindus, who had left East Pakistan before 15 October 1947 due to the communal frenzy, were excluded from the previously mentioned official definition. At that time, the 'passport system' was yet to be launched, and it was regarded as a special case since the refugees had citizenship rights in both the states. Therefore, the Indian Government probably thought the term 'displaced' more suitable than 'refugee'.

furthermore, although India became independent on 15 August 1947, the extended period of two months was given to the people for setting themselves in the country of their choice. However, in the later phase these 'displaced' people were referred to as 'migrants' and were divided into two broad categories – the 'old migrants' and 'new migrants'.

To quote the *Manual of Refugee, Relief and Rehabilitation* of the Government of West Bengal: "(a) Those who migrated between October 1946 and 31 March 1958 are known as 'old migrants'. Their rehabilitation was governed by the West Bengal Act XVI of 1951... (b) Those who came between 1 January 1964 and 25 March 1971, are known as 'new migrants'."

One be supposed to not forget that, many people crossed over to West Bengal between 1958 and 1964, who were excluded from the definition of 'migrants'. Moreover, although many people came from East Pakistan to India with 'migration certificates', they were treated like refugees and in many cases they were sent to the camps because they need rehabilitation and relief for their survival.

East remained East India

While West Bengal was the largest recipient of refugees for her geographical and cultural proximity to East Pakistan, not all districts of the state were equally affected by the problem. In most cases, the refugees from the western parts of East Pakistan came to the adjacent districts of West Bengal, whereas, the displaced from the central and eastern parts of East Bengal preferred to resettle themselves in 24 Parganas (then undivided), and in and around Calcutta. However, the refugees from the northern part of East Bengal tried to remain in the adjacent districts of the northern part of West Bengal.

Though the Annual Report of the Department of Rehabilitation of the Government of India pointed out that, in the first phase of the refugee flow during the year 1946 to 1952 2.52 million refugees arrived in West Bengal, the year between 1953 and 1956 were marked as crucial. Gradually, by December 1957 the refugee influx reached the highest point in the east. The number of the refugees crossing the international border went up to 3,16,000. Now, these figures can hardly give one any idea of the pain, trauma and agony through which the displaced might have gone due to the ruptured economic, social and cultural ties with their original homeland. Nevertheless, they are important to understand the scale and magnitude of the post-partition displacement in the East.

Initially, the Government of India attempted to discourage the migration of East Bengalis to India. It became clear from the instruction given by Mohanlal Saksena, the then Rehabilitation Minister of the Government of India to the representatives of Tripura, Assam, Bihar, Orissa and West Bengal, in a meeting held in the Writers' Buildings on March 2, 1950 that the Government's work would be restricted to relief only rather than to rehabilitation. Moreover, Saksena was in favour of establishing the relief camps in the border areas to facilitate their quick return to their homeland.

But, the refugee state of affairs in the East did not improve at all even in the late 1950s. As a result of the Nehru-Liaquat Pact (1950), a large number of Muslims who had left West Bengal before March 31, 1951, came back to West Bengal, and reclaimed their land already occupied by the Bengali Hindu refugees from East Pakistan. While the Muslim evacuees returned to West Bengal, there was hardly any reverse population flow of the Hindus from West Bengal to East Pakistan.

But, during the initial phase, the Government of India was primarily concerned about the resettlement of the refugees from West Pakistan, and the national leadership was ambivalent regarding its responsibilities toward the Bengali Hindu refugees from East Pakistan. Nehru's letter to Bidhan Chandra

Roy, the then Chief Minister of West Bengal reflected that kind of ambivalence. To quote him:

"It is incorrect to encourage any large scale migration from East Bengal to the west. Indeed, if such a migration takes place, West Bengal and to some extent the Indian union would be overwhelmed ... If they come over to West Bengal, we must look after them. But it is no service to them to encourage them to join the vast mass of refugees who can at best be poorly cared for". It made one thing obvious that the Indian Government's policy toward rehabilitation of the Bengali Hindu refugees was not only inadequate, but also discriminatory in nature.

Prafulla K. Chakrabarty, the author of *The Marginal Men,* and a major chronicler of the partition refugees in the East, identified two basic reasons behind the discriminatory attitude of the Indian Government. First, the refugees in the west were more close to Delhi, the capital of India, where any trouble might destabilize the Government, whereas the geographical distance from Delhi put the refugees in the east in a vulnerable situation; and second, there was a large number of Punjabis in the armed forces, and a military mutiny was possible, if their kith and kin were ignored.

According to the report of the Planning Commission on the Rehabilitation of the Displaced Persons, the larger part of the task of rehabilitating West Pakistani displaced persons was accomplished before the end of the first Five Year Plan. Despite that, the Second Five Year Plan provided Rs.187 million for the rehabilitation of the refugees. Funds were quite liberally available for the completion of the housing scheme already approved, and for mitigating unemployment in the townships and colonies of displaced persons through schemes for setting up industries. The continuation of the training and education schemes for the displaced people also remained crucial to the policy of the government.

The Report of the Planning Commission admitted at the end of the First Five year plan that, the continuing influx of the displaced persons from East Pakistan made the problem of rehabilitation in the eastern states particularly difficult. Although the Second Five Year Plan altogether provided Rs.668 million for the rehabilitation schemes of the displaced persons in the eastern states, the Government of India decided to review the financial provision in the third year of the Second Plan, and it was said, "if needed", provisions for the additional fund would be made. But, the sanction of this sum of money was not adequate enough to manage the entire refugee situation in West Bengal. Through and large, there was an immediate recognition of the gravity and magnitude of the refugee problem in the West, and therefore, new townships of Faridabad, Rajpura and Tripuri were constructed to permanently rehabilitate the displaced in the *pucca houses.*

Work centres and industry were also set up with the government help in those areas along with the basic amenities, like schools and hospitals. East did not witness any such development, except may be a small township in Fulia. Even the reception centres for the refugees in the West were of superior quality than their counterparts in the East. Whereas the cash dole was given in a standardised form in the West, that was not the case in the East. Some work centres in the West were only training centres without provision for residence, but each home was a complete unit providing not only residence but also education in different stages, professional or practical training and employment for at least a short length of time, as it was in Hoshiarpur. No such facility was available in the East. The rate of grants in the West was also in a way of a generous scale compared to that in the East. It was seldom below Rs.30 per month and was sometimes at a higher rate according to the professional training chosen. The rate of grant in the East was almost the same but several categories were excluded from this privilege. Women refugees taking a course of training in teaching or nursing in a recognised institution or hospital were not given any stipend but were only allowed to attend the vocational training centres specially set up for refugees. In addition to the stipends amounting to Rs.30 per head to the trainees, the government provided the houses, the establishment and equipment cost and a revolving cost of raw materials in the West. On the other hand, except in Titagarh and Gariahat work centres (which were for men), the grants for women under these heads in West Bengal were very meagre.

In short, both the Governments (Government of India as well as the State Government of West Bengal) were slow in responding to the refugee crisis in West Bengal. Under the circumstances, relief and rehabilitation process was mainly restricted to those, who registered themselves in the official records and took shelter in relief and transit camps. In other words, the problem as a displaced was, in a way, sometimes more acute for those who crossed over to West Bengal in the early years of the partition-related crisis.

'GOVERNMENT OF AGITATION' AND JABAR DAKHAL COLONIES

Permit us first consider the case of those refugees who crossed over to West Bengal from East Pakistan from the late 1940s and early '50s, and who primarily belonged to the upper or middle classes. Due to their class character, their natural destination was Calcutta where they hoped to find jobs or professional opportunities suitable for them.

Many of them had friends, relatives and acquaintances in Calcutta, who initially helped them to resettle here. In a way, a social network system of these displaced people played an important role to reconstruct their lives in the other side of the border. Neither of these two groups of people was interested to go to the relief camps. Even those who belonged to the middle class and comparatively worse off families, and did not possess much resources, did not want to settle in the refugee camps mainly because of their *maan* (honour).

Against this backdrop, the squatters' colonies, an important part of the life and landscape of West Bengal, definitely a significant part of Calcutta, mushroomed. In some cases, where the land was acquired through legal means and procedures, the government termed the areas of refugee settlement as 'private colonies'. But, in other cases, apparently vacant land, owned by the government or by big landowners, was acquired through forcible occupation. This process of 'collective takeover' was known as *jabar dakhal*.

Although the squatters' colonies flourished in other parts of West Bengal, in December 1950, there were about 149 squatters' colonies, all of which grew up in Calcutta, 24 Parganas, Howrah and Hooghly districts. A large concentration of these squatters' colonies was found in the southeastern portion of the Calcutta Metropolitan District, especially in the areas like Jadavpur, Tollygange, Kasba and Behala. Approximately 40 such colonies were established by the year 1950.

The refugees built up their own shelters in these areas virtually without any government aid. In order to link the habitation with livelihood, the colonies were set up near the towns or industrial areas. But, the squatters' colonies were not limited to the cities and suburbs. In rural areas, the refugee peasants took over the uncultivated wasteland. Such land was seized not only for habitation, but also for cultivation.

This type of agricultural colonies was established in Bankura, Birbhum, Midnapore, Burdwan, Nadia, Murshidabad, 24 Parganas, West Dinajpur, Malda, Coochbihar and Jalpaiguri districts. as recollecting his memories of those days' struggle for reconstructing their lives in not so alien land like Calcutta, Himanshu Majumder, a resident of Bijoygarh colony said:

"There was no colony as such when I came here with my father from our *desh*, Barisal. Perhaps it was November or December 1947. I knew Santosh Dutta quite well due to my political connection since the pre-partition days. Santoshda sent me a message that if we want to resettle in Calcutta, we must come here as early as possible ... In fact, when I arrived here I came to know that Santoshda, with the help of others, already formed an informal group who met and decided about a piece of land, which appeared alright.

I got a plot of five or six cottah on my first night in Calcutta. We constructed a thatched hut to live in. We used *Hogla* leaves to cover our roof. The land was low-lying and marshy. We cleared the land, installed tube-well and made the place liveable ..."

Amiyaprova Debi, another resident of Bijoygarh, who came from Chittagong of East Pakistan, portrayed almost a similar picture. In her words: "There was a military barrack in the area which was constructed for the Americans during the Second World War. So, a wide concrete road already existed there connecting Jadavpur to Tollygunge. Besides the military barracks, there were huge, vacant lands, the property of the private landlords, like Layelkas.

There were sometimes fierce battles with the hired goons of the landlords, who also had the support of the police. We fought back refusing to yield. At the same time, we also carried on negotiations with the private owners of the land and the Government. The area was full of snakes. There were least possible public amenities. We had to carry drinking water on our own as there were initially no tube-wells in the area, no electricity, ... We were quiet well-off there in our *desh*, and here we had to start our lives again like beggars living in a *basti* (slum)-like area without electricity, water supply, drainage and other basic sanitary amenities ..." It became clear to the shelter-seekers in the *jabar dakhal* colonies by the early '50s that, they had no other option but to raise their voice to get justice so far as relief and rehabilitation was concerned – what Anil Sinha calls as 'the epic battle of Kurukshetra' in order to attain 'just and legitimate' demands.

Sinha argued that, these *jabar dakhal* colonies were classic examples of the organised resentment of the East Pakistani refugees against the rehabilitation policies of the Congress government.

In 1948, with the formation of the Nikhil Banga Bastuhara Karma Parishad (All Bengal Refugee Council for Action), the politics of agitation among the refugees of the squatters' colonies took a concrete shape for the first time. In the initial phase, the Parishad had two groups of members: the pro-Congress group wanted permanent rehabilitation of the refugees without antagonising the government authorities at the Centre and the State, and the other group comprised mostly Left-minded members. In 1949, those Left-minded members took over the leadership of the Parishad, except the post of the President, which was occupied by a 'Hindu Mahasabha sympathiser'. Since then, the Parishad organised meetings and demonstrations in the squatters' colonies, and this sort of 'unionisation' helped the refugees to launch the protest movement in an organised manner.

In fact, the introduction of the Eviction of Persons in Unauthorised Occupation Land Bill (later known as Eviction Bill), which after subsequent modifications became Act XVI of 1951, triggered off the politics of agitation of the refugees in full scale against the anti-refugee policies of the Congress Government. The Government felt that, the forcible and unauthorised occupation of private and government lands and premises requisitioned by the Central and State Governments and other public bodies had created problem that could not be resolved by the normal process of legal action. In other words, the squatters' colonies violated the sanctity of private property guaranteed by the Constitution. But, Dr. B.C. Roy, Chief Minister of West Bengal, argued that the Government possessed virtually no power to evict a squatter in unauthorised occupation of land or premises except through a prolonged process of legal action and the enactment of the Bill sought to reconcile the demands of law with the needs of the refugees.

The United Central Refugee Council (UCRC), formed on June 4, 1950, launched a resistance movement against this Bill. The UCRC hastily outlined a three-fold programme of action:

a) to start an intensive propaganda campaign by involving all refugee organisations of the colonies, barracks, slums etc.;
b) to organise a volunteer force in each colony area with a sizable refugee population for the safety and security of the refugees; and
c) to mobilize fund for the campaign.

In this method, the UCRC tried to help the refugees to increase their consciousness about their rights and thereby made the civil society more vibrant for the first time since independence, which Nilanjana Chatterjee has termed as a dynamic interplay between 'official discourse' and the refugee counter-discourse. Although in this way the Leftists gradually became influential among the squatters, the refugees never became puppets of the Communists. Rather, the UCRC worked as the mouthpiece of the helpless, displaced persons from East Pakistan. In other words, the politics of rehabilitation by the Government triggered off a new politics, which may be termed as 'the politics of agitation.' This politics of agitation was an active resistance to the politics of rehabilitation initiated by the Governments (the Government of India and that of West Bengal together). Moreover, this politics of agitation by the displaced persons along with their shared memories provided the shelter-seekers a specific identity.

Life and Period in the Refugee Camps

After briefly considering the struggle of the displaced in the *jabar dakhal* colonies to reconstruct their lives, let us now turn our attention to some of the camps that were set up to provide shelter to the incoming displaced persons. As the cross-border influx continued interminably in the 1950s, the helpless, uprooted people reached the reception and interception centres at the Sealdah station. From there, they were subsequently sent to the transit camps. Although many of these refugees were supposed to be sent to other parts of the country, instant arrangements could not be made possible for their travel. Therefore, the relief and transit camps were set up in different parts of West Bengal to provide immediate help to these people.

At the peak of the inflow of refugees from across the border with East Pakistan, the government mainly set up three types of camps, namely, women's camps, worksite camps and Permanent Liability (PL) Camps. The inmates of the women's camps comprised mostly women and children who had no male member of their family to look after them. Bhadrakali and Bansberia women's camp in Hooghly district, Ranaghat Women's Home in 24 Parganas district were such women's camps. As time passed by, many of the inmates of these women's camps were permanently rehabilitated along with their family members in and around the camp area.

Second, in order to counteract the demoralising effect of the prolonged stay in the camps, the government introduced a system of keeping able-bodied men engaged in useful work for the development of the area, where they were supposed to be rehabilitated. Accordingly, 32 such worksite camps were set up in West Bengal. Bagjola camp and Sonarpur R5 scheme in 24 Parganas are examples of such worksite camps. The refugees were also kept engaged in many Central Government-aided projects like the Damodar Valley Corporation projects etc.

Finally, the PL camps were for those refugees who were considered unfit for any kind of gainful employment through which they could be rehabilitated. They were mainly old, infirm, invalid and orphans. These PL camps were located in Dudhkundi in Midnapore district, Bansberia in Hooghly, Chandmari, Cooper's Camp (partially), Chamta and Dhubulia in Nadia district, Habra, Ashoknagar and Titagarh in 24 Parganas district. On November 30, 1952, the population of these camps and the homes was 34,000, including the population of the orphanages. The number soon increased to 37,000. According to the report on the Relief and Rehabilitation of the displaced persons in West Bengal, in 1953, the number of camp admission of the refugees was 10,474, in 1954, the number was 46,904, and in 1955, the number increased to 1,09.834.

In most cases, the military barracks and tunnel-shaped huts made of iron constructed for Allied soldiers (during the World War II) were converted originally into camps for the refugees. Thousands of refugees, the displaced persons who arrived either by train or by truck from across the border, were dumped in these camps. When some of these camps became overpopulated and the government could not provide any more space in these makeshift military barracks or huts, the additional refugees got tents to live in. as a result, the camp life was not always satisfactory but sometimes subhuman in nature. While narrating her experiences in the Coopers' camp, Hironprova Das (75), a resident of the Coopers' Notified Area, said:

"Even in the dormitories of those barracks, each refugee family was allotted a little space. Each family marked its occupied area with pebbles, stones and tit-bits and sometimes did not even have a sleeping space for the members of the refugee family.

So far as the tent was concerned, each refugee family comprising four members got one tent, and a bigger family (with more than four members) got two tents to live in. Under such circumstances, there was absolutely no question of any privacy. The refugees definitely got shelter far away from their home and communal hatred, but scarcity of water, lack of proper health care, irregular supply of ration (dry doles) still made their lives unbearable. In such a situation, many children died of dysentery in the camps. Dead bodies of children were sometimes buried, but very often were simply thrown away in the jungle for paucity of funds. The government used to pay only Rs.16 for the cremation of a body."

The Government had no carefully thought-out plan for the rehabilitation of camp refugees in the East in the initial stage. It was only in 1955 and thereafter that the Government of India decided to look at the problem of the East Pakistani refugees on 'a rational basis.' Between 1947 and 1955, the Indian Government provided *ad hoc* assistance to enable the refugees to resettle themselves under the *Byanama Scheme*. Under this scheme a camp refugee was allowed to choose a plot of land that he wanted to buy with the Government loan. The Government used to grant loans for the rehabilitation of refugees in the rural and urban areas depending upon the occupational background of the displaced. However, in many cases there were tremendous irregularities to grant loan to the refugees for purchase of lands for their resettlement. Sometimes, when the refugee somehow managed to get money there was scarcity of cultivable land.

It has already been discussed that the refugees, who took shelter in the camps, were mostly cultivators. Therefore, a lack of access to the cultivable land for a long period of time naturally made them annoyed. The scarcity of cultivable land coupled with the poor living conditions in the camps, including irregular supply of food and cash doles gradually increased the grievances of the camp-dwellers. Incidents of passive and active resistance emerged in many refugee camps. According to Prangobindo Das (76), once involved in the refugee movement in the Coopers' camp:

"Initially we used to follow the non-violent methods to make the government aware about our demands for the better likelihood. At that time, we used to prefer the method of negotiation with the officers of the 'RR' Department of the Government as well as the method of *Satyagraha*. Of all the camps in West Bengal, we were more organised in the Coopers' and always took a leading part in launching any protest movement. We used to gather on the playground in front of the Kali temple (Hindu goddess of power), and all movements usually started from this place..."

though, the camp protests entered a new phase in 1958 when the Government of India took the decision to wind up the camps in the eastern region by July 1959. In view of the continuing exodus from East Pakistan, the Government of India gradually realised that it would be difficult for the cash-starved West Bengal to give shelter to all the incoming refugees from the other side of the border. Therefore, it would be wise to select some of the displaced persons who could not be rehabilitated in the economy in West Bengal, and send them to other parts of the country. After all, the Government already made it clear that there was a serious lack of available land for rehabilitation in West Bengal, especially for agriculture. In such a situation, the incoming refugees were additional liabilities for West Bengal. Against this backdrop, the Government of India decided to treat the East Pakistani refugee problem "absolutely on a national level". It is interesting here to note one of the statements of Sucheta Kripalani, a Member of Parliament, in this connection. She said:

"It was not on West Bengal's decision that this country was partitioned. This country was partitioned by a decision of India ..." "Therefore, it is a national problem and all the states should pull their weight in rehabilitating them".

This was the spirit that was perhaps responsible for the Government's decision to send the 'excess' refugees outside West Bengal to places like Dandakaranya of Madhya Pradesh and the Andaman & Nicobar Islands.

It was decided at the official level that, mainly the refugees belonging to the so-called lower castes like Namasudras, Kshatriyas, Poundra Kshatriyas, who took shelter in the refugee camps and received doles from the Government, had to go to Dandakaranya. However, the refugees, the original inhabitants of the Indo-Gangetic plains were reluctant to go to the dry, 'alien land'. In no time, the Government stopped their doles temporarily.

Anadi Mondal, a PL member of the Chamta Camp of Nadia, said in the interview with the author on 15 March 2002, that he, like other camp dwellers opposed to go to Dandakaranya and as a result, the government stopped their doles temporarily. So they did not have any other option but to go to Dandakaranya. In his own words:

"Jokhon Dandakaranyer haoa ailo, sarkar thika amago jor koira oi rukha sukha jagae pathaite chailo. Amra jol desher manush, kyamne oi pathura jagae thakum? Tai jaite raji hoilam na. Sarkar thika amago sahajyo bondho koira dilo. Jetuku khaite paitam tao gelo go! Pore oboshyo amra onek todbir korbar phole abar sahajyo paisilam, kintu tao bosor panch bade. Er modhye oboshyo amago family re Coopers thika Chamta camp e boshaisilo tenara." (When the wave of Dandakaranya came, the government tried to persuade us to go to that dry area. We are people from an area with water. How could we live in that rocky area? So, we did not agree to go there. The government stopped all assistance to us. Whatever assistance we used to get, that also was gone! We, however, managed to receive assistance once again after a lot of request, but that was after about five years. Meanwhile, our family was shifted from the Coopers to the Chamta camp.)

Gradually, the anger of the camp-dwellers in West Bengal against the Central Government's decision to send them outside the state encouraged them to raise their voice. The camp-dwellers of Bettiah in Bihar launched a peaceful *Satyagraha* movement in May 1958 for the fulfilment of their demands of improved living and economic conditions in the camp to rehabilitate them. This showed a way out to the refugees living in the camps of West Bengal. So, when the Government tried to force them to go to Dandakaranya, these refugees revolted. They launched massive civil disobedience movement in the Gandhian way and more than 30,000 camp refugees were arrested. Though this movement did not last long, it left a major impact on the psyche of the refugees. It helped them to come out of their shell.

Initially, the refugees living in the camps expected that the organisations of the squatters' colonies would join this movement, and would give it a stronger shape. Reality was not so. The squatters' colonies stood apart with their own problems. They did not intend to take part in this movement probably because of two reasons: first, they had already acquired lands through *jabar dakhal* to start their lives afresh, and second, most of them belonged to the middle class. Moreover, when the government took the decision to recognise 133 squatters' colonies in the beginning of 1958, the camp-dwellers got frustrated and felt somewhat alienated.

The role of the UCRC was very vital at this stage, whose activities mainly confined within the squatters' colonies since its inception. Initially, the leadership of the UCRC was not whole-heartedly accepted by the camp-dwellers. As many of the camp-dwellers were of so-called lower caste Namasudra community, they chose their own leaders from among themselves, and consequently, the leaders like Jogen Mondal, Hemanta Biswas, Apurbalal Mazumder and P.R.Thakur came in the forefront.

Apart from the CPI the Proja Socialist Party (PSP)-led organisation Sara Bangla Bastuhara Sammelan (SBBS), (All Bengal Refugee Conference), and the organisation called Bastuhara Kolyan Parishod (Refugee Welfare Council), led by the Revolutionary Communist Party of India (RCPI), started playing dominant role in the camps. The RCPI was more active in the camps of Nadia. Since 1958, the UCRC started to bring together the camp refugees with the help of PSP on a programme acceptable to all. Slowly but steadily, rallies and demonstrations took the place of *Satyagraha* as the weapon of refugee movement. In course of time, the 'politicisation' and 'unionisation' of the refugee movement inspired these uprooted, helpless people to become a part of the larger movement against the Union and State Governments, and the struggle of the refugees through the politics of agitation continued to counter the policies of rehabilitation since then.

Life Roll on with Dreams Devastated

Life after partition in the East was not easy at all – the displaced realised that with own experiences like no one else. Their histories have not always been lettered, but their narratives remain testimony to the nature of struggle they went through to reconstruct their lives. Life definitely was not easy for the displaced in the West. But, at least there were state initiatives to resettle and rehabilitate them in India. Government assistance could not be a substitute for their loss and agony. But, starting their lives afresh was not that difficult for many in the West.

The displaced, who crossed over to West Bengal, in particular, were not so fortunate. Few among them, who could carry along a part of their past fortune, managed to make their new dreams come true. For a large number of their fellow travellers, dream was not that easily achievable. They had to fight for their existence, their means of livelihood and for putting things together again. Some were even less fortunate and could never dream again. Their *desh* was some place else and now it is a place of no return. It can only be revisited in memories and nostalgia.

Maya Das of Bejoygarh colony in Kolkata is one of those extremely unfortunate ones. She says: *"Bhalo ghorer i to bou silam ma! Swosurer jomi-joma asilo. Chash-bash koira khaitam. Kintu dangae swami morlo. Kothae je shob haraiya gelo! Ar kaure pailam na. Gramer lokego loge ei khane ailam. Chheletar mathar byamo hoilo. Poisa silo na. Chikitsa koraite parlam na. Ekhon se to pagol, ma! Ke amago khaoaibo kao? Tai Bhikha koron chhara upay nai. Ei bhabe ei ek chilta ghore ma ar chhelete baincha asi. Ami morle or je ki hoibo, tao jani na..."* (I was indeed a bride of a well-established family! My father-in-law had some land. We used to survive on agriculture. But my husband died in the riot. I don't know where everything was gone! I could not trace anyone again. I came here with my fellow-villagers. My son became mentally unsound. I did not have money. So, I could not arrange for his treatment. Now, his situation is even worse! Who will feed us? So, I don't have any way other than begging. My son and me somehow survive in this small room. I don't really know what will happen to him after me...) Immediate Situation Post-1947 Independence and Nehru

At the time of Indian independence, India was divided into two sets of territories, the first being the territories under the control of the British Empire, and the second being the territories over which the Crown had suzerainty, but which were under the control of their hereditary rulers. In addition, there were several colonial enclaves controlled by France and Portugal.

The political integration of these territories into India was a declared objective of the Indian National Congress, which the Government of India pursued over the next decade. Through a combination of factors, Vallabhbhai Patel and V.P. Menon convinced the rulers of the various princely states to accede to India. Having secured their accession, they then proceeded to, in a step-by-step process, secure and extend the central government's authority over these states and transform their administration until, by 1956, there was little difference between the territories that had formerly been part of British India and those that had been part of princely states.

Simultaneously, the Government of India through a combination of diplomatic and military means acquired de facto and de jure control over the remaining colonial enclaves, which too were integrated into India. Although this process successfully integrated the vast majority of princely states into India, it was not as successful in relation to a few states, notably the former princely states of Kashmir, Tripura and Manipur, where active secessionist movements exist.

6

Abul Kalam Azad and Mahatma Gandhi

MAULANA ABUL KALAM AZAD

The real name of Maulana Abul Kalam Azad was Abul Kalam Ghulam Muhiyuddin. Popularly known as Maulana Azad, he was one of the foremost leaders of Indian freedom struggle. Maulana Azad was not just a prominent freedom fighter. He was also a renowned poet and scholar. He was highly educated and travelled to different countries to understand the true meaning of freedom, struggle and culture. His proficiency in many languages like Hindi, Bengali, Arabic, English, Urdu and Persian made him a leading figure in intellectual arena. Azad was his pen name that he had adopted later in his life. It represented his liberation from a narrow view of religion and life.

Born on November 11, 1888 in Mecca, Maulana Abul Kalam Azad received his primary education at home. He was first taught by his father and then eminent scholars. His family had left India during the Sepoy Mutiny but came back to India in 1890 and settled in Calcutta. His father ensured, he received best of traditional Islamic education. His visit to diverse countries like Syria, Afghanistan, Turkey, Egypt and Iraq had taught him valuable lessons about freedom struggle and Pan-Islamic spirit. His meeting with political members, freedom fighters and scholars of great repute left an indelible mark on his life. His return to India found him converted into a nationalist revolutionary. He met similar minded freedom fighters in Calcutta and decided to devote his life to freedom struggle of India.

His biggest contribution was in convincing Islamic revolutionaries to fight for India's freedom struggle. Maulana Azad explained the futility of fighting for anti-Muslim causes and urged his community to present a united front for the freedom struggle of India. His idea of freedom was based on Hindu-Muslim unity and for that he started a weekly journal which later became a big threat to British rule. Maulana Abul Kalam Azad was an active participant of Non-Cooperation Movement, Khilafat Movement and Salt Satyagraha movement. British rulers kept putting him into prison every now and then and yet his spirit found him coming back to freedom struggle.

He was appointed president of Congress party in 1940 and he continued in that post till 1946. He was a staunch supporter of Hindu-Muslim unity and partition of the country left him devastated. Maulana Azad was appointed as independent India's first education minister. He died on February 22, 1958 of a stroke. Maulana Abul Kalam Azad was posthumously awarded India's highest civilian honour, Bharat Ratna in 1992 for his invaluable contribution to the nation.

AZAD, CONGRESS AND GANDHI

Abul Kalam Azad was Congress leader and scholar of Koranic theology; twice president of the Congress; Education Minister, Government of India. He was a generalist and he edited Urdu Weekly Al Hilal. He participated in Khilafat movement and later he joined congress. He elected president of congress twice in 1923 and 1940 respectively. Mahatma Gandhi wrote, "The arrest of Maulana Abul Kalam Azad is an event of importance equal with the arrest of the President elect. Maulana Abul Kalam Azad has an all-India reputation, especially among the Mussulmans. He is a seasoned soldier having been interned for years in Ranchi. He stands high in the ranks of the learned men of Islam. His arrest must sink deep in the hearts of the Mussulmans of India. What answer will the Hindus and Mussulmans of Bengal return? Action can only be answered by counter-action. We know what the answer should be. Will the thousands of Bengali Hindus and Bengali Mussulmans enroll themselves as volunteers and be arrested? Will Bengal wear only khadi or nothing? Will Bengali students give the answer that the President of the Congress expected from them in his moving appeal?"

Mahatma Gandhi wrote, "In the language of Maulana Abul Kalam Azad, let us think of the greater temple, namely, India, which has been defiled for so many years by our submission to slavery. And if we have stood that defilement all these long years, let us not be provoked into madness by the illegal encroachments upon local temples and their still greater defilement by the intruders' abuse of them. Is Lord Reading prepared to plead extenuation even in this case on the ground that the officials are engaged in the performance of a very trying duty?" Mahatma Gandhi wrote, "Maulana Abul Kalam Azad was arrested. She became free as soon as it became clear that repression had fallen flat and that the people were not to be deterred from forming associations and holding public meetings even though they were assaulted and flogged. Freedom was ours when we were ready to pay the price for it. The settlement of our differences with the administrators is a matter of time. We cannot be said to be free so long as we need a certificate of freedom. He is not healthy who has needed to prove his health by producing a health certificate. Every man and woman who visited the Congress pandal felt in his or her own person the glow of freedom."

Mahatma Gandhi wrote, "If Begum Abul Kalam Azad and the Maulana himself complain about the inadequacy of the sentence pronounced upon the Maulana Saheb, what must be the feeling of the President of the Congress and his devoted partner on having heard that he together with Mr. Sasmal was to have only 6 months' simple imprisonment? Why on earth the trial should have been dragged and judgment postponed if such an untheatrical sentence was to be pronounced; only the Government can tell.

The gossip that was sent to me along the rails was that the Government was seeking a suitable opportunity for discharging both the Maulana and the Deshbandhu. The latest gossip which is supposed to be authentic, I dare not disclose. Nor is it of importance for the reader to know. We must take, not even excluding the President, our lot as it comes to us. I am receiving biting letters from correspondents accusing me of simplicity, of hard-heartedness, of faintheartedness and all such kindred weaknesses. Some correspondents tell me that I have sold the cause of the prisoners. Others tell me I have thrown all my non-co-operation views to the winds and I have been faithless to the President of the Congress.

Fortunately, many years of service have given me a fairly tough hide and these shafts do not pierce it, but I do assure all these impatient critics that not a particle of the principle of non-co-operation has been surrendered by the resolutions. On the contrary, refusal to suspend mass civil disobedience in the face of grave warning from Nature would have meant a complete surrender of the fundamental principle of non-co-operation. The discharge of prisoners I purposely brought to the surface when it became a point of national honour, because with the change of issue from the immediate attainment of the triple goal to the immediate attainment of the three-fold freedom the demand for the discharge of prisoners became a natural consequence. But Chauri Chaura has raised another immediate issue, viz., terrible penance and a fierce process of purification, and this penitential purification requires the sacrifice of the imprisoned workers and the temporary sacrifice of many of our activities which have revivified the nation. But such things happen in all wars, much more frequently in spiritual warfare such as ours is claimed to be. I call it spiritual in the sense that we have resolutely declined to make use of physical force for the attainment of our end. We were in danger of being drifted away from our moorings, and it was necessary for us to return, but the return is merely meant to give us greater purity, greater perception and therefore greater strength, and if non-co-operators have to become seasoned soldiers for the nation's battle, they will doubtless understand the value of waiting and preparing. He who waits for preparation or otherwise, advances the cause as much as the warrior who stands three feet deep in the trenches. All our sufferings will have been lost upon us if we do not realize these elements of the science of war, whether it is spiritual or physical."

Mahatma Gandhi wrote, "I have not yet received the telegram although the letter of advice tells me that it was sent both to Ahmadabad and Bardoli. I am able to give the telegram to the public only because the Secretary of the Bengal Provincial Khilafat Committee has very kindly sent me a copy by letter post at the instance of the Begum Sahaba.

It is a matter of no small comfort that ladies occupying the highest station in life, are coming forward one after another to step into the breach created by the withdrawal of male national workers. I tender my congratulations to Begum Abul Kalam Azad for her having offered to take her share in the public work. The readers will take to heart the message of The Maulana. It is perfectly true that neither the Government nor the country is today prepared for any compromise. The Government will not be till we have suffered long and suffered more. Bengal has certainly led in the direction. Bardoli has yet done little. Twice has it been baulked of its privilege by cruel Nature, but it is a matter of no consequence whether it is Bengal or Bardoli which leads, so long as we get rid of a system which, as is daily becoming more and more clear, is based upon terrorism. In the present mood of the country there is little danger of the vital interests being sacrificed, as the Maulana fears, to the momentary pleasure of securing the release of How prisoners."

Mahatma Gandhi wrote, "The Punjabis wanted an outsider to preside and if at all possible Maulana Abul Kalam Azad. The Maulana Sahib however was unwilling. He said, he would gladly attend but thought he would be more useful if he remained free. The Maulana's position was appreciated. Pandit Motilalji was then approached. He was good enough to say he would preside, if he was not prevented by any untoward event, and if Pandit Motilalji was prevented from presiding, I was to fill in his place. Unfortunately the unexpected happened and Pandit Motilalji could not come. As the reasons given by him are of public importance, I set them forth in his own language."

Mahatma Gandhi wrote, "Maulana Abul Kalam Azad informs me that the newspaper reports of my speech, before the European Association, the other day, has given rise to a great deal of controversy among the Mussalman friends and even some resentment, because some Mussalman friends read into my speech the view that I could not find an able and honourable Mussalman who could occupy the Mayoral chair, and that the Maulana Sahib also had given me a similar opinion. I have now read the report of my speech from which these deductions have been made. Though it is not a verbatim report, even as it stands, I do not consider that it warrants the deductions that have been drawn from it."

Mahatma Gandhi wrote, "Maulana Abul Kalam Azad has very considerately sent me a copy of his Press message on the Hindu-Muslim question. He is one of the very few men who may be claimed to be sincerely desirous to attain unity. He has asked me to call a meeting of the Working Committee in order to consider the question. I am not doing so before the Congress week at Cawnpore because the annual function is too near to warrant an earlier meeting of the Working Committee. I wish the Committee could discover a solution of the problem. But I must frankly confess that I despair. That is not to say that I despair of a solution altogether. I despair of the Congress discovering and enforcing a solution.

Let us not conceal from ourselves the truth that the Congress does not represent the fighters in either camp. Not till those unseen ones who are behind the fighters are under the Congress influence and the newspaper editors who are fomenting dissensions are either converted to the unity doctrine or cease to have any influence, can the Congress do any useful work in the direction of unity. My bitter experience has taught me that they who take the name of unity mean disunion. The atmosphere around us is as false as was the atmosphere in Europe at the time of the last War. The newspapers never told the truth. The representatives of their respective nations had made of laying a fine art. All was fair in War. The old formula of Jehovah thirsting for the blood even of children was revived in all its nakedness. And so it is today in what may be called a miniature war between Hindus and Muslims. We may lie and cheat for saving our faiths. This has been said to me not by one mouth but many. This, however, is no cause for the slightest despair. I know that the demon of disunion is at his last gasp. A lie has no bottom. Disunion is a lie. Even if it is sheer self-interest, it will bring about unity. I had hoped for disinterested unity. But I will welcome a unity based even on mutual interest. Only it will not come in the way suggested by the Maulana Saheb. It will come, when it does come, in a way perhaps least expected by us. God is the Master Trickster. He knows how to confound us, frustrate our 'knavish tricks'. He sends death when one least expects it.

He sends life when we see no sign of it. Let us admit our abject helplessness, let us own that we are utterly defeated. Out of the dust of our humility will, I feel sure, be built up an impregnable citadel of unity. I am sorry I am unable to return a more encouraging answer to the Maulana's appeal. Let him take comfort from the fact that I share his desire for union with the same intensity that he will credit himself with. What does it matter if I feel unable to share his faith in his plan of achieving unity? I shall do nothing to hinder it. I shall pray for the success of every sincere effort in that direction. My ceasing to fret does not mean the unity is no longer an article of my creed. Let me re-declare my undying faith in it. For the sake of it I must renounce the privilege of being a maker of the unity that is coming. I have the wisdom to stand aside and wait when my interference can only disturb the wound without healing."

Mahatma Gandhi wrote, "It was received after the All-India Congress Committee session was over. But do you think that any purpose can be served by calling a special session of the Congress? It can be of use only when there is a policy or programme that requires confirmation by it. But unfortunately we have neither policy nor programme. On the contrary, the tallest among us distrust one another and even where there is no distrust there is no agreement as to facts or opinion. In the circumstances a Congress session can only accentuate the existing depression. It seems to me that time alone can solve the difficulty which seems to baffle us. I wish that it was possible for us at least to devise means of ascertaining the causes and of defining the results of each riot. But it seems that we have become incapacitated even for this very simple work." Mahatma Gandhi wrote, "At the request of Maulana Shaukat Ali I prepared a draft of the non-co-operation resolution in the train. Up to this time I had more or less avoided the use of the word non-violent in my drafts. I invariably made use of this word in my speeches. My vocabulary on the subject was still in process of formation. I found that I could not bring home my meaning to purely Muslim audiences with the help of the Sanskrit equivalent for non-violent. I therefore asked Maulana Abul Kalam Azad to give me some other equivalent for it. He suggested the word ba-aman; similarly for non-co-operation he suggested the phrase tark-i-mavalat."

Mahatma Gandhi wrote, "Of course I shall gladly see the Governor during my stay in Calcutta and do whatever is possible. Dr. Bidhan wrote to me two days ago. The fast had to come. Such was God's will. So long as He desires service from me, I shall be unhurt. I reach their 19th morning." Mahatma Gandhi wrote, "Maulana Abul Kalam Azad once said that the whole country was a gurudwara. That very moment it occurred to me that the whole country was a prison. And the States are doubly so. The facilities available in the States are those available in a jail." Mahatma Gandhi wrote, "If you have seen the enclosed I would like you're considered opinion on the points raised therein. Is such conversion valid in Islam? Is the method adopted lawful? Is the way the thing is being advertised lawful or permissible? Will you publish your opinion or permit me to publish it?" Mahatma Gandhi wrote, "I have accepted Maulana Abul Kalam Azad as my guide. My suggestion, therefore, to you is that conversation should be opened in the first instance as between you and Maulana Saheb. But in every case regard me as at your disposal."

Mahatma Gandhi wrote, "This learned company included, among several others, Maulana Abul Kalam Azad and the late Maulana Abdul Bari. Led by Maulana Abul Kalam Azad they held that belief in non-violence was not only inconsistent with Islam, but it was obligatory in the sense that Islam had always preferred it to violence. It is noteworthy that this took place before the acceptance of non-violence by the Congress in 1920. Many were the discourses given by learned Muslims on nonviolence before crowded Muslim meetings." Mahatma Gandhi wrote, "You shall address me as you like. I do not know that you addressed me differently. I have written to Lord Linlithgow as suggested by you. I quite agree with you about the Pattabhi episode. I am inclined to think that there should be a considered reply from you to the Lahore resolution." Mahatma Gandhi wrote, "I have had the privilege of being associated with Maulana Abul Kalam Azad in national work since 1920. In the knowledge of Islam he is surpasses by no one. He is a profound Arabic scholar. His nationalism is as robust as his faith in Islam. That he is today the supreme head of the Indian National Congress has deep meaning which should not be lost sight or by any student of Indian politics."

Mahatma Gandhi wrote, "Whatever the Muslim League does or does not do, it behoves thoughtful Hindus to take note of the deserved taunt and purge Hinduism of its exclusiveness. It will not be protected by artificial barriers which have no sanction in ancient Hinduism or reason. Well did Maulana Abul Kalam Azad say the other day how sick he was of hearing the cry at railway stations of Hindu and Muslim tea or water? I know this touch-magnetism is deep-rooted in Hinduism as it is practiced today. But there is no reason why it should be tolerated by Congressmen. If they will be correct in their behaviour, they will pave the way for a radical transformation of Hindu society. The message of anti-untouchability does not end in merely touching the so-called untouchables. It has a much deeper meaning." Mahatma Gandhi wrote, "There is no need for you to feel unhappy because I have said that I am your faithful dog. That quadruped brother of ours possesses great nobility. According to the commentators the dog was Dharma personified. But if the Dog has become rabid, you can and should remove him. My advice to you now is that you should set right this mistake made by me. I have exceeded my authority as a general. Either rectifies the mistake I made in allowing Raja to have his resolution twisting the meaning of ahimsa or remove me. If you rectify the mistake I have a plan for future action."

Mahatma Gandhi wrote, "In the course of discussion in the Working Committee, I discovered that I had committed a grave error in the interpretation of the Bombay Resolution. I had interpreted it to mean that the Congress was to refuse participation in the present or all wars on the ground principally of non-violence. I found to my astonishment that most members differed from my interpretation and held that the opposition need not be on the ground of non-violence. On rereading the Bombay Resolution I found that the differing members were right and that I had read into it a meaning which its letter could not bear. The discovery of the error makes it impossible for me to lead the Congress in the struggle for resistance to war effort on grounds in which nonviolence was not indispensable. I could not, for instance, identify myself with opposition to war effort on the ground of ill will against Great Britain. The resolution contemplated material association with Britain in the war effort as a price for guaranteed independence of India. If such was my view, and I believed in the use of violence for gaining independence and yet refused participation in the effort as the price of that independence, I would consider myself guilty of unpatriotic conduct. It is my certain belief that only non-violence can save India and the world from self-extinction. Such being the case, I must continue my mission whether I am alone or assisted by an organization or individuals. You will, therefore, please relieve me of the responsibility laid upon me by the Bombay Resolution. I must continue civil disobedience for free speech against all war with such Congressmen and others whom I select and who believe in the nonviolence I have contemplated and are willing to conform to prescribed conditions. I will not, at this critical period, select for civil disobedience those whose services are required to steady and help the people in their respective localities."

Mahatma Gandhi wrote, "I will write to you only in Urdu. This time you will forgive me. I had already told you in Delhi that now my health do not permit me to move around. Moreover I do not have any work there and I have convened three meetings here which I must attend. People from faraway places have been invited. You will understand my position and excuse me for my absence." Mahatma Gandhi wrote, "After that I had a long talk with Rajendra Babu, Prafulla Babu and Dev. They gave news about Allahabad. In my opinion it is better that Sardar, etc. are allowed to leave the Committee. As it is the working of the present Committee hinders our work. It is not proper to insist on staying together.

It is good that we remain together as far as possible but once a major difference of opinion emerges it is better that we part company amicably. Sardar and others also share this view. I had expressed this opinion to you even earlier. Experience has now confirmed it all the more. In my opinion you should accept the resignations of Sardar and five or six other members and form a new Committee. When it is clear that there are two factions within the Committee why should we pretend that there is only one? There is a vast difference between the resolution passed and the resolution I had sent. What I intended to tell the world through my resolution is missing here. Sardar tells me that the public opinion is in favour of my resolution. I do not think it necessary to convene a meeting of the Working Committee to clear the matter. In my opinion first we both should meet and it will be better still if Jawaharlal can join us. After that if you think proper you may convene a meeting of the Working Committee."

Mahatma Gandhi wrote, "Since there was nothing particular to write I did not reply. However, the Sind affair is worrying me. Dr. Choithram, Prof. Ghanshyam and others have written to me. I have written to them that as long as they are in the Congress, they will have to do as you say. But for how long can they be held back? There are other issues too about which I am writing in Harijan. I hope you do read Harijan. I hope you will come here after you have recovered. Jawahar is coming tomorrow." Mahatma Gandhi wrote, "I depended first upon the decisive interpretation given by the President, Maulana Abul Kalam Azad, and secondly on my own, meaning that the Jagat Narain Lal Resolution should be read together with the others bearing on the question. For these latter were not cancelled by the Jagat Narain Lal Resolution."

Mahatma Gandhi wrote, "It was by mere chance that Pyarelal happened to see you. But what you told him, if his report of the talk is accurate, is startling. The Working Committee has not given you the right or the permission to form a cabinet. You yourself told me that you could not do it without the Working Committee. That is my view too. That was why I had said that you should form a small committee with the assistance of the Working Committee, which could be given that right and then act through that committee or the Working Committee itself. Since you did not react favorably to either of the proposals, I can only conclude that I do not understand or do not know the stand of the Working Committee in the matter. I understand from what Jamnalalji says that you are going to summon the Working Committee anyhow. I consider it improper. I would not wish you to be guilty of such a grave error at this juncture.

I do not know what you have done and how you could persuade the Viceroy. Even if you have committed yourself it is, in my view, your duty to inform him that a mistake has been committed. So much for the matter between you and the Working Committee. Another thing I would like to tell you is that in anything you do, you should take with you the Congress who are present and you should put everything in writing.

The third is a personal matter. Ever since I first heard the Viceroy's proclamation, that is, while I was still at Panchgani, I have been shouting that the Congress cannot accept the principle of parity between Muslims and non-Harijan Hindus, an organization of Hindus alone. Even if I am the only one among crores to do so, I shall refuse to be a party to it. I do not care if the negotiations break down on this, for I know and believe that the moment you try to form a national government at the centre in this way you will be laying a wrong foundation. In this repect I am neither a Hindu, nor belong to any other religion. I belong to all faiths or to none. I only walk in the way shown by God. I shall be very happy if you can lend me your cooperation in this matter. But if you cannot do it wholeheartedly then I would rather do without it. I shall keep you informed. I trust you are well and the climate here has not disagreed with you."

Mahatma Gandhi wrote, "I had asked Dr. Pattabhi. I did not feel it was right to say anything when I had only seen the newspaper. Now that I have received the letter I shall be writing something. I have seen the telegram Rajaji has sent you. I agree with it. I saw something in the Press by way of a directive from you about providing for the relatives of those who died during the struggle in 1942 and afterwards. The financial help we are at present giving to such relatives for their maintenance and education is something different. In my opinion if we go by truth and non-violence we cannot give such assistance. How can we say that all of them died for the country, that they sacrificed themselves for the cause of swaraj? I feel that under no circumstances can you do that. If I may advise you, I would ask you to withdraw the statement. I do not know whether there is still time for that. I am sending you a wire today. The other thing concerns Begum Azad. Dr. Khan Saheb mentioned the matter to me at Lahore. It pricked me. I am not aware of any public service rendered by Begum Azad. If what I believe is true, there should not be any public memorial in her name. Some persons came to me. I told them to do whatever they wanted. I did not have the courage to say anything more to them. But I can speak to you. I would advise you to issue a nice Press statement saying that since Begum Azad had not rendered any public service you would not like any public memorial in her name. If my advice does not appeal to you, you will please reject it. The love we hold for each other demands no less."

Mahatma Gandhi wrote, "On receipt of your letter today, I sent you the following wire: "Your letter. I think it should not be published. Writing fully." I do not infer from your letter that you are writing about my 'Hindus'. Whatever you have in your heart has not come in your writing. But do not worry about it. When we meet next we will talk over it if you so desire. Whatever you want to say about the communal problem should not be said without consulting the Working Committee. I am also of the opinion that it would be better to be quiet. The party can give its opinion after consultation with you. They have a right to do so. Besides it is their duty. I differ from your opinion. I cannot say if I attach importance to the words 'Hindu' and 'Mussalman'. Whatever the Congress does is a different thing. At one time I do not like 'Hindu' and at another time I do not like 'Mussalman'. It means there cannot be either. All this needs pondering over. I do not feel the urge for doing anything early."

Mahatma Gandhi wrote, "I am not happy to read in the newspapers about your ill health. It is not good that you should get temperature so often. Now the weather in the Punjab should be good. Perhaps the weather in the Frontier Province would be better than in Lahore. I think you need some rest. You seem to have done good work in the Punjab." Mahatma Gandhi wrote, "I really wish I had enough time to write Urdu in a beautiful hand. It will be good indeed if you can go somewhere for rest in the beginning of November. Of course work is always there but sometimes rest is essential for work and for doing more of it. Rajkumari will be reaching there today on her way to London with Dr. Sargent and Dr. Zakir Husain Saheb. Educationists from all over the world will be meeting in London. Dr. Sargent has convened this conference, and Rajkumari and Dr. Zakir Husain were invited by him. She was not at all keen on giving her name for the conference. She had discussed the matter with me. She will be able to meet others also in London. Sardar's treatment is going on. I shall have to go to Bombay for five days."

Mahatma Gandhi wrote, "What more shall I say about your health? The sooner you go somewhere for rest the better it will be for the country. You have sent three names for the Working Committee. It will be better if in this matter you consult the present members and then announce the names. I have an impression that the Congress will have to meet some time soon. In that case will it not be better if the vacancies are filled by fresh elections? But if they have to be filled now, I think the three names that you have sent are all right. However, the members will be the best judges." Mahatma Gandhi wrote, "Read the enclosed clippings. Whatever is written about me is without foundation. I have not expressed my opinion to anybody. When one or two members of the Committee asked me about it I told them that it is not proper to have the same president. In fact I feel unhappy that a Muslim should remain president at this juncture. If you agree with this view I would like you to read the enclosed clippings. You should issue a statement announcing that you do not wish to remain the president. It would be appropriate if some other person becomes the president. Badshah Khan's name had already been proposed but I strongly opposed it. I even had a discussion with Badshah Khan. If my opinion were sought this time, I would prefer Jawaharlal. There are several reasons for it. I do not want to go into them."

Mahatma Gandhi wrote, "Lawrence told me last night that you had written to him suggesting some alterations in his letter and that he had sent you a reply. What is all this? I could not say much in the matter but I did not like it. I am perplexed. It looks like I shall have to go to Simla. The mind shrinks from the thought. I feel somewhere in some way we are committing a mistake. You must also consider what you intend to do after the British army withdraws. I cannot quite see what you could do. You have announced that the present Working Committee will continue till November and you will continue as president till then. If you must continue, it does not seem proper that you should do so by a ruling. Giving such a ruling seems to me dangerous thing to do. If it becomes a duty to continue this can be done only through fresh elections. This matter deserves consideration." Mahatma Gandhi wrote, "I know you are in Calcutta in Dr. Bidhan Roy's good and able hands. At this time you ought to be spared all the trouble from friends who seek your assistance and advice. But I thought that you would perhaps know the facts much more than anybody else and give truer guidance. Hence, this trouble. I have telegraphed to Jawaharlal, Sardar, the President of the Congress and Dr. Khan Saheb. I purposely refrained from sending a wire to you in Calcutta. This too will be delivered to you by hand. I have seen your statement to the Press about your acceptance of office in the Interim Government. It is quite good and I have not the slightest doubt that your presence in the Cabinet will be of great service at this very critical juncture. I hope you will make rapid and solid recovery. Please do not hurry over the treatment. A medical adviser is entitled to consideration from a patient. That he happens to be a close friend of the patient should prove no disqualification from title to consideration if only because consideration shown to a medical adviser is really consideration shown to oneself. About movement here I dare say you glance at the newspaper reports of my words at the prayer meetings. I have put myself on trial as to whether I am an exponent of true ahimsa or only ahimsa so called. I am not relying upon Pyarelal or Sushila for my Urdu work though I see them often enough. Pyarelal is with me today, this being the last of the fifth village within his beat. If I do not follow this rule, the whole superstructure will come to pieces and the distribution of the party in affected villages will be a mockery. Mahatma Gandhi wrote, "If the ahimsa about which I have written so much and which I have striven to realize in practice all these years does not answer in a crisis, it ceases to have any value in my eyes. Your affection prompts you to say that if only I were near you, all would be well. The truth however is that so long as I cannot make good here, I can be of no use anywhere."

GANDHI AND INDIAN MUSLIMS: OVERLAPS AND CONFLICTS

What did Indian Muslims think of Mohandas Karamchand Gandhi? When Khan Abdul Ghaffar Khan (1891–1989), the stern Pathan leader who became known as the "Frontier Gandhi," left India on July 30, 1947, he said: "Mahatmaji has shown us the true path. Long after we are no more, the coming generations of Hindus will remember him as an Avatar." At the other end of the spectrum of opinion Mohammed Ali Jinnah wrote to Gandhi on the eve of the fateful Nagpur Congress meeting, December 1920, "Your methods have already caused split and division in almost every institution that you have approached hitherto, and in the public life of the country not only amongst Hindus and Muslims but between Hindus and Hindus, and Muslims and Muslims, and even between fathers and sons." Between these extreme views there are many other opinions, some of which fall into the definition of critiques. Is there a pattern to Indian Muslim critiques of Gandhi? And who are the Indian Muslims that we are considering?

I will quickly get the second question out of the way. For the purpose of this chapter I will restrict myself to Indian Muslims who knew and worked with Gandhi. Moreover, with the exception of Malayalam materials, I will confine myself to a selection of those who wrote in English or are translated. My attempt to profile those viewpoints is conditioned by four factors. The first is the historical development of the Freedom movement which brought together Indian Muslims and Gandhi within a daunting complexity. The second is the developing nature of Muslim self-consciousness, both political and religious, and the psychological involvement of Indian Muslims in the wider events of the Muslim world. At the political level they took changing directions, and at the religious level the situation compelled them to explore unfamiliar theoretical possibilities. The third factor is the intimate nature of the personal relations that existed within a fairly confined coterie of leaders. Some of the relationships were deeply affectionate ones, while others were abrasive. The final factor is that Gandhi's own pilgrimage was very much a progressive one, and Muslims who found his position agreeable at one stage did not so find it at other times. These factors in combination meant that Indian Muslim views of Gandhi were marked by a "stutter-step," even a "flip-flop" quality, rather than by an even flow.

Accepting these limitations, let us examine the Indian Muslim (hereafter simply Muslim) critiques of Gandhi. They can be organized into four major categories. The first I refer to as the mild disagreements of close colleagues that tend to be minor criticisms set within an overarching friendship. The second category has to do with the theory of ahilsa, and the conviction of Muslims that this could be maintained only as a policy and not as a creed. The third category relates to the suspicion that Gandhi was leading India to a kind of "Ram Raj" or Hindu state. The final category takes up the issue of priorities, and the alleged shift in Gandhi's approach. Running through the categories, but especially applicable to the final one, is Muslim uneasiness, sometimes articulated, with Gandhi's personal style. That includes his unpredictability, his stubbornness, his tendency to take unilateral and utilitarian positions that in the Muslim perspective left them high and dry.

I will approach the critiques by way of the opinions of individuals, but for the ahimsa discussion I will also utilize Gandhi's involvement with the Mappila Muslims of Malabar............

Abul Kalam Azad: The Critique of Silence

Hakim Ajmal Khan was six years older than Gandhi, and Ansari was eight years younger. We can think of them as Ghandi's contemporaries. Abdul Kalam Azad (1888–1958) was nineteen years his junior, making their relationship a marvel. Moreover, he was a Muslim religious scholar belonging to a class that did not ordinarily mingle with Hindu leaders. The wonder increases when we note the difference in their personalities. Both were ambitious, and to a degree flamboyant. But Azad was the reserved and private Quranic specialist, with an air of mystery, while Gandhi was the public icon of the masses.

Did the age differential play a role in the fact that Azad's critiques of Gandhi were not very explicit? Or was it his personality that took no delight in recrimination? Or was it the reality of their agreement in many fundamental issues? Yet we know that Azad disagreed with Gandhi, most notably in the final acceptance of India's division, a moment when Azad's silence spoke louder than words.

Abul Kalam Azad's public history is well-known. He developed from his precocious editorship of the revivalist Calcutta Muslim journals al-HiLal and al-Balagh, to his emergence as one of the acknowledged leaders of the Freedom movement. He became a stalwart leader in the Indian National Congress, serving as its president in 1923 and 1940, and thereafter. From his dashed hopes in 1947 he emerged to become free India's first minister of education. In the course of that career Azad went through major shifts in his point of view—

from his early optimistic spirit of pan-Islamism to his final and consistent endorsement of the secular democratic approach for free India. His famous remark concerning a "Sabbath rest," which alluded to ten years spent in British jails, passes lightly over the extent of his suffering, which included the repeated losses of manuscripts of his scholarly works. He succeeded Dr. Ansari as leader of the Nationalist Muslims in the Congress, and "dragged the ulama." into liberation politics.

Azad was not hesitant as others were in using the word mahatma, and he spoke openly of "the great soul" of Gandhiji. He disagreed with the latter at times, but did so respectfully. In 1945 Gandhi wrote to Azad asking him to refrain from putting up inscribed plaques in honor of individuals who gave their lives in the 1942 agitation, on the grounds that it was not possible to know who really died for swaraj. He also asked Azad not to endorse a memorial for Begum Shah because she had not really done any public service. Gandhi ended the letter by saying: "If my advice does not appeal to you, you will please reject it. The love we hold for each other demands no less." Azad accepted the advice in regard to Begum Shah, but rejected it in the case of the other memorials.

Azad agreed with Gandhi in most of the core issues of the Freedom movement. Hasan suggests that "even though religion and moral fervour bound the Mahatma and the Maulana in a common quest for swaraj, they did not share a common perspective on and outlook towards sociopolitical issues." It could just as well be said that though the two had different religious contexts and vocabularies their common struggle for swaraj produced a surprising commonality of outlook on major issues. Thus Azad's critiques are related to specific issues or decisions rather than to underlying themes........

The Mappila Rebellion, 1921: Critiques Rise From The Flames

The idea of ahimsa as a policy that could be adopted and discarded left the door open for local Muslim interpretation. The Mappila Rebellion illustrated how far grassroots Muslims were from accepting it as a controlling principle. The rebellion, however, also revealed Gandhi's selective utilitarianism in relation to Muslims, a critique that continues to be alive. In 1918 Gandhi had written to Mohamed Ali: "My interest in your release is quite selfish. We have a common goal and I want to utilize your services to the uttermost in order to reach that goal. In the proper solution of the Mohammedan question lies the realization of Swaraj." In the case of the Mappilas there is a sense that Gandhi first aroused them and then abandoned them. On November 25, 2000, when I interviewed a revered leader of the Mappila intellectual renaissance and a former university vice chancellor he stated that there were three things that bothered Kerala Muslims about Gandhi: his stubbornness, his religious revivalism, and his virtual abandonment of the Mappilas.

The Mappilas of Kerala, now constituting approximately 7.6 million and approximately 21.5 percent of the state, had experienced the negative impact of foreign rule long before the British arrived. Vasco da Gama, landing in Calicut, Malabar, in 1498, had led the Portuguese incursion, introducing the age of European dominance. The Portuguese distorted a centuries-long period of harmony among Hindus, Christians, and Muslims, a process that I have described elsewhere. The end result was a disaffected and volatile Mappila community, whose members were the victims of a repressive landownership system, were suffering from impoverishment, and were given to frequent violent uprisings against what they deemed to be oppression. The noncooperation movement in its Khilafat aspect dropped like a spark into this tinderbox. A key event was a conference of the Kerala Congress in Manjeri, Malabar, April 28, 1920.

The conference brought the Khilafat movement to the attention of the Mappilas. In an action that some have regarded as the seed of the rebellion activists passed a resolution supporting that movement, a decision opposed by Annie Besant and other moderates. In the short run it resulted in many startling expressions of Muslim–Hindu amity, but in the longer run the Khilafat agitation aroused the religious and emotional fervor of the Mappilas to a high degree. On August 18, 1920, Mahatma Gandhi and Shaukat Ali addressed a large public meeting at Calicut. Exhortations to join action against the British and rosy promises of quick results were in the air. While Gandhi urged Hindus to support Muslim demands for justice within the context of appropriate means, Shaukat Ali was not so restrained, and those who were there recalled the stirring impact of his words.

Shaukat Ali (1873–1938), the first secretary of the Khilafat Committee, who operated in the shadow of his younger brother Mohamed Ali, deserves greater notice than he ordinarily receives for his leadership role. He was a bluff and hearty man rather than a reflective type, and was able to rouse people easily. Moved by his pro-Turkish sentiments and by governmental tardiness in granting Aligarh, his alma mater, university status, he left government service and went into opposition. Gandhi traveled extensively with him after his release from prison in 1919, and became very fond of him. He said of his companion: "There are many good and stalwart Muslims I know. But no Muslim knows me through and through as Shaukat Ali does." Shaukat Ali, on the other hand, was quite outspoken on his disagreement with Gandhi in regard to ahimsa. Before coming to Calicut, in a speech at Shajahanpur on May 5, 1920, Shaukat

Ali stated, "I tell you that to kill and to be killed in the way of God are both satyagraha. To lay down our lives in the way of God for righteousness and to destroy the life of the tyrant who stands in the way of righteousness, are both very great service to God. But we have promised to co-operate with Mr.Gandhi who is with us. . . . If this fails, the Mussalmans will decide what to do."

We must assume that Gandhi realized that the basic Muslim view of violence differed from his own. Did he think that the experience of working together would modify the Muslim opinion and bring it into closer harmony with his own? Or, as is more likely, did he simply accept the limited possibilities, taking the practical approach? He seemed to recognize his own utilitarianism. Peter Hardy quotes him as saying, "I have been telling Maulana Shaukat Ali all along that I was helping to save his cow [i.e., the caliphate] because I hoped to save my cow thereby."

There is no need to go into the details of the Mappila Rebellion and the suffering that it entailed for both Hindus and Muslims. The events came like a pail of cold water on the flame of Muslim–Hindu harmony. The Mappilas not only turned violently against their British overlords, but also against the landowning Hindu establishment in a six-month uprising beginning August 20, 1921. Hindu leaders shocked by the Mappila militance drew back from what had been initially regarded as a joint effort. The Mappila sense of betrayal was a major factor in the anti-Hindu nature of the rebellion in its latter stages. As some Hindus even aided British forces, Mappilas responded with killings, arson, robberies, and forced conversion. While the rebellion did not begin as a communal outbreak it ended as one. After six months the Mappilas were severely repressed, and suffered most with 2,266 slain, 252 executed, 502 sentenced to life imprisonment, thousands jailed in different parts of India, and many exiled to the Andaman Islands. The fact that the Mappilas later rose like a phoenix from the ashes to become a changed community that has become positively and dynamically involved in societal development is a marvel of Indian Muslim history. At the close of the rebellion though, they were stunned and silent. There were others, however, who were not silent.

Some of them were Muslims. The cultured and educated northern leaders of Indian Muslims felt trapped by the situation, damned if they did, and damned if they didn't. Hakim Ajmal Khan took the middle ground, as the majority of Muslims did, in his 1921 presidential address to the Congress Assembly in Ahmedabad. He said, "I cannot close without referring to the tragic events that are daily taking place in Malabar and the prolonged agonies of our unfortunate Moplah brethren." He blamed the government for provoking the disturbances and denounced the British "pacification," but he also condemned the forcible conversion of Hindus. "There will be no Muslim worthy of the name who will not condemn the entire un-Islamic act in the strongest possible terms." But the opinion that Gandhi had to deal with directly was that of Hasrat Mohani (1878–1951), the pen name of Syed Fazlul Hasan. An Aligarh graduate, Urdu poet, fiery worker for the Freedom movement, advocate of a forceful approach, and critic of ahimsa, he found no fault in the essential Mappila approach. As to their attack on the Hindus he argued that it occurred because of Hindu support for the British.

Gandhi made frequent references to the Mappilas in his letters and speeches between 1921 and 1924. His reaction ranged from criticizing some Mappilas to blaming the British to pointing to Hindu failure to a bare recognition of possible responsibility on the part of the Non-cooperation movement. In a Madras speech in the middle of the rebellion he had said, "I would like you to swear before God that we shall not resort to violence for the freedom of our country or for settling quarrels between Hindus and Mussulmans . . . that in spite of the madness shown by some of our Moplah brethren we Hindus and Mussulmans shall remain united forever." He repeated the phrase "Moplah madness" frequently, and he advised Hasrat Mohani not to defend their actions. But he also blamed the British saying, "They have punished the entire Moplah community for the madness of a few individuals and have incited Hindus by exaggerating the facts." As for the Hindu responsibility he declared, "The Moplahs have sinned against God and have suffered grievously for it. Let the Hindus also remember that they have not allowed the opportunity for revenge to pass by." He gave the following advice to Hindus: "We must do away with the communal spirit. The majority must therefore make a beginning and thus inspire the minorities with confidence. . . . Adjustment is possible only when the more powerful take the initiative without waiting for response from the weaker."

In regard to the crucial question of whether there was responsibility on his own part, or on the part of the Non-cooperation movement or whether his theory was at fault, Gandhi was not very forthcoming. He acknowledged the critiques saying, "Many letters have been received by me, some from wellknown friends telling me that I was responsible even for the alleged Moplah atrocities in fact, for all the riots which Hindus have or are said to have suffered since the Khilafat agitation." Yet he felt that the significance of the Mappilas should not be overstated because they constitute a special case. Their response cannot undermine the validity or cause of nonviolence. He declared, "The Moplahs themselves had not been touched by the noncooperation spirit. They are not like other Indians nor even like other Mussalmans. I am prepared to admit that the movement had an indirect effect upon them. The Moplah revolt was so different in kind that it did not affect the other parts of India." A Muslim historian, I. H. Qureshi, gives a less sanguine perspective: "The Moplah rebellion confirmed Hindu fears and provided the first nail in the coffin of Hindu amity."

The Opinion of Sir Muhammad Iqbal: A Mild Critique

The most biting critiques of Gandhi's Hindu orientation came in connection with the Pakistan issue, but Muhammad Iqbal (1876–1938) had passed from the scene before that idea had fully flowered. In fact, Iqbal and Gandhi pay each other surprisingly little attention. On reflection the reasons become evident. On the one hand Iqbal's poetic line well describes them both:

In servitude life is reduced to a tiny stream,

In freedom it is like the boundless ocean.

Yet Iqbal's first priority, the revitalization of Islam, was quite different from Gandhi's. Moreover, the poetic and philosophic aspects of Iqbal's multisided career overshadowed political involvements. His practical politics were largely confined to the Punjab scene, and he chose not to participate in the Khilafat Movement that drew together Gandhi and other Muslim leaders. Gandhi respected Iqbal's love of India and his poetry, and in later years more than once quoted the ghazal line: "Religion does not teach us to bear ill will toward one another." Iqbal, in turn, recognized Gandhi's special role as "the apostle" of Indian nationhood, although he did not appreciate the hero-worship attached to it. Muhammad Daud Rahbar points out how Iqbal once refused to rise for Gandhiji at a meeting presided over by the viceroy on the grounds that such veneration was Islamically inappropriate.

Iqbal's primary critique of Gandhi is associated with his own vision of a Muslim territory within northwest India where Muslims could freely develop their life along modern lines, a vision that in his perspective required separate electorates. He did not regard this approach as a conflict with his commitment to religious harmony. In his presidential address to the Allahabad Session of the All-India Muslim League on December 29, 1930, Iqbal made his famous proposal for such a territorial alignment in India (which later evolved into Pakistan):

> Communalism, in its higher aspect, then, is indispensable to the formation of a harmonious whole in a country like India . . . which instead of stifling the respective individualities of the component whole, affords them choice of fully working out the possibilities that may be latent in them . . . thus possessing full opportunity of development within the body politic of India.

The issue he presented became concrete in connection with the negotiations of the Second Round Table Conference in London in 1931, and the British government's Communal Award in 1932. Iqbal, who was present at the former, opposed Gandhi's view that the Congress represented all the people of India and that in the future Indians should vote only "as Indians." With his view of a "higher" communalism, Iqbal could not and did not criticize Hindu self-consciousness, but rather Hindu unawareness of Muslim needs. Iqbal saw Gandhi's opposition to the Communal Award as a demand "for safeguarding the interests of Hindus."

He declared, "If separate electorates for Untouchables means disintegration of the Hindus, the joint electorate will mean political death for the minorities. In my opinion, it has become clear from the attitude of Mahatma Gandhi that the minorities who are keen to maintain their separate identity should not abandon separate electorate." In Iqbal's view Gandhi should have been attacking the Hindu oppression of the Untouchables more rigorously and not the protective award. But we must turn to Muhammad Ali Jinnah for the strongest critique of Gandhi's orientation.

THE GANDHI ERA

Expansion and Re-organization

In the years after the World War, the membership of the Congress expanded considerably, owing to public excitement after Gandhi's in Champaran and Kheda. A whole new generation of leaders arose from different parts of India, who were committed Gandhians-Sardar Vallabhbhai Patel, Jawaharlal Nehru, Rajendra Prasad, Chakravarti Rajagopalachari, Narhari Parikh, Mahadev Desai-as well as hot-blooded nationalists aroused by Gandhi's active leadership-Chittaranjan Das, Subhas Chandra Bose, Srinivasa Iyengar.

Gandhi transformed the Congress from an elitist party based in the cities, to an organization of the people:

- Membership fees were considerably reduced.
- Congress established a large number of state units across India-known as *Pradesh Congress Committees*-based on its own configuration of India's states on basis of linguistic groups. PCCs emerged for *Maharashtra, Karnataka, Gujarat*-states that did not yet exist and were spread over hundreds of princely states outside British India.
- All former practices distinguishing Congressmen on basis of caste, ethnicity, religion and sex were eliminated-all-India unity was stressed.
- Native tongues were given official use and respect in Congress meetings-especially *Hindustani*, which was adopted for use by the All India Congress Committee.

- Leadership posts and offices at all levels would be filled by elections, not appointments. This introduction of democracy was vital in rejuvenating the party, giving voice to ordinary members as well as valuable practice for Indians in democracy.
- Eligibility for leadership would be determined by how much social work and service a member had done, not by his wealth or social standing.

Social Development

During the 1920s, M.K. Gandhi encouraged tens of thousands of Congress volunteers to embrace a wide variety of organized tasks to address major social problems across India. Under the guidance of Congress committees and Gandhi's network of ashrams in Gujarat, Maharashtra, Uttar Pradesh, Bihar and Tamil Nadu, the Congress attacked:

- Untouchability and caste discrimination
- Alcoholism
- Unhygienic conditions and lack of sanitation
- Lack of health care and medical aid
- Purdah and the oppression of women
- Illiteracy, with the organization of national schools and colleges
- Poverty, with proliferating khadi cloth, cottage industries.

Ascendance to Power (1937-1942)

When under the Government of India Act 1935, the Congress first tasted political power, its internal organization bloomed in the diversity of political attitudes and ideologies. The focus would change slightly from the single-minded devotion to complete independence, to also entertaining excitement and theorizing about the future governance of India. The radical followers of Subhash Chandra Bose, believers in socialism and active revolution would ascend in the hierarchy with Bose's 1938 election to the Congress presidency.

The "Traditionalists"

According to one approach, the traditionalist point of view, though not in a political sense, was represented in Congressmen like Sardar Vallabhbhai Patel, Rajendra Prasad, C.Rajagopalachari, Purushottam Das Tandon, Khan Abdul Ghaffar Khan and Maulana Azad, who were also associates and followers of Gandhi. Their organizational strength, achieved through leading the clashes with the government, was undisputed and proven when despite winning the 1939 election, Bose resigned the Congress presidency because of the lack of confidence he enjoyed amongst national leaders. A year earlier, in the 1938 election, however, Bose had been elected with the support of Gandhi. Differences arose in 1939 on whether Bose should have a second term.

Jawaharlal Nehru, who Gandhi had always preferred to Bose, had a second term earlier. Bose's own differences centred on the place to be accorded to nonviolent as against revolutionary methods. When he set up his Indian National Army in South-east Asia during the Second World War, he invoked Gandhi's name and hailed him as the Father of The Nation. It would be wrong to suggest that the so-called traditionalist leaders looked merely to the ancient heritage of Indian, Asian or, in the case of Maulana Azad and Khan Abdul Ghaffar Khan, Islamic civilization for inspiration.

They believed, along with educationists like Zakir Husain and E W Aryanayakam, that education should be imparted in a manner that enables the learners also to be able to make things with their own hands and learn skills that would make them self-supporting.

This method of education was also adopted in some areas in Egypt. Zakir Husain was inspired by some European educationists and was able, with Gandhi's support, to dovetail this approach to the one favoured by the Basic Education method introduced by the Indian freedom movement.

They believed that the education system, economy and social justice model for a future nation should be designed to suit the specific local requirements.

While most were open to the benefits of Western influences and the socio-economic egalitarianism of socialism, they were opposed to being defined by either model.

The Final Battles

The last important episodes in the Congress involved the final step to independence, and the division of the country on religious lines.

Quit India

Chakravarthi Rajagopalachari, the most prominent leader from Tamil Nadu resigned from the Congress to actively advocate supporting the British war effort.

Indian National Army Trials

During the INA trials of 1946, the Congress helped to form the INA Defence Committee, which forcefully defended the case of the soldiers of the Azad Hind government. The committee declared the formation of the Congress' defence team for the INA and included famous lawyers of the time, including Bhulabhai Desai, Asaf Ali, and Jawaharlal Nehru.

Royal Indian Navy Mutiny

Some members of the Congress initially supported the sailors who led the Royal Indian Navy Mutiny. However they withdrew support at the critical juncture, when the mutiny failed.

Partition of India

Within the Congress, the Partition was opposed by Khan Abdul Ghaffar Khan, Saifuddin Kitchlew, Dr. Khan Sahib and Congressmen from the provinces that would inevitably become parts of Pakistan. Maulana Azad was opposed to partition in principle, but did not wish to impede the national leadership.

PRINCIPLES OF SWADESHI

Gandhi's vision of a free India was not a nation-state but a confederation of self-governing, self-reliant, self-employed people living in village communities, deriving their right livelihood from the products of their homesteads. Maximum economic and political power - including the power to decide what could be imported into or exported from the village - would remain in the hands of the village assemblies. In India, people have lived for thousands of years in a relative harmony with their surroundings: living in their homesteads, weaving homespun clothes, eating homegrown food, using homemade goods; caring for their animals, forests, and lands; celebrating the fertility of the soil with feasts; performing the stories of great epics, and building temples.

Every region of India has developed its own distinctive culture, to which travelling storytellers, wandering 'saddhus', and constantly flowing streams of pilgrims have traditionally made their contribution. According to the principle of swadeshi, whatever is made or produced in the village must be used first and foremost by the members of the village. Trading among villages and between villages and towns should be minimal, like icing on the cake. Goods and services that cannot be generated within the community can be bought from elsewhere. Swadeshi avoids economic dependence on external market forces that could make the village community vulnerable.

It also avoids unnecessary, unhealthy, wasteful, and therefore environmentally destructive transportation. The village must build a strong economic base to satisfy most of its needs, and all members of the village community should give priority to local goods and services. Every village community of free India should have its own carpenters, shoemakers, potters, builders, mechanics, farmers, engineers, weavers, teachers, bankers, merchants, traders, musicians, artists, and priests. In other words, each village should be a microcosm of India - a web of loosely inter-connected communities. Gandhi considered these villages so important that he thought they should be given the status of "village republics". The village community should embody the spirit of the home - an extension of the family rather than a collection of competing individuals.

Gandhi's dream was not of personal self-sufficiency, not even family self-sufficiency, but the self-sufficiency of the village community. The British believed in centralized, industrialized, and mechanized modes of production. Gandhi turned this principle on its head and envisioned a decentralized, homegrown, hand-crafted mode of production. In his words, "Not mass production, but production by the masses." By adopting the principle of production by the masses, village communities would be able to restore dignity to the work done by human hands. There is an intrinsic value in anything we do with our hands, and in handing over work to machines we lose not only the material benefits but also the spiritual benefits, for work by hand brings with it a mediative mind and self-fulfilment. Gandhi wrote, "Its a tragedy of the first magnitude that millions of people have ceased to use their hands as hands. Nature has bestowed upon us this great gift which is our hands. If the craze for machinery methods continues, it is highly likely that a time will come when we shall be so incapacitated and weak that we shall begin to curse ourselves for having forgotten the use of the living machines given to us by God. Millions cannot keep fit by games and athletics and why should they exchange the useful productive hardy occupations for the useless, unproductive and expensive sports and games." Mass production is only concerned with the product, whereas production by the masses is concerned with the product, the producers, and the process.

The driving force behind mass production is a cult of the individual. What motive can there be for the expansion of the economy on a global scale, other than the desire for personal and corporate profit? In contrast, a locally based economy enhances community spirit, community relationships, and community well-being. Such an economy encourages mutual aid. Members of the village take care of themselves, their families, their neighbours, their animals, lands, forestry, and all the natural resources for the benefit of present and future generations.

Mass production leads people to leave their villages, their land, their crafts, and their homesteads and go to work in the factories. Instead of dignified human beings and members of a self-respecting village community, people become cogs in the machine, standing at the conveyor belt, living in shanty towns, and depending of the mercy of the bosses. Then fewer and fewer people are needed to work, because the industrialists want greater productivity. The masters of the money economy want more and more efficient machines working faster and faster, and the result would be that men and women would be thrown on the scrap heap of unemployment. Such a society generates rootless and jobless millions living as dependants of the state or begging in the streets. In swadeshi, the machine would be subordinated to the worker; it would not be allowed to become the master, dictating the pace of human activity. Similarly, market forces would serve the community rather than forcing people to fit the market.

Gandhi knew that with the globalization of the economy, every nation would wish to export more and import less to keep the balance of payments in its favour. There would be perpetual economic crisis, perpetual unemployment, and perpetually discontented, disgruntled human beings. In communities practising swadeshi, economics would have a place but would not dominate society. Beyond a certain limit, economic growth becomes detrimental to human well-being. The modern worldview is that the more material goods

you have, the better your life will be. But Gandhi said, "A certain degree of physical comfort is necessary but above a certain level it becomes a hindrance instead of a help; therefore the ideal of creating an unlimited number of wants and satisfying them, seems to be a delusion and a trap. The satisfaction of one's physical needs must come at a certain point to a dead stop before it degenerates into physical decadence. Europeans will have to remodel their outlook if they are not to perish under the weight of the comforts to which they are becoming slaves."

In order to protect their economic interests, countries go to war - military war as well as economic war. Gandhi said, "People have to live in villages communities and simple homes rather than desire to live in palaces." Millions of people will never be able to live at peace with each other if they are constantly fighting for a higher living standard.

We cannot have real peace in the world if we look at each other's countries as sources for raw materials or as markets for finished industrial goods. The seeds of war are sown with economic greed. If we analyse the causes of war throughout history, we find that the pursuit of economic expansion consistently leads to military adventures. "There is enough for everybody's need, but not enough for anybody's greed," said Gandhi. Swadeshi is thus a prerequisite for peace. The economists and industrialists of our time fail to see when enough is enough. Even when countries reach a very high material standard of living, they are still caught up with the idea of economic growth. Those who do not know when enough is enough will never have enough, but those who know when enough is enough already have enough.

Swadeshi is the way to comprehensive peace: peace with oneself, peace between peoples, and peace with nature. The global economy drives people toward high performance, high achievement, and high ambition for materialistic success. This results in stress, loss of meaning, loss of inner peace, loss of space for personal and family relationships, and loss of spiritual life. Gandhi realized that in the past, life in India was not only prosperous but also conducive to philosophical and spiritual development. Swadeshi for Gandhi was the spiritual imperative.

The Rise of English Colonialism

Historically, the Indian local economy was dependent upon the most productive and sustainable agriculture and horticulture and on pottery, furniture making, metal work, jewelry, leather work, and many other economic activities. But its basis had traditionally been in textiles. Each village had its spinners, carders, dyers, and weavers who were the heart of the village economy.

However, when India was flooded with machine-made, inexpensive, mass-produced textiles from Lancashire, the local textile artists were rapidly put out of business, and the village economy suffered terribly. Gandhi thought it essential that the industry be restored, and started a campaign to stem the influx of British cloth. Due to his efforts, hundreds of thousands of untouchables and caste Hindus joined together to discard the mill-made clothes imported from England or from city factories and learned to spin their own yarn and weave their own cloth. The spinning wheel became the symbol of economic freedom, political independence, and cohesive and classless communities. The weaving and wearing of homespun cloth became marks of distinction for all social groups.

Also responsible for the destruction of India's home economy in the eighteenth century was the introduction of British education under colonial rule. Lord Macaulay, introducing the Indian Education Act in the British Parliament, said, "A single shelf of a good European library was worth the whole native literature of India... Neither as a language of the law, nor as a language of religion has the Sanskrit any particular claim to our engagement... We must do our best to form a class of persons, Indian in blood and colour but English in taste, in opinions, in morals and in intellect."

This aim was pursued with the entire might of the British Raj. Traditional schools were replaced by colonial schools and universities. Wealthy Indians were sent to public schools such as Eton and Harrow and universities such as Oxford and Cambridge. Educated Indians increasingly learned English poetry, English law, and English customs to the neglect of their own culture. Reading Shakespeare and the 'London Times' became much more fashionable than reading Indian classics such as the 'Ramayana', the 'Mahabarata', the 'Vedas', and the 'Upanishads'. Educated Indians saw their own culture as backward, uncivilized, and old-fashioned. They wanted to become rulers of India, but they wanted to rule like the British.

If there was any one person who represented this type of Western-educated Indian it was Jawaharlal Nehru, who became the first prime minister after independence. Nehru sought to promote the industrialization of India not via the capitalist route but by centralized planning. His inspiration came from the intellectuals of the London School of Economics and the Fabian Society - the labour Party's think tank.

Gandhi, on the other hand, believed that India's essential contribution to the world was simply het India-ness. He felt that Indians should recognize their own genius and not try to copy Western culture, which was simply a tool of colonization. Economics and politics should not simply be concerned with material things but should be the means to the fulfilment of cultural, spiritual, and religious ends. In fact, economics should not be separated from the deep spiritual foundations of life. This can be best achieved, according to Gandhi, when every individual is an integral part of the community; when the production of goods is on a small scale; when the economy is local; and when homemade handicrafts are given preference. These conditions are conducive to a holistic, spiritual, ecological, and communitarian pattern of society.

In Gandhi's view, spiritual values should not be separated from politics, economics, agriculture, education, and all the other activities of daily life. In this integral design, there is no conflict between spiritual and material.

It is no good for some people to close themselves in a monastic order practising religion and for other people to say that a spiritual life is only for saints and celibates. Such a separation of religion from society will breed corruption, greed, competition, power mania, and the exploitation of the weak and poor. Politics and economics without idealism will be a kind of prostitution, like sex without love.

Someone asked Gandhi, "What do you think of Western civilization?" He simply replied, "It would be a good idea." For Gandhi a machine civilization was no civilization. A society in which workers had to labour at a conveyor belt, in which animals were treated cruelly in factory farms, and in which economic activity necessarily lead to ecological devastation could not be conceived of as a civilization.

Its citizens could only end up as neurotics, the natural world would inevitably be transformed into a desert, and its cities into concrete jungles. In other words, global industrial society, as opposed to society made up of largely autonomous communities committed to the principle of swadeshi, is unsustainable. Swadeshi for Gandhi was a sacred principle - as sacred for him as the principle of truth and nonviolence. Every morning and evening, Gandhi repeated his commitment to swadeshi in his prayers.

Unfortunately, within six months of independence, Gandhi was assassinated, and Nehru gained a free hand in shaping the economy of India. Nehru found Gandhian thinking too idealistic, too philosophical, too slow, and too spiritual.

He gathered around him Western-educated bureaucrats, and the enterprise to which they were jointly committed made them the unwitting agents of economic colonization. They pressed ahead with the construction of large dams and big factories, which for them were the temples and cathedrals of the new India.

The spirit of dedication, idealism, and self-sacrifice that had been paramount under the leadership of Gandhi was quickly replaced by a lust for power, privilege, comfort, and money. Nehru and his colleagues followed the opposite path to that of swadeshi, and since that time, the history of India has been the history of corruption and political intrigue at the highest level. The political colonization of India might have ended officially with independence in 1947, but her economic colonization continued unabated and at an even greater pace. She has been turned into a playground for global economic forces.

Colonialism without the Colonialists

Now, India continues to be ruled in the English way, but without English rulers. This is the tragedy of India, and there is no end in sight. The industrialists, the intellectuals, and the entrepreneurs in collusion with the government still see the salvation of India in her subordination to the policies of the World Bank and GATT. They see India as part of the global economy working hand in glove with the multinational corporations. However, discontent among the Indian people is growing rapidly. The failures of the Congress Party under Nehru, his daughter, Indira Gandhi, and her son, Rajiv Gandhi, are fully evident to all. As Mahatma Gandhi predicted, the body politic is seething with corruption. The poor are poorer than ever, and the growing middle classes are turning away from the Congress Party. The farmers are agitating against the patenting of their seeds by multinational companies. The global economy of GATT is built on sand. Even though it may appear that its grip is firm, it has no grassroots support, and as its true implications become apparent, the people of India, among whom the teachings of Gandhi are still very much alive, will react against it and will return to swadeshi for the reenchantment of their local culture, their community, and their lives. In fact, the lessons of swadeshi may bring hope for an economics of permanence even among Westerns, once the fraudulent promise of economic growth and industrialism is exposed.

CONGRESS AND 'NATIONALIST' MUSLIMS

IT was not only Jinnah whom Gandhi and the Congress spurned. They spurned also Muslims within their own ranks. V.P. Menon noted: "Nationalist Muslims found themselves in a particularly difficult position. They felt that, unless the Congress could reassure the Muslims, it would not be possible to win their support in the coming elections [in 1946]. Towards the end of August 1945, Abul Kalam Azad approached Gandhiji with a plan for a settlement." Menon summarised the plan and remarked that he was unaware of the Congress' response. The Working Committee's resolution in September accepted the right of secession; only vaguely hinted at the partition of Punjab and Bengal - which Jinnah could notice but not his followers - and declared that the Congress would approach Muslims *directly*.

In his memoirs, Azad suppressed his letter of August 2, 1945, and Gandhi's reply of August 16. They were published in 1976 in Vol. VI of *Transfer of Power* (pages 155-157; Seervai's *Partition of India;* 1994; pages 38-39). Like Rajaji, Azad proposed "to leave entirely to Muslims the question of their status in the future Constitution of India". Gandhi replied on August 16: "I did not infer from your letter that you are writing about my Hindus. Whatever you have in your heart has not appeared in your writing. But don't worry. We will talk the matter over when next we meet if you so desire. Whatever you want to say about the communal problem should not be said without consulting me and the Working Committee. I am also of the opinion that it would be better to keep quiet.... My opinion differs from your (sic)" (*Transfer of Power,* Vol. VI, page 172). Both letters had been intercepted by the government.

Azad wrote to Sardar Patel on August 13, urging acceptance of the right to secede. "Time has now come when the Muslim Nationalists should recognise themselves and place their point of view before the Muslims in general." Patel asked him on August 29 to put it before the Working Committee (*Sardar's Letters Mostly Unknown*; Vol. 4, pages 171-172).

Azad had nothing to offer to the Muslim voter. Neither had Nehru and Patel. The League swept the polls. M. Asaf Ali's memoirs explain how marginalised Azad and he were. In December 1943, Azad reviewed with him and Syed Mahmud "the Congress-Muslim position". "Personally I [Asaf Ali] think it is time that merciless self-criticism was undertaken by nationalist Muslims and Hindu Congressmen. Indian Muslims as a bulk are dissatisfied with the policies of the Congress, howsoever well intentioned they may have been. A practical politician would take note of it and alter the course of his policies... ." In July 1944, Asaf Ali noted that "certain persons [that is, Jinnah] and policies are like the red rag to him [Nehru] and the very mention of them sends him into an unreasonable outburst of passion, expressed more in his tense face... the impression of a proud and unreasoning victim of volcanic emotions".

He asked what was the solution to the communal issue "if not the one proposed by Jinnah? Could any political progress be made without solving this question?... He [Nehru] was frankly not hopeful of any deal with Jinnah, who he thought was not aware of the world forces and economic developments... "

Patel made no secret of his contempt for Congress Muslims even in prison. "Patel & Co. have time and again, spoken in a manner rather ironical, indicating that Mahmud, I and (less marked) Maulana don't come up to their mark," Asaf Ali wrote.

In January 1948, Patel questioned Azad's patriotism. But the unkindest cut was Gandhi's stance. On July 24, 1947, he wrote to Nehru opposing Azad's membership of the first Cabinet of free India. "Sardar is decidedly against his membership." So, "name another Muslim for the Cabinet".

That was Azad's lot; insulted by Jinnah as "a show-boy" and distrusted by Gandhi and Patel for his espousal of Muslim interests from a nationalist viewpoint. The nationalist Muslim had no role to play. The Congress left the field to the League.

INDIAN NATIONAL CONGRESS

Founded in 1885 by a narrowly based national elite, the Indian National Congress (INC) gradually transformed into a broadbased nationalist organisation from the beginning of the 20th century. The Anglo-Indian agitation against the Ilbert Bill during ripon's viceroyalty served to underline the efficacy of an all-India political organisation as India's English educated politicians wished to speak effectively and authoritatively to the British rulers. Surendranath Benerjee, who had been playing a key role in organising nationalist forums like the Indian association (1876) and the National Conference (1883), welcomed the move of AO Hume, a retired British ICS officer, for establishing an organisation by the western educated upper class Indians to function as a 'safety valve' for the escape of growing resentment of Indians against British rule. Hume had the blessings of viceroy dufferin who accepted the idea of such an organisation as the 'loyal opposition' to the British Raj.

Barrister WC Banerjee was chosen as the first president of the INC's inaugural session in Bombay in December 1885.

Surendranath Benerjee joined the INC at its second session in Calcutta in 1886. The INC was then not a full-fledged political party, rather a loose association of influential men in provincial politics trying to build up a national platform. Leading public figures such as Dadabhai Naoroji, Feroze Shah Mehta, Badruddin Tayabji, KT Telang and others associated themselves with the INC.

The Indian National Congress initially had little year round activity and was active only in its annual gatherings. Its delegates were mostly upper caste Hindus and its leaders primarily came from the legal profession. Known for their loyalty to the Raj, they did not like radical sort of political or social change and were interested in having some say in government administration and structures of political life. Until 1905 these moderate leaders confined themselves to political agitation by 'prayer-petition-protest'.

At the beginning the Muslims were not attracted to INC in significant numbers. Sir Sayyed Ahmad advised the Muslims to keep themselves away from INC in the interest of furthering Muslim solidarity. Aswini Datta, the mass leader of Barisal, described each of the sessions of the INC as 'three-day opera'. The moderate leaders of the INC believed that British rule in India was a good dispensation, which can be made better through negotiations. They shunned the violence of small groups of terrorists and revolutionaries in Bengal, the Punjab and Bombay provinces.

Viceroy Curzon's measure of partitioning the province of Bengal in 1905 evoked strong protest from the Bangali Hindu leaders and ultimately gave rise to militant politics of aurobindo ghosh, Bipin Chandra Pal, Bal Gangadhar Tilak and Lala Lajpat Rai. The Calcutta-based swadeshi movement and the programme of boycotting British goods were instrumental in creating the extremist faction within the INC. The moderate and extremist leaders openly and violently clashed in the Surat session (1907) over the 'policy of mendicancy' pursued by the moderates. The INC suffered a split as the extremists came out of it. Congressmen were divided by personal animosities, and factionalism became endemic within the INC at national, provincial and local levels. Meanwhile, the Muslim league (ML) was formed in 1906 to protect the interests of the Muslims.

When the British government involved India in Britain's war efforts in 1914 without consulting Indian opinion, strong Indian resentment against this policy brought the INC and the ML closer. The leaders of INC and ML entered into 'Lucknow Pact' (1916) to strengthen India's demand for self-government. The growing popularity of the Home Rule Leagues led by Annie Besant and

B.G Tilak and the 'Lucknow Pact' persuaded the British government to promise in 1917 self-government on a gradual basis. But the political situation suddenly changed for the worse in the wake of the Jalianwala Bagh massacre in 1919.

By the 1920s the old uncertainties of imperial paternalism were gone. There were clear signs of the beginning of a more popular politics, being welded into a nationalist movement by a new leader Mohandas Karamchand Gandhi, who had experience of launching nonviolent *Satyagraha* movement in South Africa and had emerged in Indian politics at this hour with his new technique of offering resistance to injustice. He received support from the Congress leadership and also from the national revolutionaries who agreed to give him a chance of realising his stated goal of achieving 'Swaraj' (self-government) in one year's time. Gandhi utilised the grievances of the Indian Muslims over the issue of *Khilafat* for forging unity among the Hindus and the Muslims against British imperialism.

Gandhi launched in 1920 his non-cooperation movement which was the first truly national and popular political campaign against the British government. Gandhi's strategy boosted the significance of the INC in Indian politics. The INC undoubtedly owed much of its success into building itself as the organisations of mainstream nationalism in the 1920s to Gandhi and a number of other leaders like Motilal Nehru, Madan Mohan Malavya and Chitta Ranjan Das. Later emerged a new generation of leaders who were content to work with Gandhi and submit to his authority. Prominent among this group were C Raja Gopalachari, Rajendra Prasad, Jawaharlal Nehru, Abul Kalam Azad and Sardar Vallabbhai Patel. Subhas Chandra Bose was initially a part of this group but soon was unwilling to submit to Gandhi. Though the INC accepted in 1929 complete independence of India as its goal, its main aim was to force concessions from the British imperialists. Through the non-cooperation movement (1920-22) and the civil disobedience movement (1930-34) Gandhi exercised his charisma over millions of men and women to make INC a mass-based political forum.

When the British government arranged the Round Table conferences and offered the 'communal award' for reservation of seats in legislatures for different communities and scheduled castes, Gandhi resisted it by undertaking a fast unto death, but the superior skill of political dialogue and divisive strategy of the British imperialism ultimately got Gandhi and the INC outwitted. The Government of India Act (1935) did not introduce full responsible government at the central level but introduced responsible autonomy at the provincial level. There was much resentment within the INC against the proposed federation with the 'native states' and the formidable 'special power' in the governor general's hand.

An inner pressure group of leftists and socialists within the INC was formed in 1934 styled as the Congress Socialist Party (CSP) with Acharya Narendra Dev as chairman and Jayaprakash Narayan as general secretary. Nehru and Subhas Bose sympathised with the cause of socialism but did not formally join the CSP. The leaders and workers of the Communist Party of India, which was banned at that time, worked through the CSP. The group of MN Roy and the Krishak Sabha maintained close contact with the INC and the CSP. The consolidation of leftist forces within the INC caused some consternation in Gandhi and the rightist camp of the INC.

In the elections held in 1937 under the Government of India Act 1935, the INC achieved great successes in the general seats and formed its own government in six Hindu-majority provinces. It failed electorally in Sindh and the Punjab and became the single largest party in Assam, Bengal and NWFP. In Bengal the INC's decision to reject the coalition offer from Ak Fazlul Huq's Krishak Praja party paved the way for the Muslim League-Krishak Praja Party coalition. The ML's desire to form a coalition government with the INC in UP was also sabotaged by Nehru's insistence on ML accepting the 'congress creed'. In order to take the wind out of the leftist sail Gandhi nominated the leftist leader Subhas Bose as the Congress president at the Haripura session (1938). Bose refused to be an obedient disciple of Gandhi, and showed dynamic leadership bent on a massive struggle against imperialism and laying the broad principles of planned economic development of India. Gandhi and the rightist leaders refused to re-elect Bose for the next year, but their nominee was defeated by Bose with the help of the leftists. This confrontation eventually pushed Bose out of the INC. Meanwhile, the ML adopted the Lahore resolution (1940) calling for establishing independent Muslim states in the subcontinent. In 1941, Bose left India to Europe and from there to the East Asian war theatres to launch armed struggle against British imperialism.

Gandhi launched the quit India movement in August 1942, which went in a violent way and was suppressed quickly. This was followed by a series of negotiations between the British government, the INC and the ML for transfer of power. Viceroy Wavell called all concerned parties to the Simla Conference in June-July 1945, but nothing concrete emerged. The search for a consensus between the INC and ML proved illusive.

Between December 1945 and February 1946 fresh elections were held in which the Indians were found to be clearly divided in their allegiance to the INC and the ML. Meanwhile there was a massive popular upsurge against British rule in the wake of the trial of the officers of Indian National Army of Subhas Bose, followed by revolts in the Royal Indian Navy in February 1946 and also wide discontent in the army, police and civil service. The British Prime Minister Attlee announced the appointment of a high power cabinet mission for negotiation with the Indian leaders. The mission recommended a Constituent Assembly and a responsible interim government to be formed by Indian ministers. The ML's demand for Pakistan was not accepted, but a grouping of provinces was recommended to accommodate the demand for powerful provinces on the communal divide. Both the Congress and the League grudgingly accepted the recommendations, but the whole plan was ruined as Nehru indiscreetly asserted the INC's rights to proceed on constitution making without any precondition. This attitude alienated Mohammed Ali Jinnah and the ML which began sabotaging Nehru's interim cabinet and organised violent campaigns to force the British government to concede the demand for partition of India in early 1947. Attlee sent lord Mountbatten as the new viceroy and set the deadline of June 1948 for ending British rule in India. Things now began moving fast. The partition of India took place on 14 August 1947.

FREEDOM AND PARTITION OF INDIA

Gandhi advised the Congress to reject the proposals the British Cabinet Mission offered in 1946, as he was deeply suspicious of the grouping proposed for Muslim-majority states-Gandhi viewed this as a precursor to partition. However, this became one of the few times the Congress broke from Gandhi's advice (though not his leadership), as Nehru and Patel knew that if the Congress did not approve the plan, the control of government would pass to the Muslim League. Between 1946 and 1947, over 5,000 people were killed in violence. Gandhi was vehemently opposed to any plan that partitioned India into two separate countries.

An overwhelming majority of Muslims living in India, side by side with Hindus and Sikhs, were in favour of Partition. Additionally Muhammad Ali Jinnah, the leader of the Muslim League, commanded widespread support in West Punjab, Sindh, NWFP and East Bengal. The partition plan was approved by the Congress leadership as the only way to prevent a wide-scale Hindu-Muslim civil war. Congress leaders knew that Gandhi would viscerally oppose partition, and it was impossible for the Congress to go ahead without his agreement, for Gandhi's support in the party and throughout India was strong. Gandhi's closest colleagues had accepted partition as the best way out, and Sardar Patel endeavoured to convince Gandhi that it was the only way to avoid civil war. A devastated Gandhi gave his assent.

On the day of the transfer of power, Gandhi did not celebrate independence with the rest of India, but was alone in Calcutta, mourning the partition and working to end the violence. After India's independence, Gandhi focused on Hindu-Muslim peace and unity. He conducted extensive dialogue with Muslim and Hindu community leaders, working to cool passions in northern India, as well as in Bengal. Despite the Indo-Pakistani War of 1947, he was troubled when the Government decided to deny Pakistan the Rs. 55 crores due as per agreements made by the Partition Council. Leaders like Sardar Patel feared that Pakistan would use the money to bankroll the war against India. Gandhi was also devastated when demands resurged for all Muslims to be deported to Pakistan, and when Muslim and Hindu leaders expressed frustration and an inability to come to terms with one another.

He launched his last fast-unto-death in Delhi, asking that all communal violence be ended once and for all, and that the payment of Rs. 55 crores be made to Pakistan. Gandhi feared that instability and insecurity in Pakistan would increase their anger against India, and violence would spread across the borders. He further feared that Hindus and Muslims would renew their enmity and precipitate into an open civil war. After emotional debates with his life-long colleagues, Gandhi refused to budge, and the Government rescinded its policy and made the payment to Pakistan. Hindu, Muslim and Sikh community leaders, including the Rashtriya Swayamsevak Sangh and Hindu Mahasabha assured him that they would renounce violence and call for peace. Gandhi thus broke his fast by sipping orange juice.

Assassination: On January 30, 1948, on his way to a prayer meeting, Gandhi was shot dead in Birla House, New Delhi, by Nathuram Godse. Godse was a Hindu radical with links to the extremist Hindu Mahasabha, who held Gandhi responsible for weakening India by insisting upon a payment to Pakistan. Godse and his co-conspirator Narayan Apte were later tried and convicted, and on 15 November 1949, were executed.

Gandhi's memorial (or Samadhi) at Raj Ghat, New Delhi, bears the epigraph, which may be translated as "Oh God". These are widely believed to be Gandhi's last words after he was shot, though the veracity of this statement has been disputed by many. Jawaharlal Nehru addressed the nation through radio: "Friends and comrades, the light has gone out of our lives, and there is darkness everywhere, and I do not quite know what to tell you or how to say it. Our beloved leader, Bapu as we called him, the father of the nation, is no more. Perhaps I am wrong to say that; nevertheless, we will not see him again, as we have seen him for these many years, we will not run to him for advice or seek solace from him, and that is a terrible blow, not only for me, but for millions and millions in this country." According to his wish, the majority of Gandhi's ashes were immersed in all the major rivers of the world such as The Nile,

Volga, Thames, etc. Also, a small portion was sent to Paramahansa Yogananda from Dr. V.M. Nawle, (a publisher and journalist from Poona, India) encased in a brass & silver coffer. The ashes were then enshrined at the Mahatma Gandhi World Peace Memorial in the Self-Realization Fellowship Lake Shrine within a thousand-year-old stone sarcophagus from China.

Cabinet Mission

The War ended in 1945. After an election, Labour Party's Government came to power in England. England had been extremely weakened financially and militarily. The Azad Hind Sena had shown that even the army was not untouched by nationalism.

Mutiny of the naval ratings in February 1946 gave the same indication. The people were in an agitated mood. The British rule had lost legitimacy in the eyes of the people.

The British, therefore, decided to withdraw from India. Cabinet Mission was sent to India to help in the formation of Interim Government and to purpose a scheme regarding the transfer of power. The mission proposed that the provinces be divided in three groups, in one of which Hindus were in the majority while in the other two Muslims. Subjects like defence, foreign affairs, communications etc., were to be with the Central Authority and the groups were to be free to frame constitutions about other subjects. Gandhi found the proposals defective. Muslim League declared 'Direct Action' to get Pakistan. 'Direct Action' meant unleashing of violence. The Hindus retaliated. In Calcutta alone, over 6000 people were killed 4 days. The Hindu communalism too became stronger.

The Noakhali Massacre

In the Noakhali area of East Bengal, where Muslims formed 82% of the population, a reign of terror was let loose in a planned and systematic way in October 1946. The Hindus were killed and beaten, their property was burnt, thousands of Hindus were forcibly converted and thousands of Hindu women were abducted and raped. Temples were defiled and destroyed. The League Government in Bengal aided the goondas. Even ex-serviceman joined in committing the atrocities. In Noakhali, about three-fourth of the land belonged to the Hindu landlords and the tenants were mostly Muslims. The peasant unrest was naturally there. It was now turned along communal channels. The Noakhali massacre had few parallels in the history. It showed to what level communal politics could stop to. It was meant to terrorise, kill, convert or drive away the Hindus from Muslim-majority areas so that Pakistan could become a reality.

Gandhi's Noakhali March

Gandhi was deeply shocked. He could not bear the defeat of his long-cherished principles. On 6th November 1946, he rushed to Noakhali. It was to be his final and perhaps the most glorious battle. Gandhi reached Shrirampur and camped there for a few days. He sent his associates including Pyarelal and Sushila Nayyar to different villages which were mostly deserted by the Hindus. He did all his personal work himself. He worked like a possessed man. He walked barefooted, went from house to house, talked to Hindus and Muslims, heard their points of view, and reasoned with them and addressed meetings.

He wanted to instill fearlessness into the Hindus. He exhorted them to die nonviolently, if need be, but not to submit to terror. He did not appease the Muslim. He told the truth bluntly. He wanted to win their confidence and make them see reason and earn the confidence of the Hindus. He did not only preach, he served the village poor. He was testing his Nonviolence. It was very difficult to establish mutual trust. The League had made poisonous propaganda against him. But Gandhi's mission began to yield results. It boosted the morale of Hindus. Passions began to subside. Some evacuees started returning home. Some even returned to their original faith. Gandhi gradually succeeded in earning the love and confidence of even the Muslims.

India wins Independence

Noakhali had its reaction in Bihar, where Hindus resorted to violence. The country was seized by communal madness. Gandhi went to Bihar and brought the situation under control. The situation in the country was explosive. Civil War was imminent. The Congress ultimately consented to the partition of India. Despite Gandhi's bitter opposition, he could not do anything to prevent the partition. While the country was celebrating the Independence. Day on 15th August 1947, Gandhi was in Bengal to fight communal madness. Partition was followed by riots, a massacre of unparalleled dimensions. It witnessed movement of about one crore persons and killing of at least six lakh persons. Calcutta was once more on the verge of riots. Gandhi under-took a fast which had a magical effect. Lord Mountbatten described him as 'one-man peace army'. Gandhi continued to plead for sanity in those turbulent days.

Gandhi's Death

It was January 1948. Communal feelings were high due to the partition of the country. Hindu communalists thought that Gandhi was pro-Muslim. His fast for communal amity which resulted in the Government of India honouring its obligation of giving Rs. 50 Crores to Pakistan had further angered them.

Gandhi was staying at the Birla house in New Delhi. He used to hold evening prayer meetings regularly. He used to speak on various issues. Once a bomb was thrown during his prayer meeting. Still, Gandhi did not permit security checks. On 30th of January 1948, about 500 people had gathered for the prayer meeting on the lawns of the Birla House. Gandhi was a bit late as Sardar Patel had come to see him. At 5.10 p.m. he left the room and walked to the prayer ground. He was supporting himself on the shoulders of Abha and Manu, his grand daughter-in-law and granddaughter respectively. People rushed forward to get his darshan and to touch his feet.

Gandhi folded his hands to greet them. When he was a few yards away from the prayer platform, a young man came forward. He saluted Gandhi, suddenly took out a small pistol and fired three shots. The bullets hit Gandhi on and below the chest. He fell to the ground with the words. 'Hey Ram' on his lips. He died within minutes. The crowd was shocked. The assassin was Nathuram Godse,' a worker of Hindu Mahasabha. He was caught and handed over to the Police. Gandhi's body was taken to Birla House. People thronged the place and wept bitterly. The whole world was plunged in sorrow. The next morning, Gandhi's body was placed on a gun-carriage and taken to Rajghat. Millions of people joined the procession to have the last darshan (glimpse) of the Mahatma. His son Ramdas lit the funeral pyre. The Mahatma had become a martyr for communal unity.

7

Azad, Jinnah and Cabinet Mission Plan

1946 CABINET MISSION TO INDIA

The United Kingdom Cabinet Mission of 1946 to India aimed to discuss the transfer of power from the British government to the Indian leadership, with the aim of preserving India's unity and granting it independence. Formulated at the initiative of Clement Attlee, the Prime Minister of the United Kingdom, the mission had Lord Pethick-Lawrence, the Secretary of State for India, Sir Stafford Cripps, President of the Board of Trade, and A. V. Alexander, the First Lord of the Admiralty. Lord Wavell, the Viceroy of India, did not participate in every step but was present.

Purposes and proposals

The British wanted to keep India and its Army united so as to keep it in their system of 'imperial defence' even after granting it independence. To preserve India's unity the British formulated the Cabinet Mission Plan.

The Cabinet Mission's role was to hold preparatory discussions with the elected representatives of British India and the Indian states so as to secure agreement to the method of framing the constitution, to set up a constitution body and to set up an Executive Council with the support of the main Indian parties.

The Mission held talks with the representatives of the Indian National Congress and the All-India Muslim League, the two largest political parties in the Constituent Assembly of India. The two parties planned to determine a power-sharing arrangement between Hindus and Muslims to prevent a communal dispute. The Congress, under Gandhi and Nehru, wanted to obtain a strong central government, with more powers than state governments. The

All India Muslim League, under Jinnah, wanted to keep India united but with political safeguards provided to Muslims like parity in the legislatures because of the wide belief of Muslims that the British Raj was simply going to be turned into a Hindu Raj once the British departed, and since the Muslim League regarded itself as the sole spokesman party of Indian Muslims, it was incumbent upon it to take the matter up with the Crown.

After initial dialogue, the Mission proposed its plan over the composition of the new government on 16 May 1946. In its proposals, the creation of a separate Muslim Pakistan was rejected.

Plan of 16 May

1. A united Dominion of India would be given independence.
2. The Muslim-majority provinces would be grouped, with Sind, Punjab, Baluchistan and North-West Frontier Province forming one group, and Bengal and Assam would form another.
3. The Hindu-majority provinces in central and southern India would form another group.
4. The central government, stationed in Delhi, would be empowered to handle nationwide affairs, such as defence, currency, and diplomacy, and the rest of powers and responsibility would belong to the provinces, coordinated by groups.

Plan of 16 June

The plan of 16 June 1946 had a united India, in line with Congress and Muslim League aspirations, but that was where the consensus between the two parties ended since Congress abhorred the idea of having the groupings of Muslim-majority provinces and that of Hindu-majority provinces with the intention of balancing one another at the central legislature. The Muslim League could not accept any changes to this plan since they wanted to keep the safeguards of British Indian laws to prevent absolute rule of Hindus over Muslims.

Reaching an impasse, the British proposed a second plan on 16 June 1946 to arrange for India to be divided into Hindu-majority India and a Muslim-majority India that would later be renamed Pakistan since Congress had vehemently rejected 'parity' at the centre. A list of princely states of India, which would be permitted to accede to the dominion or attain independence, was also drawn up.

The Cabinet Mission arrived in India on 23 March 1946 and in Delhi on 2 April 1946. The announcement of the Plan on 16 May 1946 had been preceded by the Simla Conference in the first week of May.

Reactions

The approval of the plans determined the composition of the new government. The Congress Working Committee officially did not accept either plan. The resolution of the committee dated 24 May 1946 concluded that

The Working Committee consider that the connected problems involved in the establishment of a Provisional Government and a Constituent Assembly should be viewed together... In absence of a full picture, the Committee are unable to give a final opinion at this stage.

And the resolution of 25 June 1946, in response to the June plan concluded

In the formation of a Provisional or other governance , Congressmen can never give up the national character of Congress, or accept an artificial and unjust parity, or agree to a veto of a communal group. The Committee are unable to accept the proposals for formation of an Interim Government as contained in the statement of June 16. The Committee have, however, decided that the Congress should join the proposed Constituent Assembly with a view to framing the Constitution of a free, united and democratic India.

On 10 July, Jawaharlal Nehru, who later became the first prime minister of India, held a press conference in Bombay declaring that the Congress had agreed only to participate in the Constituent Assembly and "regards itself free to change or modify the Cabinet Mission Plan as it thought best." The Congress ruled out the June 16 plan, seeing it as the division of India into small states.

Following consultations, the Viceroy invited 14 men to join the interim government on 15 June 1946. They were Jawaharlal Nehru, Sardar Vallabhabhai Patel, Rajendra Prasad, C. Rajagopalachari and Hari Krishna Mahtab of the Indian National Congress; Mohammed Ali Jinnah, Liaqat Ali Khan, Mohammed Ismail Khan, Khwaja Sir Nazimuddin and Abdul Rab Nisthar of the Muslim League; Sardar Baldev Singh (representing the Sikhs), Sir N.P. Engineer (representing the Parsis), Jagjivan Ram (representing the scheduled castes) and John Mathai (representing the Christians). The Congress proposed Zakir Hussain among its quota of 5 nominees to the interim council. Objecting to the decision, on 29 July 1946, Jinnah announced that his party would not participate in the process to form the Constituent Assembly.

The Viceroy began organising the transfer of power to a Congress-League coalition but League president Muhammad Ali Jinnah denounced the hesitant and conditional approval of the Congress and rescinded League approval of both plans. Thus Congress leaders entered the Viceroy's Executive Council or the Interim Government of India. Nehru became the head, vice-president in title, but possessing the executive authority. Patel became the home member, responsible for internal security and government agencies. Congress-led governments were formed in most provinces, including the NWFP, in Punjab (a coalition with the Shiromani Akali Dal and the Unionist Muslim League). The League led governments in Bengal and Sind. The Constituent Assembly was instructed to begin work to write a new constitution for India.

Coalition and breakdown

Jinnah and the League condemned the new government, and vowed to agitate for Pakistan by any means possible. Disorder arose in Punjab and Bengal, including the cities of Delhi, Bombay and Calcutta. On the League-organized Direct Action Day, over 5,000 people were killed across India, and Hindu, Sikh and Muslim mobs began clashing routinely.

Wavell stalled the Central government's efforts to stop the disorder, and the provinces were instructed to leave this to the governors, who did not undertake any major action. To end the disorder and rising bloodshed, Wavell encouraged Nehru to ask the League to enter the government. While Patel and most Congress leaders were opposed to conceding to a party that was organising disorder, Nehru conceded in hope of preserving communal peace.

League leaders entered the council under the leadership of Liaquat Ali Khan, the future first Prime Minister of Pakistan who became the finance minister, but the council did not function in harmony, as separate meetings were not held by League ministers, and both parties vetoed the major initiatives proposed by the other, highlighting their ideological differences and political antagonism.

At the arrival of the new (and proclaimed as the last) viceroy, Lord Mountbatten of Burma in early 1947, Congress leaders expressed the view that the coalition was unworkable. That led to the eventual proposal, and acceptance of the partition of India. The rejection of cabinet mission plan led to a resurgence of confrontational politics beginning with the Muslim League's Direct action day and the subsequent killings in Noakhali and Bihar. The portioning of responsibility of the League, the Congress and the British Colonial Administration for the breakdown continues to be a topic of fierce disagreement.

JINNAH, IN A CLASS OF HIS OWN

Mohammad Ali Jinnah is an enigma of modern history. His aristocratic English lifestyle, Victorian manners, and secular outlook rendered him a most unlikely leader of India's Muslims. Yet, he led them to separate statehood, creating history and, in Saad R. Khairi's apt phrase, 'altering geography'.

Several scholars, among them H.M. Seervai, Aisha Jalal and Saad R. Khairi, help explain his shift from Indian nationalism to Muslim separatism but the mystery of Jinnah's appeal remains. After all, neither Muslim nationalism nor the idea of Pakistan originated with him; he embraced them somewhat reluctantly.

There is another way of viewing the matter. In the twentieth century, two extraordinary personalities competed for the leadership of Indian Muslims. They were Abul Kalam Azad and Mohammed Ali Jinnah. As a point of departure in comprehending the aspirations of Muslims in India, we might review their biographical profiles.

The contrasts in their family background, education, culture, and styles of leadership were remarkable. Azad's ancestors belonged since Emperor Babar's time to the Persian and Urdu-speaking Muslim aristocracy of India. His great-grandfather was one of the last Ruknul Mudarrasin, a position roughly analogous to today's 'minister of education', in Mughal India. After the War of 1857 his family migrated to Madina where it intermingled with the Sharifain aristocracy. Azad's mother was a daughter of Sheikh Mohammed Zaher Watri, in his time Madina's best known 'Alim'. His father Maulana Khair al-Din gained much fame in the Muslim world for his ten-volume work on Islam, and for his central role in the restoration of Nahr Zubeida, Makkah's main source of water. Among Indian Muslims who were still wistful over a lost empire, and reeling from the excesses of British colonisation, it is hard to envision a family with better credentials than Abul Kalam Azad's.

Abul Kalam was a most worthy scion of an extraordinary family with roots deep in the duality—Indian and pan-Islamic—to which South Asia's Muslims have been historically linked both psychologically and culturally. Born in Makkah, he was fluent in Arabic, at ease in Persian, and a most gifted writer of Urdu prose. He was deeply immersed in the mystical tradition of Islam. As early as 1919 he wrote on Sarmad Shaheed and the grand dichotomy between state and civil society in Islam. His later commentaries on the Holy Qura'an are still regarded as among the best in the world.

"Who is your master among the mufassareen?" I asked the late Maulana Kausar Niazi some years ago. "Abul Kalam" he replied reflexively. Al-Hilal, the magazine Azad founded in 1912, at age 22, marked the beginning of serious, mass circulation Urdu journalism. With its successor al-Balgah, it remains a milestone in the development of Urdu as a popular vehicle of political and social discourse. Azad was a spellbinding speaker and, like Jinnah, an ardent nationalist. In 1923, at age 35, he was the youngest man to be elected president of the Indian National Congress, a record Nehru will break later. An overwhelming majority of India's Ulema supported him. The man we shall later revere as the Quaid-i-Azam was a contemporary of Azad, and a most unlikely contender for Muslim leadership.

He was born in 1876; Azad in 1890. But beyond the proximity of age, the two stood in sharp contrast to each other. While Azad's aristocratic roots lay in the Muslim heartland of UP and Bengal, Jinnah was born to a middle class business family in the port town of Hindu-dominated Karachi. At age 21 he moved to England, thence to Bombay, the modern gateway to British India. Unlike Azad who belonged to the majority Sunni denomination of Islam, Jinnah came from the minority Shi'a community. He was the prototypical westernized Indian, tutored at Lincoln's Inn, tailored at Saville Row, in his youth a Shakepearian actor, a constitutionalist barrister in the Anglo-Saxon tradition, married to a Parsi woman. More at home in English than his native Gujrati, Jinnah spoke little Urdu which he would later designate as Pakistan's official language, knew neither Persian nor Arabic, and had only the rudimentary knowledge of Islam which is common to western educated Muslims. He was anathema to an overwhelming majority of the Ulema of the subcontinent, including so grand a figure as Maulana Husain Ahmed Madani and such ideologue as Abul Ala Maudoodi.

Mr. Jinnah made little effort to overcome his obvious handicaps. Unlike Barrister M.K. Gandhi with whom Jinnah shared similarities of language, class, and education, and who donned the Mahatma's home spun dhoti, Jinnah stuck to his western ways and pin-stripe suits. He bowed but rarely to populist symbols, appearing only occasionally at political ralies, and shunning the display of emotion in public. Reasoned arguments and cold logic were the hallmark of Jinnah's discourse. He spoke at political rallies as though he were addressing a courtroom, or a conference of lawyers. This is not the populist style anywhere, least of all in South Asia. Yet, in less that a decade of his return from London in 1935, he had eclipsed his political foes no less than colleagues in the Muslim League, and successfully established himself and the League as the sole spokesman of India's Muslims. In the elections of 1937 the Muslim League barely survived as a minor political party; in 1940 it set Pakistan as its goal. Barely seven years later the new state was born.

In the Introduction to this first volume of Jinnah papers Professor Zaidi has asked this central question: "What then turned Jinnah into the embodiment of Muslim hopes and aspirations?" One answer, admirably documented by Saad Khairi and H.M. Seervai, is that the leadership of the Indian National Congress allowed Jinnah no alternative even though he constantly probed for one. But a deeper explanation offered in Professor Zaidi's Introduction worth quoting:

"What distinguished Jinnah from his great contemporaries is that he was quite self-consciously a modern man – one who valued, above all, reason, discipline, organisation, and economy. Jinnah differed from other Muslim Leaders in so far as he was uncompromisingly committed to substance rather than symbol, reason rather than emotion, modernity rather than tradition."

But how could this apparently modern figure so powerfully appeal to a people laden with tradition and religious inertia? I should summarise Professor Zaidi's answer to this question: Jinnah's peculiar appeal worked because collectively Indian Muslims had an instinctive if inarticulate grasp of recent history.

"It was a community conscious of its declining condition, and it had experienced the ineffectiveness of old remedies. After all, neither the revivalist prescriptions of Shah Waliullah, nor the fiery war cries of Syed Ahmed Shahid, nor the flamboyant, though confused, demarche of the Khilafat movement – with which Abdul Kalam Azad had become associated and from which Jinnah kept a pronounced distance – provided relief from the ills which afflicted Muslim society in India. Restorationist alternatives had nearly exhausted when Jinnah re-entered the second act of contemporary Muslim tragedy in India. On their part, leaders of the Indian National Congress were so overcome with hubris that they refused to open viable political doors to this wounded and bewildered people.

Significantly, by then the modernist view of the causes of Muslim decline and of the remedies it required, especially as articulated by Sir Syed Ahmed Khan and his ideological successors, including Iqbal, had seeped into the consciousness of the Muslim intelligentsia. There was to this phenomenon also a pan-Islamic context: In the 1930s the Muslim world as a whole had entered what Albert Hourani has described as the Liberal Age when Muslim nationalism grew exponentially on the premises of modernism and reform. Mr Jinnah returned from England in 1935 to find himself swept to the crest of this wave.

In the four decades that have followed his passing, Pakistan has moved precipitously away from the country its founding father had envisioned, and the people had created at costs beyond counting. The two volumes of Jinnah Papers and the archives from which they are drawn do not tell the story of the cowardice and betrayals which followed the Quaid-i-Azam. What they do tell us is who he was, how he waged a difficult and deeply painful struggle for statehood, the vision he nourished, and the hopes he had for this country. I would like to recall him and remind us in passing of what we have done with his legacy. I am sorry if in the process I cause some discomfort to some of you readers.

BRITISH STRATEGIC INTERESTS IN INDIA AND THE CABINET MISSION

The Cabinet Mission sought to solve the problem of British strategic interests in India by 'giving both the claimants some part of what they wanted...'a Pakistan trimmed to the bone [Scheme B], or a central government stripped of most of its real powers, and not 'worth much' [Scheme A]...

Once the Cabinet had given the go-ahead [in March-April 1946], the way was clear to offer Jinnah the alternatives of a small Pakistan with sovereign rights and treaty relations with Hindustan, or a larger Pakistan (with some minor boundary adjustments and only excluding Assam) inside a federation with Hindustan.

The great merit was that in such a federation 'Pakistan' would have equal status with Hindustan in those two matters over which a rather emasculated all-India centre was to be given authority. There was to be no union legislature and any question at the centre on which the two federal units failed to agree would be referred back to their respective group legislatures. Agreement would not be imposed by central dictate, but by agreement between two federated governments.

To make this all-India federation even more attractive for Jinnah, it was clearly stated that the Muslim-majority areas would have complete control over all their affairs except those specifically given to the centre; and at the centre 'they would meet the Hindus on a level where it was States which counted and not the number of individuals in them.' This principle of equality, which was exactly what Jinnah had been fighting for all along was, he was now told [by Lord Pethick Lawrence], 'the essence of the proposal'.

Now the [Cabinet] Mission offered [Jinnah] the substance of what he was really after. It was not the impractical 'Pakistan' of fantasy for which the man in the street or the mullah in the mosque was wont to cry, nor was it the 'mutilated and motheaten' Pakistan which was outlined in Scheme B and which finally emerged in 1947.

His Pakistan did not intend to throw the advantages of an undivided Punjab and Bengal to the winds, nor did it plan to leave the Muslims in Hindustan unprotected. Undivided provinces and protection for minority Muslims could only be achieved inside the framework of an union with an effective centre where the League had an equal say.

So we must carefully assess why Jinnah did not jump more openly and more enthusiastically at what the Mission now offered in its Scheme A...It was only by pressing for even more than he had been offered that Jinnah hoped to persuade the Congress to accept the Mission's proposed all-India federal scheme as a lesser evil. Then there were his own followers to consider. Few among them would understand that the Mission had dealt them a royal flush or that equality at an all-India federal centre outweighed the advantages which a sovereign but truncated Pakistan would bring.

So the game was played in Jinnah's usual manner. He argued that equality at the centre was all very well on Cabinet paper, but would never work in Khadi practice. Equality could hardly be assured inside a system of government where one party had the big battalions, and the other the small.

What Jinnah needed was to get all the parties to agree to dissolve the existing centre, in principle if not in fact, and then immediately to recreate it on the basis of a sovereign Pakistan. In his opinion, this alone would ensure Muslims equal treatment at the centre, since it would be an equality underwritten by the law of nations:a treaty between sovereign states. In return he was prepared to give up parts of the six Muslim provinces (though Assam could hardly be considered a Muslim province) to which he had laid claim.

But unless and until Congress came forward with a clear 'yes'. he would not say what he was willing to give up'. He wanted to make terms with the Congress, but only if it gave him a 'viable' state, not if it 'struck at the heart of Pakistan'. If Congress refused to budge, then Jinnah wanted the Mission to impose a settlement, and thought they were in a 'position to do it'.

In fact he would have preferred the British to give him what they had offered and what he was ready to accept by an award, since the Congress was unlikely in the end to concede such a degree of sovereignty to Pakistan which his scheme demanded. So the British should impose their solution and stay on for a few years to make it stick. Union here and now between the League and Congress provinces was all very well only provided the British remained to supervise fair play to the weaker partner represented by the League..

[As revealed later in the Simla conference in May 1946].. Both parties had diametrically different conceptions of what power the union centre should possess. Finance was the nub of the matter, since power comes out of the drawers of the till. Congress wanted a self-supporting centre, with control over subjects to do with revenue. Jinnah claimed he wanted a centre with no real financial powers, a mere agent for the federations, dependent on doles from the provinces. He did not want the centre to have authority to levy taxes upon the groups.

The union would have to be given a budget for defence, but that budget was to be kept to the minimum in line with previous expenditure by the two federations who would have to agree on what to give. If the union needed more money, Jinnah wanted its budget to go to the group legislatures for their approval. Not surprisingly, Nehru retorted that the Congress could never accept such a 'vague and airy Centre'.

By his implacable opposition to an union legislature, Jinnah showed what he was really after. He would have preferred even foreign affairs and defence, the union centre's two responsibilities, to be discussed and settled in the group legislatures and he conceded with reluctance that this was neither logical nor practical.

But if there was to be a union legislature, parity for the League was of the essence: different legislatures would be entitled to elect an equal number of representatives to the union legislature, and the balance between the League and the Congress would be made immune to any changes, even if the princes were to come in later...

Cabinet Mission Plan (2). Congress-League positions on 12 May 1946.

Documents included:

- Terms of the offer made by the Muslim League as a basis of agreements 12 May 1946.
- Terms of Offer made by the Indian National Congress as a basis of agreement, 12 May 1946.
- Note by the Indian National Congress on the terms of the offer made by the Muslim League, 12 May 1946.

[For Maulana Azad and M.A. Jinnah's positions on 8-9 May see CMP (7B)]

From 'Speeches and Documents on the Indian Constitution 1921-1947', Selected by Sir Maurice Gwyer and A. Appadorai, OUP, 1957 Vol. II.

(C) Terms of the offer made by the Muslim League as a basis of agreements 12 May 1946.

1. The six Muslim Provinces (Punjab, North-West Frontier Province, Balochistan, Sind, Bengal and Assam) shall be grouped together as one group and will deal with all other subjects and matters except Foreign Affairs, Defence and Communications necessary for Defence, which may be dealt with by the constitution-making bodies of the two groups of Provinces-Muslim Provinces (hereinafter named Pakistan Group) and Hindu Provinces-sitting together.

   [blogger's comment:Assam had in fact a non-Muslim majority!! The Cabinet Mission listed Assam as having 3.44 million Muslims and 6.76 million non-Muslims yet they grouped it with Bengal]

2. There shall be a separate constitution-making body for the six Muslim Provinces named above, which will frame Constitutions for the group

and the Provinces in the group and will determine the list of subjects that shall be Provincial and Central (of the Pakistan Federation) with residuary sovereign powers vesting in the Provinces.

3. The method of election of the representatives to the constitution-making body will be such as would secure proper representation to the various communities in proportion to their population in each Province of the Pakistan Group.
4. After the constitutions of the Pakistan Federal Government and the Provinces are finally framed by the constitution-making body it will be open to any Province of the Group to decide to opt out of its group, provided the wishes of the people of that Province are ascertained by a referendum to opt out or not.
5. It must be open to discussion in the joint constitution-making body as to whether the Union will have a Legislature or not. The method of providing the Union with finance should also be left for decision of the joint meeting of the two constitution-making bodies, but in no event shall it be by means of taxation.
6. There should be parity of representation between the two groups of Provinces in the Union Executive and the Legislature, if any.
7. No major point in the Union Constitution which affects the communal issue shall be deemed to be passed in the joint constitution-making body, unless the majority of the members of the constitution-making body of the Hindu provinces and the majority of the members of the constitution-making body of the Pakistan Group, present and voting, are separately in its favour.
8. No decision, legislative, executive or administrative, shall be taken by the Union in regard to any matter of controversial nature, except by a majority of three-fourths.
9. In Group and Provincial Constitutions fundamental rights and safeguards concerning religion, culture and other matters affecting the different communities will be provided for.
10. The Constitution of the Union shall have a provision whereby any Province can, by a majority vote of its Legislative Assembly, call for reconsideration of the terms of the Constitution, and will have the liberty to secede from the Union at any time after an initial period of ten years.

These are the principles of our offer for a peaceful and amicable settlement and this offer stands in its entirety and all matters mentioned herein are interdependent.

(D) Terms of Offer made by the Indian National Congress as a basis of agreement, 12 May 1946.

1. The Constituent Assembly to be formed as follows:
   (i) Representatives shall be elected by each Provincial Assembly by proportional representation (single transferable vote). The number so elected should be one-fifth of the number of members of the Assembly and they may be members of the Assembly or others.
   (ii) Representatives from the States on the basis of their population in proportion to the representation from British India. How these representatives are to be chosen is to be considered later.
2. The Constituent Assembly shall draw up a Constitution for the Federal Union. This shall consist of an all-India Federal Government and Legislature dealing with Foreign Affairs, Defence, Communications, Fundamental Rights, Currency, Customs and Planning as well as such other subjects as, on closer scrutiny, may be found to be intimately allied to them. The Federal Union will have necessary powers to obtain for itself the finances it requires for these subjects and the power to raise revenues in its own right. The Union must also have power to take remedial action in cases of breakdown of the Constitution and in grave public emergencies.
3. All remaining powers shall vest in the Provinces or Units.
4. Groups of Provinces may be formed and such groups may determine the Provincial subjects which they desire to take in common.
5. After the Constituent Assembly has decided the Constitution for the all-India Federal Union as laid down in paragraph 2 above, the representatives of the Provinces may form groups to decide the Provincial Constitutions for their group and, if they wish, a group Constitution.
6. No major point in the all-India Federal Constitution which affects the communal issue shall be deemed to be passed by the Constituent Assembly unless a majority of the members of the community or communities concerned present in the Assembly and voting are separately in its favour. Provided that in case there is no agreement on any issue, it will be referred to arbitration. In case of doubt as to whether any point is a major communal issue, the Speaker will decide, or, if so desired, it may be referred to the Federal Court.
7. In the event of a dispute arising in the process of constitution-making, the specific issue shall be referred to arbitration.

8. The Constitution should provide machinery for its revision at any time subject to such checks as may be desired. If so desired, it may be specifically stated that this whole Constitution may be reconsidered after 10 years.

(E) Note by the Indian National Congress on the terms of the offer made by the Muslim League, 12 May 1946.

The approach of the Muslim League is so different from that of the Congress in regard to these matters that it is a little difficult to deal with each point separately without reference to the rest. The picture as envisaged by the Congress is briefly given in a separate note. From a consideration of this note and the Muslim League's proposal the difficulties and the possible arrangement will become obvious.

The Muslim League's proposals are dealt with below briefly:

(1) We suggest that the proper procedure is for one constitution-making body or Constituent Assembly to meet for the whole of India and later for groups to be formed if so desired by the Province concerned. The matter should be left to the Provinces and if they wish to function as a group they are at liberty to do so and to frame their own Constitution for the purpose.

    In any event Assam has obviously no place in the group mentioned and the North-West Frontier Province, as elections show, is not in favour of this proposal.

(2) We have agreed to residuary powers, apart from the Central subjects, vesting in the Provinces. They can make such use of these as they like and, as has been stated above, function as a group. What the ultimate nature of such group may be cannot be determined at this stage and should be left to the representatives of Provinces concerned.

(3) We have suggested that the most suitable method of election would be by single transferable vote. This would give proper representation to the various communities in proportion to their present representation in the legislatures. If the population proportion is taken, we have no particular objection, but this would lead to difficulties in all the Provinces where there is weightage in favour of certain communities. The principle approved of would necessarily apply to all the Provinces.

(4) There is no necessity for opting out of a Province from its group as the previous consent of the Provinces is necessary for joining the group.

(5) We consider it essential that the Federal Union should have a Legislature. We also consider it essential that the Union should have power to raise its own revenue.

(6, 7) We are entirely opposed to parity of representation as between groups of Provinces in the Union Executive or Legislature. We think that the provision to the effect that no major communal issue in the Union Constitution shall be deemed to be passed by the Constituent Assembly unless a majority of the members of the community or communities concerned present and voting in the Constituent Assembly are separately in its favour, is a sufficient and ample safeguard of all Minorities.

We have suggested something wider and including all communities than has been proposed elsewhere. This may give rise to some difficulties in regard to small communities, but all such difficulties can be got over by reference to arbitration. We are prepared to consider the method of giving effect to this principle so as to make it more feasible.

(8) The proposal is so sweeping in its nature that no Government or Legislature can function at all. Once we have safeguarded major communal issues other matters, whether controversial or not, require no safeguard. This will simply mean safeguarding vested interests of all kinds and preventing progress, or indeed any movement in any direction. We, therefore, entirely disapprove of it.

(9) We are entirely agreeable to the inclusion of fundamental rights and safeguards concerning religion, culture and like matters in the Constitution. We suggest that the proper place for this is the All-India Federal Union Constitution. There should be uniformity in regard to these fundamental rights all over India.

(10) The Constitution of the Union will inevitably contain provisions for its revision. It may also contain a provision for its full reconsideration at the end of ten years. The matter will be open then for a complete reconsideration. Though it is implied, we would avoid reference to secession as we do not wish to encourage this idea.

CMP (3) Cabinet Mission Plan issued on 16 May 1946

Document included:

- The Cabinet Mission Plan from *'Speeches and Documents on the Indian Constitution 1921-1947'*, Selected by Sir Maurice Gwyer and A. Appadorai, OUP, 1957 Vol. II. (excerpts)

Statement by the Cabinet Mission to India and His Excellency the Viceroy, 16 May 1946 (excerpts)

4. It is not intended in this statement to review the voluminous evidence which has been submitted to the Mission; but it is right that we should

state that it has shown an almost universal desire, outside the supporters of the Muslim League, for the unity of India.

5. This consideration did not, however, deter us from examining closely and impartially the possibility of a partition of India; since we were greatly impressed by the very genuine and acute anxiety of the Muslims lest they should find themselves subjected to a perpetual Hindu-majority rule. This feeling has become so strong and widespread amongst the Muslims that it cannot be allayed by mere paper safeguards. If there is to be internal peace in India it must be secured by measures which will assure to the Muslims a control in all matters vital to their culture, religion or other interests.
6. We therefore examined in the first instance the question of a separate and fully independent sovereign state of Pakistan as claimed by the Muslim League. Such a Pakistan would comprise two areas: one in the North-West consisting of the Provinces of Punjab, Sind, North-West Frontier, and British Balochistan; the other in the North-East consisting of the Provinces of Bengal and Assam. The League were prepared to consider adjustment of boundaries at a later stage, but insisted that the principle of Pakistan should first be acknowledged.

The argument for a separate state of Pakistan was based, first, upon the right of the Muslim majority to decide their method of government according to their wishes, and, secondly, upon the necessity to include substantial areas in which Muslims are in a minority, in order to make Pakistan administratively and economically workable.

The size of the non-Muslim Minorities in a Pakistan comprising the whole of the six Provinces enumerated above would be very considerable as the following figures [from the recent 1941 census] show:

Northwestern Area

	Muslim	Non-Muslim
Punjab	6,217,242	12,201,577
North-West Frontier Province	2,788,797	249,270
Sind	3,208,325	1,326,683
British Baluchistan	438,930	62,701
TOTAL	22,653,294	13,840,231
	62.07 per cent	37.93 per cent

Northeastern Area

	Muslim	NonMuslim
Bengal	33,005,434	27,301,091
Assam	3,442,479	6,762,254
TOTAL	36,447,913	34,063,245
	51.69 per cent	48.31 per cent

The Muslim Minorities in the remainder of British India number some 20 million dispersed amongst a total population of 188 million.

These figures show that the setting up of a separate sovereign state of Pakistan on the lines claimed by the Muslim League would not solve the communal minority problem; nor can we see any justification for including within a sovereign Pakistan those districts of Punjab and of Bengal and Assam in which the population is predominantly non-Muslim. Every argument that can be used in favour of Pakistan can equally, in our view, be used in favour of the exclusion of the non-Muslim areas from Pakistan. This point would particularly affect the position of the Sikhs.

7. We, therefore, considered whether a smaller sovereign Pakistan confined to the Muslim-majority areas alone might be a possible basis of compromise. Such a Pakistan is regarded by the Muslim League as quite impractical because it would entail the exclusion from Pakistan of (a) the whole of Ambala and Jullundur divisions in the Punjab; (b) the whole of Assam except the district of Sylhet; and (c) a large part of Western Bengal, including Calcutta, in which city the percentage of the Muslim population is 23.6 per cent. We ourselves are also convinced that any solution which involves a radical partition of Punjab and Bengal, as this would do, would be contrary to the wishes and interests of a very large proportion of the inhabitants of these Provinces. Bengal and the Punjab each has its own common language and a long history and tradition. Moreover, any division of the Punjab would of necessity divide the Sikhs, leaving substantial bodies of Sikhs on both sides of the boundary. We have therefore been forced to the conclusion that neither the larger nor the smaller sovereign state of Pakistan would provide an acceptable solution for the communal problem.

8. Apart from the great force of the foregoing arguments there are weighty administrative, economic and military considerations. The whole of the transportation and postal and telegraph systems of India have been established on the basis of a united India. To disintegrate them would

gravely injure both parts of India. The case for a united defence is even stronger. The Indian armed forces have been built up as a whole for the defence of India as a whole, and to break them in two would inflict a deadly blow on the long traditions and high degree of efficiency of the Indian Army and would entail the gravest dangers. The Indian Navy and Indian Air Force could become much less effective. The two sections of the suggested Pakistan contain the two most vulnerable frontiers in India and for a successful defence in depth the area of Pakistan would be insufficient.

9. A further consideration of importance is the greater difficulty which the Indian States would find in associating themselves with a divided British India.

10. Finally there is the geographical fact that the two halves of the proposed Pakistan State are separated by some seven hundred miles and the communications between them both in war and peace would be dependent on the goodwill of Hindustan.

11. We are therefore unable to advise the British Government that the power which at present resides in British hands should be handed over to two entirely separate sovereign states.

12. This decision does not, however, blind us to the very real Muslim apprehensions that their culture and political and social life might become submerged in a purely unitary India, in which the Hindus with their greatly superior numbers must be a dominating element.

    To meet this the Congress have put forward a scheme under which Provinces would have full autonomy subject only to a minimum of Central subjects, such as Foreign Affairs, Defence and Communications.

    Under this scheme Provinces, if they wished to take part in economic and administrative planning on a large scale, could cede to the Centre optional subjects in addition to the compulsory ones mentioned above.

13. Such a scheme would, in our view, present considerable constitutional disadvantages and anomalies. It would be very difficult to work a Central Executive and Legislature in which some Ministers who dealt with compulsory subjects were responsible to the whole of India while other Ministers, who dealt with optional subjects, would be responsible only to those Provinces who had elected to act together in respect of such subjects. This difficulty would be accentuated in the Central Legislature, where it would be necessary to exclude certain members from speaking, and voting when subjects with which their Provinces are not concerned are under discussion.

Apart from the difficulty of working such a scheme, we do not consider that it would be fair to deny other Provinces, which do not desire to take optional subjects at the Centre, the right to form themselves into a group for a similar purpose. This would indeed be no more than the exercise of their autonomous powers in a particular way.

14. Before putting forward our recommendation we turn to deal with the relationship of the Indian States to British India. It is quite clear that with the attainment of independence by British India, whether inside or outside the British Commonwealth, the relationship which has hitherto existed between the Rulers of the States and the British Crown will no longer be possible. Paramountcy can neither be retained by the British Crown nor transferred to the new Government. This fact has been fully recognised by those whom we interviewed from the States. They have at the same time assured us that the States are ready and willing to cooperate in the new development of India. The precise form which their cooperation will take must be a matter for negotiation during the building up of the new constitutional structure, and it by no means follows that it will be identical for all the States. We have not therefore dealt with the States in the same detail as the Provinces of British India in the paragraphs which follow.

15. We now indicate the nature of a solution which in our view would be just to the essential claims of all parties and would at the same time be most likely to bring about a stable and practicable form of Constitution for all India.

We recommend that the Constitution should take the following basic form:

(1) There should be a Union of India, embracing both British India and the States which should deal with the following subjects: Foreign Affairs, Defence, and Communications; and should have the powers necessary to raise the finances required for the above subjects.

(2) The Union should have an Executive and a Legislature constituted from British Indian and States' representatives. Any question raising a major communal issue in the Legislature should require for its decision a majority of the representatives present and voting of each of the two major communities as well as a majority of all members present and voting.

(3) All subjects other than the Union subjects and all residuary powers should vest in the Provinces.

(4) The States will retain all subjects and powers other than those ceded to the Union.

(5) Provinces should be free to form groups with Executives and Legislatures, and each group could determine the Provincial subjects to be taken in common.

(6) The Constitutions of the Union and of the groups should contain a provision whereby any Province could by majority vote of its Legislative Assembly could call for a reconsideration of the terms of the Constitution after an initial period of ten years and at ten-yearly intervals thereafter.

16. It is not our object to lay out the details of a constitution on the above lines, but to set in motion the machinery whereby a constitution can be settled by Indians for Indians.

It has been necessary however for us to make this recommendation as to the broad basis of the future constitution because it became clear to us in the course of our negotiations that not until that had been done was there any hope of getting the two major communities to join in the setting up of the constitution making machinery.

17. We now indicate the constitution-making machinery which we propose should be brought into being forthwith in order to enable a new constitution to be worked out.

18. In forming any assembly to decide a new constitutional structure the first problem is to obtain as broad-based and accurate representation of the whole population.. After a most careful consideration of the various methods by which these points might be corrected, we have come to the conclusion that the fairest and most practicable plan would be-

(a) to allot to each Province a total number of seats proportional to its population, roughly in the ratio of one to a million, as the nearest substitute for representation by adult suffrage

(b) to divide this provincial allocation of seats between the main communities in each Province in proportion to their population

(c) to provide that the representatives allocated to each community in a Province shall be elected by members of that community in its Legislative Assembly.

We think that for these purposes it is sufficient to recognise only three main communities in India: General, Muslim, and Sikh, the 'General' community including all persons who are not Muslims or Sikhs. As smaller Minorities would upon a population basis have little or no representation..we have made the arrangements set out in paragraph 20 below to give them a full representation upon all matters of special interest to Minorities.

19. (i) We therefore propose that there shall be elected by each Provincial Legislative Assembly the following numbers of representatives, each part of the Legislative Assembly (General, Moslem or Sikh) electing its own representatives by the method of proportional representation with single transferable vote:

Table of Representation

Section A			
Province	*General*	*Muslim*	*Total*
Madras	45	4	49
Bombay	19	2	21
United Provinces	47	8	55
Bihar	31	5	36
Central Provinces	16	1	17
Orissa	9	0	9
TOTAL	167	20	187

Section B				
Province	*General*	*Muslim*	*Sikhs*	*Total*
Punjab	8	16	4	28
North-West Frontier Province	0	3	0	3
Sind	1	3	0	4
TOTAL	9	22	4	35

Section C			
Province	*General*	*Muslim*	*Total*
Bengal	27	33	60
Assam	7	3	10
TOTAL	34	36	70

(iii) Representatives thus chosen shall meet in New Delhi as soon as possible.

(iv) A preliminary meeting will be held at which the general order of business will be decided, a chairman and other officers elected and an Advisory Committee (see paragraph 20 below) on the rights of citizens, minorities, and tribal and excluded communities set up. Thereafter the Provincial representatives will divide up into three Sections shown under A, B and C in the Table of Representation in sub-paragraph (i) of this paragraph.

(v) These Sections shall proceed to settle Provincial Constitutions for the Provinces included in each Section and shall also decide whether any group constitution shall be set up for those Provinces and if so with what Provincial subjects the group should deal.

Provinces should have power to opt out of groups in accordance with the provisions of subclause (viii) below.

(vi) The representatives of the Sections and the Indian States shall reassemble for the purpose of settling the Union Constitution.

(vii) In the Union Constituent Assembly resolutions varying the provisions of paragraph 15 above or raising any major communal issue shall require a majority of the representatives present and voting of each of the two major communities. The Chairman of the Assembly shall decide which, if any, resolutions raise major communal issues and shall, if so requested by a majority of the representatives of either of the major communities, consult the Federal Court before giving his decision.

(viii) As soon as the new constitutional arrangements have come into operation it shall be open to any Province to elect to come out of any group in which it has been placed. Such a decision shall be taken by the Legislature of the Province after the first general election under the new Constitution.

20. The Advisory Committee on the rights of citizens, minorities, and tribal and excluded areas should contain full representation of interests affected, and their function will be to report to the Union Constituent Assembly upon the list of Fundamental Rights, the clauses for the protection of minorities, and a scheme for the administration of the tribal and excluded areas, and to advise whether these rights should be incorporated in the Provincial, Group, or Union constitution.

21. His Excellency the Viceroy will forthwith request the Provincial Legislatures to proceed with the election of their representatives and the States to set up a Negotiating Committee. It is hoped that the process of constitution-making can proceed as rapidly as the complexities of the task permit so that the interim period may be as short as possible.

22. It will be necessary to negotiate a Treaty between the Union Constituent Assembly and the United Kingdom to provide for certain matters arising out of the transfer of power.

23. We attach the greatest importance therefore to the setting up at once of an Interim Government having the support of the major political parties...The Viceroy has already started discussions to this end and hopes soon to form an Interim Government in which all the portfolios, including that of War Member, will be held by Indian leaders having full confidence of the people...

24. To the leaders and people of India who now have the opportunity of complete independence we would finally say this. We and our Government and countrymen hoped that it would be possible for the Indian people themselves to agree upon the method of framing the new constitution under which they will live. Despite the labours which we have shared with the Indian Parties, and the exercise of much patience and goodwill by all, this has not been possible. We therefore now lay before you proposals which, after listening to all sides and after much earnest thought, we trust will enable you to attain your independence in the shortest time and with the least danger of internal disturbances and conflict. These proposals may not, of course, completely satisfy all parties, but you will recognise with us that at this supreme moment in Indian history statesmanship demands mutual accommodation.

We ask you to consider the alternative to these proposals. After all the efforts which we and Indian Parties have made together for agreement we must state that in our view there is small hope of peaceful settlement by agreement of the Indian Parties alone. The alternative would therefore be a grave danger of violence, chaos, and even civil war. The result and duration of such a disturbance cannot be foreseen; but it is certain that it would be a terrible disaster for many millions of men, women and children. This is a possibility which must be regarded with equal abhorrence by the Indian people, our own countrymen, and the world as a whole.

We therefore lay these proposals before you in the profound hope that they will be accepted and operated by you in the spirit of accommodation and goodwill in which they are offered. We appeal to all who have the future good of India at heart to extend their vision beyond their own community or interest to the interests of the whole four hundred millions of the Indian people.

Comments

[The Cabinet Mission was composed of three members of the British Cabinet, Sir Stafford Cripps, Lord Pethick-Lawrence and A. V. Alexander].

The reason why the lengthy paragraph 19 has been included in these excerpts is that one key element of the stated disagreements between Congress and Muslim League/Cabinet Mission over the 'long-term' part of the Mission Plan lay in paragraphs (v) (viii) and (vii) (there were serious disagreements over the 'short-term' part, the Interim government, as well).

In my opinion, either with intentions to keep the Plan alive or with intention to grant Jinnah parity between 'Hindustan' and Pakistan by hook or crook (as they had promised), the British did try to fudge the issue by saying one thing in public and promising another in private while blaming everyone else for intransigence. Many historians have tried to fudge the issue as well, but it was really quite simple.

Assam and N.W.F.P provinces had Congress-majority legislatures at the time and moreover Assam had non-Muslim majority population. The Congress could not support forcing Assam to remain within Section C without the option to opt out of it, and similarly could not support forcing N.W.F.P to remain in Section B. The Sikhs were also included against their stated will in Section B.

Muslim League and the Mission however insisted that given the above paragraphs, no changes were possible in the Plan and that the Congress must accept the Plan on those terms. This meant that under the Cabinet Mission Plan, only after the separate Section Constitutions were brought into force, and then, only if a majority of the combined Bengal and Assam representatives had previously agreed to it while writing their Section Constitution, could Assam have the choice to opt out of Section C. This was unlikely to happen since the Section C would be Muslim majority. If a sovereign independent Pakistan did finally come into being (as Jinnah and the Muslim League kept asserting throughout this period that it would) the Mission Plan compelling Assam to remain in the Pakistan-intended grouping Section C was inconsistent with the statement on freedom of provinces to form groups which the Mission expressed in para (15 (5)) and that on 'self-determination' in para (6). This was true with respect to the Sikhs as well. Clearly, the Mission Plan was meant to placate Jinnah by keeping alive the option for the League to walk away with two wings (Section B and C) of the country at a time of its choosing. It is interesting to note the limits placed by the Mission on self-determination and rights of minorities.

It is also interesting to note when a majority was considered a legitimate majority by Jinnah and when it was not. A majority was considered legitimate by Jinnah only when it was a Muslim majority. He labelled it yet another sign of Congress and Hindu perfidy when the Assam legislature passed by majority a resolution opposing joining Section C - clearly he thought it just that the Section C majority should prevail over Assam. But I am getting ahead of my excerpts

CMP (4) Jinnah's and Muslim League's responses to the Cabinet Mission Plan on 22 May 1946 and 6 June 1946.

Documents included below:

- Statement by Mr. M. A. Jinnah on the Cabinet Mission Plan, 22 May 1946. From 'Speeches and Documents on the Indian Constitution 1921-

1947', Selected by Sir Maurice Gwyer and A. Appadorai, OUP, 1957 Vol. II. (excerpts)

- Jinnah's Speech at the Secret Session of the All India Muslim League Council, New Delhi, June 6 1946. From 'Speeches, 'Statements and Messages of the Quaid-e-Azam', Vol IV, Khurshid Yusufi, Bazm-i-Iqbal, Lahore.
- Resolution passed by the Council of the All-India Muslim League, 6 June 1946, Gwyer and Appadorai (excerpts)

Comment

The point to note is that the League and Jinnah stated clearly that the Plan took them closer to their final goal of a sovereign Pakistan and that is why they accepted it. It was clearly stated that a united India was not their final goal, nor was it the reason for their acceptance. Any historian who asserts otherwise needs to explain why.

Statement by Mr. M. A. Jinnah on the Cabinet Mission Plan, 22 May 1946. (excerpts)

I regret that the Mission should have negatived the Muslim demand for the establishment of a complete sovereign state of Pakistan, which we still hold is the only solution of the constitutional problem of India and which alone can secure stable Governments and lead to the happiness and welfare not only of the two major communities, but of all the peoples of this subcontinent.

It is all the more regrettable that the Mission should have though fit to advance commonplace and exploded arguments against Pakistan and resorted to special pleadings couched in deplorable language which is calculated to hurt the feelings of Muslim India. It seems that this was done by the Mission simply to appease and placate the Congress, because when they come to face the realities, they themselves have made the following pronouncement embodied in paragraph 5 of the statement..

I shall now deal with some of the important points in the operative part of the statement:

(1) They have divided Pakistan into two-what they call Section B (for the North-Western Zone) and Section C (for the North-Eastern Zone).

(2) Instead of two constitution-making bodies only one constitution-making body is devised with three Sections A, B and C.

(3) They lay down that : 'There should be a Union of India, embracing both British India and the States.... "

There is no indication at all that the Communications would be restricted to what is necessary for Defense nor is there any indication as to how this Union will be empowered to raise finances required for these three subjects, while our view was that finances should be raised only by contribution and not by taxation.

(4) It is laid down that : 'The Union should have an Executive and a Legislature

While our view was:

(a) that there should be no Legislature for the Union, but the question should be left to the Constituent Assembly to decide;

(b) that there should be parity of representation between the Pakistan group and the Hindustan group in the Union Executive and Legislature, if any; and.

(c) that no decision, legislative, executive or administrative, should be taken by the Union in regard to any matter of a controversial nature, except by a majority of three-fourths; all these three terms of our offer have been omitted from the statement...

(5) Our proposal that the Pakistan group should have a right to succeed from the Union after an initial period of ten years, although the Congress had no serious objection to it, has been omitted and now we are only limited to a reconsideration of terms of the Union Constitution after an initial period of ten years.

(7) With regard to the constitution-making body for the purpose of framing the proposed Union Constitution, it will have an overwhelming Hindu majority as in a House of 292 for British India the Muslim strength will be 79 and, if the number alloted to Indian states (93) is taken into account, it is quite obvious that the Muslim proportion will be further reduced as the bulk of the States representatives would be Hindus..

This raises a very serious question indeed, for if it is left to the Union Constituent Assembly to decide these matters by a majority vote, whether any of the recommendations of the Advisory Committee should be incorporated in the Union Constitution, then it will open a door to more subjects being vested in the Union Government. This will destroy the very basic principle that the Union is to be strictly confined to three subjects.."

Jinnah's Speech at the Secret Session of the All India Muslim League Council, New Delhi, June 6 1946 Speeches, 'Statements and Messages of the Quaid-e-Azam', Vol IV, Khurshid Yusufi, Bazm-i-Iqbal, Lahore.

I advised you to reject the Cripps proposal, I advised you to reject the last Simla Conference formula. But I cannot advise you to reject the British Cabinet

Mission's proposal. I advise you to accept it."..Mr Jinnah added "The Lahore resolution did not mean that when Muslims put forward their demand, it must be accepted at once. It is a big struggle and a continued struggle. The first struggle was to get the representative character of the League accepted. That fight they had started and they had won. Acceptance of the Mission's proposal was not the end of their struggle for Pakistan. They should continue their struggle till Pakistan was achieved."

Mr. Jinnah said that they could create a deadlock in the Constituent Assembly if anything was done against their wishes. They would continue to fight in the Constituent Assembly for their objective. They would also fight for the right of the Units or Groups to rejoin the Group from which they seceded.

As regards groupings, Mr. Jinnah is reported to have expressed satisfaction and said : The Groups should have power on all subjects except defence, communications and foreign affairs. But so far as defence is concerned, it would remain in the hands of the British till the new constitution was enforced. So they need not worry about it now. They would fight in the Constituent Assembly to restrict "Communications" to what was absolutely necessary for defence only.

Resolution passed by the Council of the All-India Muslim League, 6 June 1946, (excerpts)

1. This meeting of the Council of the All-India Muslim League, after having carefully considered the statement issued by the Cabinet Mission and the Viceroy on 16th May 1946... places upon record the following views for the guidance of the nation and direction of the Working Committee.
2. That the references made, and the conclusions recorded in paras 6,7,8,9,10 and 11 of the statement concerning the Muslim demand for the establishment of a full sovereign Pakistan as the only solution of the Indian constitutional problem are unwarranted, unjustified and unconvincing, and should not therefore have found a place in a state document issued on behalf and with the authority of the British Government.

   These paragraphs are couched in such language, and contain such mutiliations of the established facts, that the Cabinet Mission have clearly been prompted to include them in their statement solely with the object of appeasing the Hindus, in utter disregard of Muslim sentiments.

   In order that there may be no manner of doubt in any quarter, the Council of the All-India Muslim League reiterates that the attainment of the goal of a complete sovereign Pakistan still remains the unalterable objective of the Muslims in India for the achievement of which they will, if necessary, employ every means in their power, and consider no sacrifice or suffering too great.

3. That notwithstanding the affront offered to Muslim sentiments by the choice of injudicious words in the preamble to the statement of the Cabinet Mission, the Muslim League, having regard to the grave issues involved, and prompted by its earnest desire for a peaceful solution, if possible, of the Indian constitutional problem, and inasmuch as the basis and the foundation of Pakistan are inherent in the Mission's plan by virtue of the compulsory grouping of the six Muslim provinces in Sections B and C, is willing to cooperate with the constitution-making machinery proposed in the scheme outlined by the Mission, in the hope that it would ultimately result in the establishment of complete [ly] sovereign Pakistan, and in the consummation of the goal of independence for the major nations, Muslims and Hindus, and all the other people inhabiting the vast subcontinent.

   It is for these reasons that the Muslim League is accepting the scheme, and will join the constitution-making body, and it will keep in view the opportunity and right of secession of Provinces or groups from the Union, which have been provided in the Mission's plan by implication. The ultimate attitude of the Muslim League will depend on the final outcome of the labours of the constitution-making body, and the final shape of the Constitutions which may emerge from the deliberations of the body jointly and separately in its three Sections.

The Muslim League reserves the right to modify and revise the policy and attitude set forth in this resolution at any time during the progress of the deliberations of the constitution-making body, or the Constituent Assembly, or thereafter if the course of events so require, bearing in mind the fundamental principles and ideals herebefore adumbrated, to which the Muslim League is irrevocably committed.

CMP (5) Jinnah's discussions with the Cabinet Mission on April 4 1946, before the Plan was issued .

Document included.

- Record of Interview between Cabinet Delegation, Field Marshal Viscount Wavell and Mr. Jinnah on Thursday, 4 April 1946 at 10 am (full text)

The India Office's secret official records were declassified and published in 1977 in 'The Transfer of Power 1942-7', Volume VII The Cabinet Mission 23 March - 29 June 1946, Eds., Nicholas Mansergh and Penderel Moon.

April 4th 1946 meeting (full text) - 48 page 118

Record of Interview between Cabinet Delegation, Field Marshal Viscount Wavell and Mr. Jinnah on Thursday, 4 April 1946 at 10 am

The Delegation invited Mr. Jinnah in the first place to give them his reasons why he thought it better for the future of India that India should have a Pakistan.

Mr. Jinnah said that throughout her history from the days of Chandra Gupta there had never been any Government of India in the sense of a single Government. The Muslim Mughal Empire had the largest control but even in those days the Mahrattas and the Rajputs were not under Muslim rule. When the British came they gradually established their rule in a large part of India but, even then, India was only one-third united. The big States and sovereign States were constitutionally and legally already Pakistans.

The only limitation of this is the Paramount Power of the Crown. The effect of Paramountcy is that the Paramount Power in the last resort maintains internal order in the States but as a counterpart of this has a duty to prevent gross maladministration. Nowadays we talk of British India and say India is one. Mr. Jinnah considered that could not stand examination for a moment. India is really many and is held by the British as one.

Now we have strong Hindu-Muslim tension. This began to develop at the first transfer of a small amount of power about 1906. The British Government to meet it gave separate electorates. The same troubles arose at the time of the Montagu-Chelmsford reforms and the British Government gave a constitution which they thought best suited to India. In the discussions of 1930-35 no agreement could be reached on the communal question and the British Government gave a decision. No doubt the present constitution was an advance and gave more contact with power than ever before, but it showed that the grave apprehensions of Muslims had come true. In the 1935 discussions the Muslims insisted that Sind should be separated and the Frontier made a full Province so that there would be at least four Muslim majority Provinces. All this was decided by the British Government.

Now we have come to the stage when the British Government say they will give complete independence to India inside or outside the Empire. To whom is the government of this subcontinent, with its fundamental differences, to be transferred? It is no use saying "transfer power and we will settle who exercises it afterwards." The question is how to transfer power.

The differences in India are far greater than between European countries and, compared to those, are of a vital and fundamental character. Even Ireland provides no parallel. The Muslims have a different conception of life from the Hindus. They admire different qualities in their heroes; they have a different culture based on Arabic and Persian instead of on Sanskrit origins. Their social customs are entirely different. A Hindu will wash his hands after shaking hands with a Muslim. No Hindu will let Mr. Jinnah have a room in his building. Hindu society and philosophy are the most exclusive in the world. Muslims and Hindus have been side by side in India for a thousand years but if you go into any Indian city you will see separate Hindu and Muslim quarters. They have different names and use a different calendar. The Hindus worship the cow and even today in certain States a 10-year sentence is imposed for killing a cow. This means nothing to the Muslims. You cannot make a nation unless there are essential united factors.

How are you to put 100 millions of Muslims together with 250 millions whose way of life is so different. No Government can ever work on such a basis and if this is forced upon India it must lead us to disaster. No Government can survive unless there is a dominant element which can provide a "steel frame". At present this frame is provided by the British who have always retained the key posts. It is true that this is beginning to cease but already the consequences are apparent. Only one Indian has been a Chief Justice, Sir Shadi Lal in the Punjab. The post of Chief Presidency Magistrate in Bombay has always been held by a British officer because the situation there is so delicate that an un-impartial officer can cause great trouble.

The present Government of India is, of course, not a Parliamentary Government but is a bureaucratic system under which ultimately the British are responsible. Indians can vent their feelings in the Central Legislature but it is powerless. The British could never have run the administration without their own officers in the key positions in the Civil Service, the Police and the Army. Little progress has been made in the Indianisation of these key posts. It has already become difficult because Hindu officials everywhere (of this there is unimpeachable evidence) have both sympathy and feeling for the Hindus and Muslim officials for the Muslims. Every day this is noticeable and becoming more prominent.

Therefore you must have a "steel frame" for an independent India. Mr. Jinnah could see none and had therefore definitely come to the conclusion, after years of experience that there is no other solution than the division of India. Any scheme for this has obvious objections which can be raised against it. But there must be division so that in each of the two parts there will be a dominant community which can provide the "steel frame". Where you have three Muslims and one Hindu your "steel frame" is there.

Sir S. Cripps asked whether 51 per cent. Muslims to 49 per cent of others would provide a "steel frame". Mr. Jinnah said that there would then be no "steel frame". You must choose the area with a clear and dominant majority. It need not necessarily be as high to three to one. If there were no "steel frame", the Civil Service, the Police and the Army would not stand loyally to the Cabinet and the Legislature and the State could not survive. Fortunately, in India the Muslims have their homelands and so let us divide India.

Sir S. Cripps asked whether Mr. Jinnah thought the difference between the Hindu and the Muslim in Bengal was greater than the difference between the Pathan and the Muslim in Sind. Mr. Jinnah said that the fundamentals were common to Muslims all over India. He had travelled everywhere and he knew. The Muslims believed in one God. They believed in equality of men and in human brotherhood. The Hindus believe in none of those principles. Wherever a Muslim goes in India he would not say that everyone understood him but a very large body of Musalmans do. Even in the remote rural areas of Bengal the Muslims understood him.

Mr. Alexander asked whether the difference was essentially racial or religious. Mr. Jinnah said that he readily admitted that 70 per cent. of Muslims were converts from Hindus. A large body were converted before any Muslim conqueror arrived. Muslim missionaries came from Arabia and converted large numbers of Hindus, not singly but by whole sub-Castes together, 10 to 20 thousand people at a time. These Muslim converts were made outcasts by the Hindus. They were thrown out of every department of social life. Therefore you find millions who have stood for centuries under the umbrella of a totally different civilization of their own. There are in India two different civilizations with deep roots side by side. They are totally different. The only solution is to have two "steel frames", one in Hindustan and one in Pakistan.

His Excellency the Viceroy said that he thought that Mr. Jinnah had once agreed with him that from the point of view of practical economic considerations one India would be desirable if that were possible. Mr. Jinnah said that if he had said that it was only in the sense that it was an ideal but an impracticable ideal like a world federation. Sir S. Cripps said that a federation of Europeans for example was quite different. That was bringing together separate sovereign States but India already had common governmental institutions.

Mr. Jinnah said that this unity was not a unity of the people. It was imposed by the British Government. He agreed that common railways, customs, and so forth were convenient but the question was by what Government would those services be controlled. If we have Pakistan and Hindustan it does not follow that they will be in isolation. He certainly contemplated treaties and agreements governing such matters. As soon as the fundamentals of Pakistan are agreed to these things can be settled.

The Secretary of State said that up to a point he accepted the view that India was united at present by British control and by the British Army, Navy and Air Force. But he would not go so far as to say that it was solely so united. He thought that Hindus and Muslims had not only acquiesced in but had cooperated in supporting that unity. The Cabinet Mission had come to decide the ways and means by which the domination of British authority in India was to come to an end. Therefore they had to decide in whose keeping the repository of force is to be given. What they wanted to know was whether there was any agreement as to the repository to which this power should be transferred.

In pursuance of that we ask Congress, the Muslim League and the Princes whether they themselves can work out an agreed solution. The Congress say "unite India" as the solution, but do also say that they cannot compel any large section. The Rulers say they might join an all-India federation. Mr. Jinnah, however, says there must be two Indias with nothing more than treaties and agreements between them. The British Government consider that if they were to withdraw their forces and their Government from India they are entitled to know what the situation in India is. Will they find themselves faced with a major head on collision between the two main communities? If we can find no answer except that situation we shall have to consider what we shall do, but it should be understood that the British would not stay here to pull chestnuts out of the fire.

The Cabinet Mission also came as the representatives of one of the world's great powers. They had to look at the position in India as part of the world situation and they had a vital interest in the preservation of peace in this large area of the world. They were entitled to ask whether India would be able to stand up for itself in the world. It would not be able to stand up at all at sea and as a land power only to some extent.

Therefore the British Government presume that they will be invited to assist in India's defence since the logic of events will make this necessary. We shall then have to consider the conditions on which we should be prepared to do this and we might expect some return, for example, India's help in the defence of adjacent territories, such as Malaya, Burma and Ceylon. But also there must be a solution of India's affairs which makes effective provisions for India's own defence against external aggression, and the British Government are entitled to know whether the new setup in India will be of a kind with which we can in practice cooperate.

The Cabinet Mission are not here to dispute as to whether there should be one or two Indias. They ask the Muslims and the Hindus to consider these matters but, before they do withdraw, the British wish to find out how far the Hindus and Muslims are agreed. If they were to withdraw before an agreement and when India was still in its present state, the consequences would be disastrous. He therefore thought that before the British withdrew the greatest possible efforts should be made by Indians to reach agreement amongst themselves. Mr. Jinnah said that the Muslim League started on the basis that there was going to be Hindustan and Pakistan, each one of them a completely sovereign State. As regards defence, he contemplated, of course, that some arrangement should be made between the two but this could only be on the basis of two sovereign States with treaty relations. The same sort of relations subsisted between the United Kingdom and the Dominions.

His Excellency the Viceroy pointed out that the Indian case was different in that the defence of the North-East Frontier required defence in depth which must be organized in both States. Mr. Jinnah said that only made it the more inevitable that there should be suitable treaty relations between the two. The Viceroy said that no two foreign States had ever made successful mutual arrangements in peace time for their defence, and Sir S. Cripps pointed out that in the case of the Dominions there were Prime Ministers Conferences and common foreign policy all of which operated under the nexus of allegiance to the Crown.

Mr. Jinnah said that they must assume that they would be handing over power to responsible people. The Muslims had not decided that they would have nothing to do with the British Commonwealth. It might be in the mutual interests of Pakistan and Great Britain for them to remain within it. It was an accepted basis that Hindustan and Pakistan must have common defence arrangements, but he could not agree to any machinery which would derogate the sovereignty of Pakistan.

Sir S. Cripps said that a treaty derogated from sovereignty but Mr. Jinnah contented that a treaty was a voluntary exercise of sovereignty which remains unimpaired since the treaty could be terminated. It was pointed out that the United Nations Organization involved the permanent surrender of sovereignty.

The Secretary of State asked Mr. Jinnah why he objected to work in with some all-India machinery for defence. Mr. Jinnah asked what sort of machinery was envisaged. Sir S. Cripps said some common organization with a secretariat, Chiefs of Staff, and which had a machinery by which policy and administration could be concerted. It would be an advisory body except in so far as there were agreement. The United Nations Organization has executive authority but only where there is agreement on the Security Council. Mr. Jinnah said he saw no reason why Pakistan and Hindustan should not join the United Nations and uses its machinery.

The Secretary of State said that the Mission was here to explore the position. They were exploring the possibility of Pakistan and its viability both in peace and war. If Mr. Jinnah could not convince the Delegation of the defensibility of Pakistan he was rather driving the Mission into the solution of handing over authority to a United India. Mr. Jinnah said that if he had not convinced the Delegation he could not do so. He could not agree to anything which would derogate from the sovereignty of Pakistan. He was not there to persuade the Cabinet Mission or as a plaintiff. India was neither united not divided -it was a British possession. Great Britain proposed to transfer power; he had been asked to say how he thought this could be done. The only way in his opinion it could be done with safety was by division. On certain matters he could say that he would make agreements.

Sir S. Cripps said, could Mr. Jinnah not suggest the content of a treaty? For example, would Mr. Jinnah agree that there should be provision for mutual defence? Mr. Jinnah said that he would agree to defensive alliance. Sir S. Cripps said, would he agree to mutual consultation in regard to foreign policy? Mr. Jinnah said that would naturally be covered. Sir Stafford asked what the position was about inter-running communications of all kinds. Mr. Jinnah said that could be arranged. He was not able to express any view about sea customs.

Sir S. Cripps said that if we were to try to persuade the Congress to meet Mr. Jinnah's views it would be important to specific on these matters, but Mr. Jinnah said that he could not consider anything more unless a proposal was made to him. The Government and the Congress had powerful secretariats which could do that kind of work better than the Muslim League.

His Excellency the Viceroy asked Mr. Jinnah what were the boundaries of Pakistan as he (Mr. Jinnah) conceived it. Mr. Jinnah said that he wanted a viable Pakistan which would not be carved up or mutilated. He drew the line on the five Provinces, but said he was quite willing to consider mutual adjustments. But Pakistan must be a live State economically. He was not insisting on including a large number of Hindus in Pakistan but if it were said to him that only the number of heads could be considered, he could not agree to that. Sir S. Cripps said that on any principle of self-determination the counting of heads must be a primary factor.

The Secretary of State pointed out that the inclusion of any considerable area in which there was majority of non-Muslims might very well not strengthen but weaken the viability of Pakistan. Mr. Jinnah said that he was not opposing the view but said that suppose it were suggested that Calcutta should be added to Bihar he would say that was an impossibility. He contemplated that there would be territorial adjustments, but he could not agree that Calcutta could be taken away merely because it was a Hindu-majority city. Much of the Hindu population of Calcutta was not indigenous but brought there from outside. Sir S. Cripps said that the Hindus might say it was impossible for them to live without Calcutta but Mr. Jinnah replied that they had Bombay and Madras and could have a new port in Orissa. Pakistan without Calcutta would be like asking a man to live without his heart.

He did not want to keep Hindus in Pakistan against their will and they could migrate but he could not reduce the area of Pakistan below the point on which the State could live. Sir S. Cripps pointed to the danger that if there were large Hindu elements they would form a dominant political element making for instability because the Muslims would be divided amongst themselves on social and economic questions and the Hindus might secure the balance. Areas like Burdwan might develop a secessionist movement.

Mr. Jinnah said that he agreed that areas like Burdwan, if they were not essential to the economic life, could go into Pakistan [Hindustan]. In reply to a suggestion that Calcutta should be a free port through which goods would enter both countries free of duty and administered by a condominium, Mr. Jinnah asked what examples of this there were in the world. The cases of Danzig, Shanghai and Fiume were mentioned but Mr. Jinnah pointed out that all these had been imposed and maintained by force. What he wanted was a nucleus Muslim territory surrounded by sufficient additional territory to make it economically viable.

CMP (6) Jinnah's meeting with the Cabinet Mission on April 16 1946

Document included:

- Record of Interview between Cabinet Delegation [Viceroy Wavell was also present] and Mr. Jinnah on Tuesday, 16 April 1946 from 'The Transfer of Power 1942-7' Volume VII The Cabinet Mission 23 March-29 June 1946, Eds., Nicholas Mansergh and Penderel Moon, 1977 (full text)

116 page 280 (full text)

Record of Interview between Cabinet Delegation [Viceroy Wavell was also present] and Mr. Jinnah on Tuesday, 16 April 1946 at 11 am.

The Secretary of State said that the Delegation had now heard all points of view, that they recognized the importance of the case which Mr. Jinnah had put to them and of the claims of his community.

They felt it was essential to reach an agreement between the parties. If this could be done on the main issue, other matters would fall in place. If there was no agreement, the prospects for the people of India, for Great Britain and for the world would be gravely affected. A breakdown of the administration in India might result. In particular there would be a breakdown of the food administration.

Therefore the Delegation were anxious that the gap between Congress and the Muslim League should be closed by both parties moving towards each other, and they were approaching Mr. Jinnah on the one hand and the Congress on the other to that end. He felt sure that Mr. Jinnah would help provided it was clear that we were not asking for all the concessions to be made from his side.

After considering with the greatest care the case which Mr. Jinnah had put forward, the Delegation had come to the conclusion that the full and complete demand for Pakistan in the form in which Mr. Jinnah had put it forward had little chance of acceptance and they thought that Mr. Jinnah could not reasonably hope to receive both the whole of the territory, much of it inhabited by non-Muslims, which he claimed and the full measure of sovereignty which he said was essential. If the full territories were insisted upon then some element of sovereignty must be relinquished if there were to be a reasonable prospect of agreement. If, on the other hand, full sovereignty is desired, then the claims to the [non-]Muslim territories could not be conceded.

The Delegation believed that the progress might be possible in one of two ways. First, agreement might perhaps be reached on a separate State of Pakistan consisting of, say, Sind, North-West Frontier Province, Balochistan, the Muslim-majority provinces of the Punjab, except perhaps Gurdaspur, [Eastern Bengal?] and the Sylhet district of Assam. Whether there would be any chance of Calcutta being a free port seemed doubtful. Its inclusion in Pakistan could not be justified on any principle of self-determination. It seemed to the Delegation that Pakistan on this basis would clearly need to contract a defensive alliance with Hindustan and enter into special Treaty relations with it. Under this scheme the Indian States would be at liberty to join Hindustan or Pakistan or to remain outside.

No doubt there would be points in this scheme which would not appeal to Mr. Jinnah but the Delegation did not think that they, for their part, could press Congress to go further than this to meet Mr. Jinnah's point of view.

The Secretary of State here emphasized that this proposal was not a scheme which the Cabinet Delegation put forward as one which they considered the best or even as desirable, but as a possible hopeful line on which agreement might be achieved.

The second and alternative suggestion was that the Congress and the Muslim League should sit down together to try to evolve an agreed scheme for an Indian Union. Opinions would no doubt differ about the details of such a plan which must be matters for negotiation. If, however, the League accepted the principle of a Union Centre for the essential subjects, say, defence, foreign affairs and communications, it might then be possible to include in one Federation the whole of the Provinces of Sind, Balochistan, North-West Frontier Province, the Punjab and Bengal, plus perhaps the Sylhet district of Assam. In such a Union the two parts might have equal representation. Whether the States would come into the Union as a separate Federation would be a matter for negotiation. There might be provision that any party to it could secede after a certain period, say 15 years. A setup of this kind would secure a very strong Muslim Federation and it was possible that it might be acceptable to the Congress.

The Delegation had asked Mr. Jinnah to come to see them in order to get his view as to which of these two alternative possible avenues of approach to an agreement would be best from his point of view.

Mr. Jinnah asked how Pakistan came in under the proposed all-India Union. The Secretary of State said that briefly there were two propositions - a small Pakistan with sovereign rights and a Treaty relation, and a larger Pakistan including broadly the present Provinces except Assam and subject perhaps to some frontier adjustment. The latter would come together with Hindustan on terms of equality within an all-India Union for the essential purposes of defence and foreign affairs.

Sir. S. Cripps said that under the second alternative two Federations would be created linked by a Union Centre. The States would come in either at the Union or at the Federation level and there would be equal representation of Hindustan and Pakistan at the Union level. The communal balance would be retained at the Centre by some means even if the States came in there.

Mr. Jinnah asked how the Union Executive would be formed. Sir S. Cripps said that the Federations would choose the members of the Union Executive. Mr. Jinnah asked how, if there were equal representation, decisions were to be reached and Sir S. Cripps said that there would be no Union Parliament. The responsibility would go back to the two Federations if agreement could not be reached and differences could only be decided by inter-Governmental agreement. Mr. Jinnah expressed doubts as to whether this arrangement would work in practice. Matters would have to be decided every day in regard to defence. From what had been said he had not been able to get anything which would enable him to say that the Union idea was worth considering.

The Secretary of State emphasized that the essence of the Union was the equality of the two component parts which made it entirely different from a Centre in which the Hindus had a majority. In so far as the Muslim League's claim as to territory of Pakistan would be conceded the Muslims would have control by majority of large areas in all except the essential Union subjects and there they would meet the Hindus on a level where it was the States which counted and not the number of individuals in them.

Of course the Secretary of State did not know whether the Congress would agree to this principle of equality but it was the essence of the proposal. Mr. Jinnah said that no amount of equality provided on paper was going to work. Equality could not exist between the majority and minority within the same Governmental system. Would there, for example, be equality of each community in the Services? A Treaty of mutual defence between our separate States was quite different. It operated in certain contingencies such as external attack, but at other times and in other matter the States were separate. He did not think that the domination of the Muslims by the Hindus could be prevented in any scheme in which they were kept together. It is only when the Muslims are the majority in Pakistan and the Hindus in Hindustan that you have sufficient united force running through the State from the top to the bottom to provide a "steel frame" which can hold it together.

The Secretary of State said that Mr. Jinnah seemed to be turning to the other alternative and asked Mr. Jinnah's views on that. Mr. Jinnah said that once the principle of Pakistan was conceded the question of territory of Pakistan could be discussed. His claim was for the six Provinces but he was willing to discuss the area. The first question was whether the principle was accepted. He claimed that the six Provinces was a reasonable demand but he could not possibly accept that Calcutta should go out merely for the sake of 5 or 6 lakhs of Hindus (largely Depressed Classes who would prefer Pakistan) most of whom were imported labour. What was the reason why Calcutta could not be given to Pakistan? The Secretary of State said that what the Delegation were doing was seeking for a basis of agreement. They did not think that the agreement could be reached on the basis that Calcutta was included in Pakistan. Mr. Jinnah said he could not in any event accept the exclusion of Calcutta.

The Secretary of State said he wished to emphasize that the Delegation did not consider that either of these two alternatives would be readily acceptable to the Congress. Both of them were some way beyond what the Congress would like. Mr. Jinnah said that the Congress were in a very strong position. Even if the whole of Mr. Jinnah's claims were granted, they got three-quarters of India. At the worst they would lose Calcutta, some part of Western Bengal (Burdwan) and the Ambala Division.

The Secretary of State said the Congress would lose much more than this. They would lose the unity of India which alone would make India a strong entity in the outside world. Further, if Pakistan were conceded the difficulty of getting the States into a united India would be greatly increased.

Mr. Jinnah said that he thought with respect that the Congress stood to lose nothing. The unity of India was a myth. All that Congress would lose was that their minority in Pakistan would cease to have its present protected position under which it enjoys at the present time a dominating position in those areas. As regards the States, if Paramountcy went the States would be bound to come into Hindu India. They could not stand out and they knew it. Sir S. Cripps said that Paramountcy would cease to be, and Mr. Jinnah said he was glad to hear that was so.

The Secretary of State said that if Mr. Jinnah got his two steel frames set up by agreement he could see the force of the case which he put forward. If, however, Mr. Jinnah did obtain otherwise than by agreement more than the Muslim-majority districts he would find himself in a very vulnerable position subsequently. He would have a large internal element of Hindu population and also external opposition from a hostile Hindustan. Pakistan would be in two parts divided by a power which would be hostile to both of them. That seemed to him to be an exceedingly difficult and dangerous position to be in.

Mr. Jinnah said that he thought this was an exaggerated statement of the position. All the non-Muslims could not be counted as Hindus. He thought that the Congress had nothing to lose and had no need of an agreement. They would get three-quarters of India anyway, whether the British Government had to make an award or not. If the Congress drove the British Government to make an award, very likely they would, in order to appease the Congress, give some part of the six Provinces of Pakistan to Hindustan. The Secretary of State said that the consequences of no agreement were much worse than that. A settlement without agreement would lead to chaos and starvation, and the whole prospect of the future for the Indian people would be blighted.

Mr. Jinnah said that those arguments should in his view be put before the Congress. If he made a concession he would have lost it before the negotiations began. It was Congress who would should make a proposal. The Secretary of State said that the Delegation was not asking Mr. Jinnah to commit himself to anything but merely to say whether he would prefer the matter to be considered on the basis of sovereignty and the small area or a Union and a larger area. Mr. Jinnah said that so far as the Union was concerned he could not accept the principle. On the other hand, he claimed the six Provinces and if Congress considered that was too much they should say what they considered he ought to have. He was not prepared to say what he was willing to give up.

Sir S. Cripps said that Mr. Jinnah was merely saying that he would not negotiate. If he could make no advance at all it made negotiation impossible. Mr. Alexander said that what the Delegation were putting to Mr. Jinnah was the maximum which they thought the Congress could be brought to agree to. They were asking Mr. Jinnah whether, if the Congress could be persuaded to come that far, he would be prepared to discuss on that basis.

Mr. Jinnah said he understood from the Delegation that there was a chance of a settlement on the basis of the first alternative. If Congress would say that on that basis they wanted certain defined areas taken from Pakistan he was willing to discuss whether what they proposed was reasonable, fair and workable. He would try his very best to reach agreement with the Congress on that basis but if what was proposed struck at the heart of Pakistan it was impossible, and if the principle of Pakistan was not accepted it was no use pursuing the matter. Ultimately, if Congress and the Muslims could not agree the Delegation would have to do what they thought right and they were in a position to do it.

The Secretary of State said that if the Delegation gave an award in the Muslim League's favour and then Great Britain withdrew her troops, the Muslims would be exposed to grave dangers. Mr. Jinnah said that he was 100% in favour of an agreement but what if there was no agreement. The situation was unprecedented. The British Government was asking the Indian people to take self-government and the Indians were unable to do so.

Sir. S. Cripps suggested that Mr. Jinnah should make some alternative suggestion as to what he would like the Delegation to get Congress to agree to. Mr. Jinnah again said that it was Congress who should say what it wanted. The Congress President had today issued a statement sticking to every point.

He (Mr. Jinnah) had never said he would not discuss the situation but the Congress President two days before he came to see the Delegation said that he would never agree to sovereignty for Pakistan. Mr. Alexander asked whether he rightly understood Mr. Jinnah to say that if the Congress would make a proposition on the basis of the first of the two alternatives he would be prepared to discuss it. Mr. Jinnah said he was ready to do anything which did not prevent Pakistan from being, in the Delegation's own word, a "viable" State economically, strategically and politically but on that he must insist. The Lahore Resolution contemplated a transitional period. He must tell the Delegation that the only way there could be a peaceful transference of power was that defence should remain in the interim period under British control. It did not mean that Britain must retain it for ever but for a period of years. Sir S. Cripps indicated that this was not a possibility.

The Secretary of State suggested that Mr. Jinnah should think the matter over further and see whether he could not revise his attitude to the second alternative, though he gathered that it was not acceptable. After the Delegation's return from Kashmir perhaps, Mr. Jinnah would let them know his position. In the meantime, had Mr. Jinnah any view to express on whether these two alternatives should be put by the Delegation to the Congress on the following day. Mr. Jinnah said that the more the Congress were encouraged to lop off parts of the Pakistan which he claimed or to reduce its sovereignty, the less possibility there would be of an agreed settlement.

CMP (7A) Maulana Azad's discussions with the Mission on 17 April 1946

Documents included:

- Record of Meeting between Cabinet Delegation and Viscount Wavell on 17 April 1946 (excerpts)
- Record of Meeting of the Cabinet Delegation and Viscount Wavell with Maulana Azad on 17 April 1946 (excerpts)

From 'The Transfer of Power 1942-7' Volume VII The Cabinet Mission 23 March-29 June 1946, Eds, Nicholas Mansergh and Penderel Moon, 1977.

Comment

Maulana Azad had issued a statement on April 15 (ref. footnote in CMP (6)) and the Cabinet Delegation asked him to explain further his ideas for Union federation in that statement. The differences between Jinnah's position and Maulana Azad's position on the structure of the Union as understood by the Delegation were summarized by them in a meeting prior to that with the Maulana.

118 Page 288 (excerpts)

Record of Meeting between Cabinet Delegation and Field Marshal Viscount Wavell on Wednesday, 17 April at 10.45 am

I. The Secretary of State said that he had been thinking over the manner of putting across the idea of an Indian Union confined to defence and foreign affairs with two federations for Pakistan and Hindustan underneath it. He thought there was some danger of selling two different articles under the same name.

Jinnah's way of arriving at a satisfactory Pakistan was to dissolve the existing apparatus and rebuild on the basis of Pakistan. When the Pakistan State existed he would be prepared to construct some sort of Agency Centre through a Treaty.

Congress on the other hand would start with the existing Centre and subtract the optional subjects. The first involved undoing the Indian Army and re-creating it as two armies, then making some arrangements for cooperation. The second meant that the main army would remain under the Central Government though Hindustan and Pakistan might have smaller forces of their own.

Sir S. Cripps thought it did not much matter how the result was reached, whether by a constitution or by a Treaty, or otherwise, provided that the result was an Executive Body controlling defence and foreign policy.

II. The Viceroy said that the positions appeared to be that Jinnah had not moved at all. Sir S. Cripps said he was seeing Jinnah that evening and that if he got no indication that Jinnah was prepared to move, he thought that the Delegation must proceed to get out its own base of settlement. This should then be shown to the two Parties confidentially who might be asked if they had any observations on it before it was published. It was essential to do something which would have the support of one side. If Jinnah would not play he inevitably drove us into the arms of the Congress.

III. It was agreed that in meeting the Congress that afternoon nothing should be said about what had passed with Jinnah except that the Delegation had put certain suggestions to Jinnah which he was thinking over and that his final reply was awaited. Sir S. Cripps said that he would like it to be indicated to Azad that we should be reaching a decisive stage soon after Easter.

The Viceroy suggested that it would be desirable to press Azad to enlarge upon his recent statement. Sir S Cripps said there was nothing new in this statement. He understood independently that the question in the minds of Congress was whether they could agree to a federation for optional subjects distinct from the Central Federation and whether there would be a Legislature at that level or only a Executive for joint administrative operations. It was agreed that it would be desirable to get the position clarified on this point.

The Viceroy that it would be desirable to put first the statements about Paramountcy and the Interim Government. He thought both these should be mentioned very broadly and as unalterable facts of the situation in order to avoid arguments being raised on them. Sir S. Cripps thought that these two matters might be dealt with as an introduction to the subject of Azad's statement and the nature of the federation.

Sir S. Cripps said that he thought that fairly soon the Congress would want to know what are the points we wish to raise in a Treaty. The meeting had before them a note of the Treaty points prepared by Sir William Croft. It was agreed that the main matter was financial obligations, including the rights of Services...

(end excerpts)

121 Page 294 (excerpts)

Record of Meeting of the Cabinet Delegation and Field Marshal Viscount Wavell with Maulana Azad on Wednesday, 17 April 1946 at 4.45 pm

The Secretary of State said that the Delegation had now practically completed hearing the views of the various parties and interests and were anxious to get on with reaching a settlement as quickly as possible. They considered that the Pakistan question was the main issue and very much hoped that it might be possible for an agreement to be reached on this subject between the Congress and the Muslim League since this was obviously the only satisfactory method. They could, however, assure the Maulana that they did not intend to allow lack of agreement between the two main parties on this issue to impede the settlement of India's independence.

The Delegation had seen Mr. Jinnah and put to him general suggestions designed to make bridge between his standpoint and that of the Congress. They were still awaiting Mr. Jinnah's final response and would prefer not to say anything about that at present except that they were sure that in any discussions on these they could count on the Congress showing a spirit of compromise.

Meanwhile, there were other matters which would have to be settled on which the Delegation felt that it would be useful to have a discussion with Congress representatives. The first of these was the future of the Indian states.

Next in importance to the settlement of the Pakistan issue was the formation of a new Executive Council at the Centre.

The Secretary of State proceeding said that the Delegation had been interested in the Maulana's recent statement on the question of federation and would like to know his views in rather more detail. They understood that his idea was that there should be a Centre for the whole of India with a Legislature and Executive and that this Centre should deal with certain compulsory and with certain optional subjects in respect of these Provinces which opt to come in for them. The Maulana would remember that Sir S. Cripps had made the suggestion that the Provinces might be grouped for the optional subjects into two federations subject to an all-India Federation. This was an interesting point which the Delegation would like to discuss further with the Maulana.

Maulana Azad said he would like to know whether the Delegation's talks with Mr. Jinnah had produced any response at all from Mr. Jinnah and whether they were expecting any further reply from him. The Secretary of State said that the Delegation expect to be seeing Mr. Jinnah again after their return from Kashmir. Mr. Jinnah had certain points to think over and they felt it better not to say anything to the Maulana on that subject at present.

With reference to the suggestion for a Council representing the States and British India in the interim period, the Maulana asked whether the Political Advisor to the Crown Representative could not during that period be an Indian. The Viceroy explained...

(approx. 1 page of discussion)

The Maulana said that before we came to discuss these points he would like to be clear about the powers of the interim Executive. Would it have plenary powers or not..

(approx. 2 pages of discussion)

The Secretary of State then asked the Maulana to deal with the last point raised in his opening statement, namely, the structure of the Union as envisaged in his recent statement.

The Maulana said that as he had already explained there would be two lists of Central subjects, optional and compulsory. The precise division of subjects between the two was a matter of detail but he agreed that the essential subjects for the compulsory list were foreign affairs and defence and that, broadly speaking, the optional list would cover all remaining Central subjects under the existing constitution.

The Secretary of State said that he would like to envisage clearly the position under this proposal. If some Provinces decided not to opt for the second list there would come into being a Centre having different relations with two sets of Provinces, some federated for a wider range of subjects than others. This seemed to the Delegation to involve the sub-division of the Centre into two parts dealing with (a) the Provinces that opt for the full range of subjects, and (b) the Provinces that are federated for the compulsory subjects only.

If there were anything in the nature of Pakistan you could not prevent those Provinces that were within it from agreeing on their own to pool some of their subjects in the optional field together and it would seem to work out in practice as a separate Centre for Pakistan and Hindustan with a super-Centre above it dealing with the compulsory subjects.

Maulana Azad said that so long as we were proceeding on the assumption of a federal constitution there would be no question of a division into two parts. There would be Provinces where the Muslims happened to have a majority and other Provinces. Some sort of legislative and executive machinery would have to be set up to deal with the two divisions of compulsory and optional subjects.

Sir S. Cripps said it might reasonably be assumed that the Hindu majority Provinces would federate for the optional subjects and that the Muslim majority Provinces would not. You would then get a Centre with a Legislature and Executive comprising all Provinces. Was it practicable for the Muslims in these two bodies to take part in the decision of optional matters for which the Provinces which they represented had not opted?

The Maulana said that the representatives of the Muslim provinces need not participate in the work of the Executive and the Legislature when the optional subjects were under consideration but Sir Stafford Cripps pointed out that it would be difficult to prevent them from attending the Legislature if they wished to do so and very difficult to define exactly which subjects of debate were optional.

Foreign Affairs, for example, might have implications in the optional field. It would be most difficult to define exactly which subjects of debate were optional. It would be most difficult to work a system of that kind. He thought you must either have a Legislature on two parts sitting together for the compulsory field, or two Legislatures with a separate Legislature for the compulsory subjects. If you allowed only the representatives of the Hindu Provinces to participate for the optional subjects you must allow the Muslim Provincial representatives to discuss the optional subjects separately if they wished to do so.

The Maulana said that this was a matter that he must consider further, and Sir Stafford Cripps said that it was a very important point which might go a long way to meet some of the Muslim objections to the Congress proposal. Provided that a Centre was kept together for the compulsory subjects the Congress might be prepared to consider the idea.

Sir S. Cripps said that the Executive would have to be in two compartments also so far as the optional subjects were concerned. You could not have the same minister for, say, education, if that were an optional subject, controlling the policy in both the Hindu and the Muslim majority Provinces.

The Maulana said there were many other matters which needed to be discussed such as the future relationships between Britain and India. The Delegation said that they would like the Maulana to let them have a list of the points which he would like to discuss so that they could consider them before they met him again.

The Maulana said that he would discuss the matters which had been put to him by the Delegation with the Working Committee. He wished to say that he was most anxious to explore ways and means of bringing the Muslim League and Congress closer together if possible. Could the Delegation make any suggestion to this end?

The Secretary of State said that at the present state they were not able to do so. As he had said in the beginning, Mr. Jinnah was considering what the Delegation had said to him and they had north The Congress's unease with parity. Exchanges between the Congress and the Cabinet Mission on 8th and 9th May.

From 'The Transfer of Power 1942-7' Volume VII The Cabinet Mission 23 March-29 June 1946, Eds, Nicholas Mansergh and Penderel Moon, 1977.

222 page 466 (full text)

Mr. Gandhi to Sir S. Cripps

"Chadwick", Simla, W., 8 May 1946

Dear Sir Stafford,

The four Congress Delegates had a warm debate over the Cabinet Mission's suggestions. The foremost point was that if the Delegates accepted the terms they would be binding on them and, therefore, on the Congress unless the latter repudiated them. The same would be the case with the Muslim League. On the strength of what you told me last night I said they were binding on no one. The Constituent Assembly would be free to throw out any of the items and the members of the two delegations were equally free to add or amend the suggestions before the Constituent Assembly. I added that they were meant only as a scaffolding by means of which the two institutions could be brought to the Constituent Assembly adumbrated in the draft. If you are able to confirm the above and are free to make a public declaration to that effect, the main difficulty would be over.

As to merits the difficulty about parity between six Hindu majority Provinces and the five Muslim majority Provinces is insurmountable. The Muslim majority Provinces represent over nine crores of the population as against over nineteen crores of the Hindu majority Provinces. This is really worse than Pakistan. What is suggested in place is that the Central Legislature should be framed on the population basis and so too the Executive. If this is considered unfair an impartial non-British tribunal should award on this as on any other matter of differences otherwise incapable of adjustment. If these two points are cleared my way would be clear.

Instead of running down to you I thought I should send this note, leaving you to decide whether we should meet before the Conference or whether an exchange of letters should suffice. I am in your hands.

Yours sincerely, M.K. Gandhi

223 page 466 (full text)

Sir S. Cripps to Mr. Gandhi

Viceregal Lodge, Simla 9 May 1946

My dear Mr. Gandhi,

Sudhir brought me your letter last night just as I had got into bed after my excellent treatment by Dr. Mehta, so I sent you back an answer verbally by him.

This is merely a note to confirm what he will have told you.

As to your first point the position, as I see it, is this:- If the Congress and Muslim League Delegates agree to a certain basis for the new constitution they will be bound as honourable men to do their utmost to see that the form agreed upon is that adopted by the Constituent Assembly. To do less than that would be to go back upon their word. As to the second point - equality at the centre, I appreciate your difficulty though not that "it would be worse than Pakistan". If this can be overcome with some form of international arbitration by agreement with the League there is, of course, nothing whatever to prevent such agreement.

I am very grateful for this further helpful advice and look forward to seeing you again this evening after the Conference has met again.

Yours very sincerely. R. Stafford Cripps.

Bibliography

Abduhu, G. Rasool : *The Educational Ideas of Maulana Abul Kalam Azad,* Sterling Publishers, 1973

Abulkalam Azad, Syeda Saiyidain Hameed, Mujib Rizvi, Sughra Mahdi: *India's Maulana Abul Kalam Azad,* Indian Council for Cultural Relations, 1990

Ahmad, Imtiaz: *State and Foreign Policy: India's Role in South Asia*, New Delhi, Vikas, 1993.

Ahmed, Waheed: *Quaid-I-Azam Muhammed Ali Jinnah : Speeches Indian Legislative Assembly 1935-1947*, Quaid-i-Azam Accademy, 1991.

Ambedkar, B. R.: *Annihilation of Caste: An Undelivered Speech,* Arnold Publishers, New Delhi, 1990.

Anand, Som. *Lahore: Portrait of a Lost City*. Lahore: Vanguard Books, 1998.

Anthony, J. Parel : *Hind Swaraj or Indian Home Rule,* Cambridge University Press, 1925.

Asghar Ali.: *Mandal Commission Controversy*, Ajanta Publications, Delhi, 1991.

Ashraf, Muhammad Arslan. *Why Partition of India?: Gandhi, Jinnah, Nehru, Azad - Congress and Muslim League,* 2016.

Ashton, S.R.: *British Policy Towards the Indian States, 1905-1939*, London: Curzon, 1982.

Bourai, Himanshu : *Gandhi and Modern Indian Liberals*, Delhi, Abhijeet Pub., 2004.

Chakrabarti, Santosh : *Studies in Tagore : Critical Essays*, New Delhi, Atlantic, 2004.

Chaudhary, M.: *Partition and the Curse of Rehabilitation*, Calcutta, Bengal Rehabilitation Organization, 1964.

Douglas, Ian Henderson: *Abul Kalam Azad: An Intellectual and Religious Biography*. Oxford University Press, 1993.

Gandhi, Rajmohan. *Eight Lives: A Study of the Hindu-Muslim Encounter*. New York: State University Press, 1986.

George, Davis : *Dynamics of Power : The Gandhian Perspective*, New Delhi, Frank Bros. & Co., 2000.

Gorhe, Neelam: *Social Development and Dalit Women*, Gyan Pub. House, New Delhi, 1995.

Green, Martin: *The Challenge of the Mahatmas*, Basic Books, New York, 1978.

Guha, Ramachandra : *India After Gandhi : The History of the World's Largest Democracy*, New Delhi, Picador, 2007.

Gupta, Manmath Nath: *Gandhi and his Times*, Lipi Prakashan, New Delhi, 1982.

Hameed, Syeda Saiyidain. *Islamic Seal on India's Independence; Abul Kalam Azad - A Fresh Look.* Karachi: Oxford University Press, 1998.

Jain, Vidya: *M.K. Gandhi, Leader of the Masses*, Deep & Deep Publications, New Delhi, 1995.

John, S.J. : *Gandhi and Gutierrez : Two Paradigms of Liberative Transformation*, New Delhi, Decent Books, 2004.

Kshirsagar, R. K.: *Dalit Movement in India and Its Leaders (1857-1956)*, MD Pub. Pvt. Ltd., New Delhi, 1994.

Kumar, S.B. : *Environmental Problems and Gandhian Solutions : The Only Ray of Hope to the Present Ailing World*, New Delhi, Deep & Deep, 2002.

Murthi, R.K. : *Discovery of Nehru*, Indian Pub., Delhi, 1993.

Narula, Sanjay : *Indian Politics*, New Delhi, Murari Lal and Sons, 2007.

Nevile, P.: *Lahore: A Sentimental Journey*, New Delhi, Penguin, 1993.

Noorani, A.G. : *Indian Political Trials : 1775-1947*, New Delhi, Oxford University Press, 2005.

Prasad, Lal Bahadur : *Indian Political System and Law*, New Delhi, Shree, 2005.

Pruthi, R.K. : *Indian Political Thought*, New Delhi, Mohit Pub., 2007.

Ravikant and Saint, Tarun K.: *Translating Partition*, New Delhi, Katha, 2001.

Ravindra Kumar: *Life and Works of Maulana Abul Kalam Azad*, Atlantic Publishers & Distributors, 1991

Ray, B.N. : *Gandhigiri : Satyagraha After Hundred Years*, New Delhi, Kaveri Books, 2008.

Saksena, N.S.: *India: Towards Anarchy, 1967-1992*, New Delhi, Abhinav, 1993.

Salim, Ahmad: *Lahore 1947*, New Delhi, India Research Press, 2001.

Sankar Ghose: *Congress Presidential Speeches*, New Delhi, 1975.

Sarkar, J.: *Caste, Occupation and Change*, B. R. Publishing Co., Delhi, 1984.

Index

C

Cabinet Mission, 13, 58, 71, 96, 111, 112, 114, 118, 166, 168, 171, 172, 173, 178, 180, 184, 192, 193, 194, 196, 197, 198, 201, 202, 203, 204, 210, 215.

Congress Leader, 9, 118, 134.

E

Education System, 2, 35, 42, 44, 46, 47, 154.

Educational Backwardness, 42.

Educational Leadership, 36, 38.

Educational Policies, 37.

Eminent Educationist, 26, 27, 28, 47.

F

Freedom, 4, 14, 15, 17, 18, 19, 20, 21, 22, 23, 25, 26, 29, 31, 33, 35, 36, 40, 41, 47, 53, 60, 61, 62, 63, 64, 68, 70, 71, 72, 73, 78, 79, 80, 89, 90, 93, 96, 98, 101, 102, 113, 116, 117, 133, 134, 135, 145, 146, 147, 150, 151, 154, 158, 166, 193.

I

Indian Education Policy, 40.

Indian National Army, 154, 165.

Indian National Congress, 1, 5, 6, 17, 20, 23, 25, 26, 57, 58, 62, 64, 65, 69, 70, 71, 77, 81, 88, 96, 103, 107, 113, 132, 139, 145, 146, 153, 162, 163, 169, 171, 173, 175, 176, 177, 178, 180, 182, 183, 184, 188, 189, 191.

J

Jawaharlal Nehru, 5, 7, 9, 16, 23, 27, 38, 96, 109, 116, 117, 118, 152, 154, 159, 164, 167, 173.

Jinnah, 9, 10, 11, 12, 13, 23, 26, 62, 65, 68, 71, 72, 86, 91, 92, 93, 94, 95, 96, 97, 98, 99, 100, 102, 103, 106, 107, 112, 116, 117, 118, 145, 152, 161, 162, 166, 171, 172, 173, 174, 175, 176, 177, 178, 179, 180, 192, 193, 194, 196, 197, 198, 199, 200, 201, 202, 203, 204, 205, 206, 207, 208, 209, 210, 211, 212, 213, 215.

M

Mahatma Gandhi, 1, 5, 16, 17, 25, 38, 40, 47, 64, 72, 75, 90, 96, 97, 106, 133, 134, 135, 136, 137, 138, 139, 140, 141, 142, 143, 144, 148, 152, 160, 168.

Mappila Rebellion, 147, 149.

Maulana Muhammad Ali Jauhar, 33, 34.

Maulana Zafar Ali Khan, 31, 32, 33.
Muhammad Iqbal, 151.
Muslim League, 6, 9, 10, 11, 13, 15, 24, 32, 34, 57, 62, 64, 66, 70, 71, 78, 81, 90, 91, 94, 95, 96, 97, 100, 107, 110, 111, 112, 118, 139, 151, 165, 166, 168, 171, 172, 173, 174, 176, 180, 183, 185, 186, 192, 193, 194, 195, 196, 197, 201, 202, 203, 205, 206, 212, 215, 216.

N

National Movement, 61, 69, 70.
Noakhali Massacre, 168.

P

Pakistan Without Partition, 92.
Partition of India, 2, 12, 13, 15, 17, 25, 26, 36, 61, 82, 95, 96, 97, 111, 155, 170, 176, 179, 184, 195.

Q

Quit India, 2, 10, 11, 22, 58, 64, 71, 72, 80, 96, 103, 121, 163, 175.

R

Refugee Camps, 14, 25, 124, 129.
Revolutionary Activities, 3, 20, 78.
Revolutionary Journalist, 23, 26.
Right to Education, 47, 56.
Role of Journalism, 28.

S

Scholar Extraordinary, 55.
Sir Syed Ahmad Khan, 30, 69.
Swarajist Strategy, 73.

❑❑❑